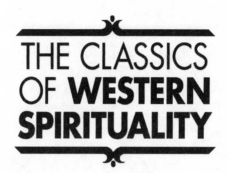

THE CLASSICS
OF **WESTERN
SPIRITUALITY**

THE CLASSICS OF WESTERN SPIRITUALITY
A Library of the Great Spiritual Masters

1900

Elisabeth Leseur

SELECTED WRITINGS

EDITED, TRANSLATED, AND INTRODUCED BY
JANET K. RUFFING, RSM

PREFACE BY
WENDY M. WRIGHT

PAULIST PRESS
NEW YORK • MAHWAH, NJ

Cover Art: Cover photograph of Elisabeth Leseur, 1910, Archives of the Dominican Province of France, Bibliotèque du Saulchoir, Paris, used with permission.

Frontispiece: The photograph of Charles Duvent's portrait of Elisabeth Leseur, 1900, is from the Archives of the Dominican Province of France, Bibliotèque du Saulchoir, Paris, used with permission.

Acknowledgments
Scripture quotations are taken from *The New Revised Standard Version: Catholic Edition of the Holy Bible*. Nashville: Catholic Bible Press, 1991, used with permission.

Permission to translate the writings of Elisabeth Leseur included in this volume from the original Gigord (Paris) French editions has been granted by Les Editions du Cerf, Paris.

Cover and caseside design by A. Michael Velthaus
Book design by Lynn Else

Library of Congress Cataloging-in-Publication Data

Leseur, Elisabeth, 1866–1914
    [Selections. English. 2005]
    Selected writings / Elisabeth Leseur ; edited, translated, and introduced by Janet K. Ruffing ; preface by Wendy M. Wright.
        p.   cm. — (The classics of Western spirituality)
    ISBN 0-8091-4329-1 (pbk. : alk. paper);
    ISBN 0-8091-0574-8 (cloth : alk. paper)
    1. Spiritual life—Catholic Church.   2. Leseur, Elisabeth, 1866–1914.
I. Ruffing, Janet, 1945- II. Title. III. Series.

BX2350.3.L4813 2005
282'.092—dc22

                                                                    2004028082

Published by Paulist Press
997 Macarthur Boulevard
Mahwah, New Jersey 07430

www.paulistpress.com

Printed and bound in the
United States of America

CONTENTS

Foreword ix

Preface xi

Introduction
    Elisabeth Leseur (1866–1914) 1
    Elisabeth Leseur's Spirituality 6
    Primary Influences on Elisabeth Leseur's Spirituality 9
    Church and Society 20
    The Women's Movement. 24
    The Communion of Saints. 27
    Personal Vocation. 31
    Suffering 33
    Friendship Within the Communion of Saints. 43
    The Writings 46
    Note on the Translation 48

The Texts
    Journal and *Daily Thoughts* 51
        The Journal: Part 1 (1899–1906). 53
        Notebook of Resolutions (1906–1912) 91
        The Journal: Part 2 (1911–1914). 117
        Daily Thoughts (1899–1906). 135
        My Spiritual Testament 162
    Writings on Christian Vocation 165
    Letters to Unbelievers 191
    Letters on Suffering 222

Notes 286

Selected Bibliography 311

Index 316

Editor and Translator of This Volume

JANET K. RUFFING is a Sister of Mercy and professor of spirituality and spiritual direction in the Graduate School of Religion and Religious Education at Fordham University. She has lectured in Australia, Ireland, India, Thailand, Guam, Belgium, France, Canada, and throughout the United States on spirituality, spiritual direction, and religious life. She is also the author of *Spiritual Direction: Beyond the Beginnings* (Paulist Press, 2000).

Author of the Preface

WENDY M. WRIGHT is professor of theology at Creighton University and holds the John C. Kenefick Faculty Chair in the Humanities. Her academic work has focused on the Salesian spiritual tradition. She is also the author of *Francis de Sales and Jane de Chantal: Letters of Spiritual Direction* (Paulist Press Classics of Western Spirituality Series, 1988).

FOREWORD

My experience with the writings of Elisabeth Leseur has been deeply moving for more than a decade. My colleague and friend at Fordham, Dr. Astrid O'Brien, introduced me to Elisabeth when I was still a non-tenured professor and invited me to write scholarly papers on her for a session at the Mystics Conference in Kalamazoo in the early 1990s. From the beginning, Elisabeth intrigued me. Who was this woman who thought women should study philosophy? Where did she come from? How was it that she had such a clear sense of her distinctly lay vocation? After three initial papers given in various academic venues, I kept returning to the *Letters on Suffering*. In them, the reader looks into Elisabeth's heart most deeply, because she is so transparent with her soul-friend, Soeur Goby. This long dormant interest was suddenly revived by a phone call from Xaverian Brother Reginald Cruz, a hagiographer tracing factual information about Soeur Goby. It was he who told me where the original documents were in Paris and reignited my interest. He also carefully read the first draft of the introduction to this volume with expert attention to historical detail. Thanks to our faculty fellowship program and research grants, I began to arrange for the translations of these letters into English for the first time, calling on Sisters Moire McQuillan, RSHM, Rita Arthur, RSHM, and Therese Grace Murray, SC. What began as a simple project of translating and introducing these letters became much larger when Christopher Bellitto of Paulist Press and Dr. Bernard McGinn became interested in featuring Elisabeth Leseur in this series. I am grateful for their encouragement and helpful suggestions in creating this greatly expanded project.

I wish to express my appreciation to Fordham University for a faculty fellowship leave in the spring of 2004. Fordham also awarded a generous archival research grant that enabled me to work in the Dominican Archives in Paris at the Bibliotèque du Saulchoir in June 2003 and January 2004, as well as in the Postulator General's

Office at Santa Sabina in Rome. In addition, Brigida Perciballi, my graduate assistant at Fordham, provided invaluable scanning service along with many other tasks that furthered the project.

Dr. Paul Philibert, OP, was invaluable in providing me with the necessary connections to gain access to these materials in both locations. In Paris, Rev. Eric de Clermont-Tonnere, OP, chief editor of Editions du Cerf, was most gracious in his support of this project and in granting permission for this new translation of Elisabeth's writings. At the Saulchoir, Archivist Rev. Michel Albaric, OP, located the necessary materials with a great deal of personal effort. Ms. Isabelle Séruzier most competently and graciously interpreted my many requests and questions and made my work in the library very pleasant. Likewise, Rev. Ricci, OP, at Santa Sabina welcomed me in the Postulator General's Office. I was also offered generous hospitality in Paris by the Sisters of Marie Reparatrix; my brother Kenneth on the second trip; and the Religious of the Sacred Heart of Mary at Via Nometana in Rome, Sisters Eileen Kearns, Francisca, de Lourdes, and Ann. Lorraine Ruffing accompanied me to Beaune and to all the sites in the vicinity related to Soeur Goby. I am also grateful to Claude Menesguen, who helped nuance the Introduction.

While working on the translations and writing the Introduction, I was also accompanying my mother, Dorothy Ruffing, during the final period of her life. She died April 20, 2004, just as I was bringing this volume to completion. I learned a great deal about the mystery of illness, death, and the communion of saints simultaneously from my mother and Elisabeth Leseur.

The Sisters of St. Joseph of Orange offered me extraordinary hospitality, friendship, and support throughout the entire eight months I stayed with them so I could be near my mother. I cannot offer enough thanks to President Katherine Gray and our longtime family friend Sister Judith Wemmer for their attentive presence and support through it all. Sister Anne Lynch helped with the final draft of the *Letters on Suffering*.

Finally, I am grateful to the Sisters of Mercy, who supported my request for the family leave I took in the fall that enabled me both to write and to spend more time with my mom, and to Sister Marilyn Gouilhardou, RSM, who expertly proofread the entire volume in many stages.

PREFACE

Wendy M. Wright

Not long ago a retired priest contacted me about a book he hoped to complete during the last active phase of his life. It would be a book about Christian saints for the journey, and he wanted to be inclusive, so, of the twenty portraits he planned to paint, he hoped to fashion ten of exemplary women. The problem, and this is why he had written to me, was that all the names he could come up with were women in vowed religious life. Could I recommend to him any well-documented stories of women enrolled in the ranks of the canonized who were lay people? Of course, I could not offer him a long list, and of the few examples I could come up with, other than some early martyrs, the spirituality of the women—Catherine of Genoa for example—was very much cast in the ascetic mold shaped by monastic life. Or a life was so singular—I think of the sickly Kateri Tekakwitha, the Lily of the Mohawks, who clung to her chosen faith despite being persecuted by members of her tribe—that it really belongs to one time and place. There is little documentation about women whose Christian Catholic faith was deeply realized precisely as lay persons.

Part of the problem in coming up with officially canonized female lay saints, of course, lies with the process by which the Roman Catholic Church recognizes those persons felt to be heroic practitioners of the Christian life. But the issue is deeper than this specifically ecclesial one. When one looks beyond the ranks of those who are formally recognized as worthy of liturgical veneration to the many other Christian holy persons whose names and stories are enthusiastically admired today, one finds that, while some are lay women, they are generally admired because of the dramatic narrative arc of their spiritual journey. Contemporary heroine Dorothy Day embraced radical poverty and offered uncompromising hospitality to the homeless and hungry on the streets of America's cities, and Maryknoll lay missioner Jean Donovan made the ultimate sacrifice of her own life for the people of El Salvador. Their witness compels admiration, even imitation, but their lives don't really mirror most of ours.

This focus on the unusual and the exceptional as characteristic of the heralded Christian life extends to the academic world as well. The last thirty years or so, with the Paulist Press Classics of Western Spirituality series leading the way, have been rich ones in the scholarly world for the discovery and recovery of the width, depth, and breadth of Christian spiritual traditions. Yet so many of the narratives and texts held up to us are of the unusual variety. As fascinating as are kataphatic visionaries, pursuers of the apophatic depths of the Godhead, bi-locators, martyrs, hermits, undaunted foundresses, and spiritual performance artists, and as important as they are for our understanding of the trajectory of the tradition, their stories rarely offer us a vision of the Christian life that finds us just where we are—in our little lives with our mundane responsibilities, so-so relationships, our probably pretty pedestrian joys and pains. Rarely do they take our breath away by a glimpse of the sheer simplicity and elegance of an ordinary life made transparent by being lived in faith.

And then there is Elisabeth Leseur.

"The Christian life is great and beautiful and full of joy," she wrote. When you begin to read the personal journal entries, letters, and writings on vocation and suffering that Elisabeth penned, you begin yourself to entertain just such a radical thought. Her story is both very ordinary and extraordinary, and it is that in a hidden, unpretentious way.

How can I describe Elisabeth Leseur in a manner that conveys some real sense of the presence captured by Janet Ruffing's lovely translation of her writings? She is very French. Her profound formation in the spirit of French-speaking Francis de Sales is evident. She studied and internalized the *Introduction to the Devout Life* that he wrote for lay women two centuries before she lived. She gave herself completely to God's animating life exactly as a wife, an aunt, a friend, a woman who struggled with illness, and as an avid student of the gospel and of contemporary thought. The Savoyard bishop's insistence that each "state in life" has its own spiritual practices and tonality shaped by the duties of that life is something she knew well. One can also hear the echo of Francis's injunction to "be what you are and be that well" as Elisabeth discovered the trajectory of her own spiritual pilgrimage: in her tenderness for her nonbelieving husband, in her silent evangelization of others through the practice of being a loving presence, in her probing correspondence with her spiritual friend Soeur Goby, in the integrity of her intelligent pursuit of her recovered Catholic faith, in the long diminishment that resulted from her breast cancer. There is as well in Elisabeth Leseur something reminiscent of two French Carmelite women whose lifespans overlapped hers. There is in her spirituality something akin to Thérèse of Lisieux's utterly simple, clear grasp of the mysteries of faith, something of Thérèse's "little way," and something reminiscent too of Edith Stein's inquiring mind, which applied itself with such penetration to matters of faith.

To read Elisabeth Leseur is to encounter the spiritual possibilities of late nineteenth-century and early twentieth-century Roman Catholicism, an era often overlooked by scholars of Christian spirituality as an age dominated by pietistic devotionalism and reactionary theology. Elisabeth Leseur did find redemptive meaning in the illness that finally claimed her life, but one cannot roll one's contemporary eyes at a distasteful "victim spirituality" or snigger at the thought that she was just mindlessly "offering it up." Rather, the depth at which Elisabeth explored the resources of the Catholic spiritual tradition of her day, both before and after her last illness, are revelatory both of her own deeply examined faith and of the inherent depth of that same tradition. Evident in her writing is the creative dynamism stirring the church of her day: the beginnings of historical criticism and liturgical renewal, the emerging Catholic social-teaching tradition and vital movements encouraging lay involvement, the artistic and philosophical explorations that would emerge in the French Catholic Revival. She also provides a stunning example of a convicted believer whose breadth of spirit and trust in the divine compassion at the root of all creation allowed her to live graciously and gratefully in a society and a marriage often hostile to or dismissive of faith.

Elisabeth Leseur's presence also seems to expand outward beyond the confines of her era and geographical location. Perhaps that is why she so rightly belongs in the Classics of Western Spirituality series. Her thought as recorded in these writings is spacious and expansive, at once balanced and pene-trating. Very little of it seems constrained by narrow or petty concerns. She was capable of a lyricism that is profoundly con-templative, sensitive to both the interior and exterior dynamics of a fully lived faith. Thus she could write expressively:

> Let us love. Let our lives be a perpetual song of love for God first of all, and for all human beings who suf-fer, love and mourn. Let deep joy live in us. Let us be like the lark, enemy of the night, who always announces the dawn and awakens in each creature the love of light and life. Let us awaken others to the spir-itual life.

Strangely, when I try to evoke her to entice readers to dis-cover her for themselves, I find myself conjuring up a man of the next generation, Dag Hammarskjöld, the Swedish secretary-general of the United Nations, whose personal spiritual note-book, *Markings*, was not made known until after his death. Elisabeth was not a public figure or an internationally known diplomat, but she, like Hammarskjöld, left a precious record of a remarkable inner spiritual journey that was all but hidden from contemporaries. Profoundly personal, the inner journeys these two undertook were not, however, privatized. They undergirded lives of intense service to others. They flowered in a spirituality at once social and intimate, sophisticated and utterly transparent.

Elisabeth's spiritual formation did not take place at the University of Uppsala, in the board rooms of international diplo-macy, or in the cradle of the Swedish Lutheran Church. Her for-mation was French and Roman Catholic, and the arena in which her wisdom was exercised was in her marriage, her extended family, and in the varied social and political circles in which she and her husband moved. Nevertheless, the spaciousness and maturity of her spiritual vision, like Hammarskjöld's, seem almost universal.

Whether or not the readers of this volume think that official ecclesial recognition of the saints—those who give witness to the Christian life in a heroic or exemplary way—is a valuable or even necessary practice, they will nevertheless be compelled by the gentle, luminous witness to that life that Elizabeth Leseur has left us.

INTRODUCTION

Elisabeth Leseur (1866–1914)

Born into the privileged Arrighi family during the last half of the nineteenth century and dying on the eve of World War I, Elisabeth Leseur creatively and originally responded to the spirit of her own times in the way she understood and practiced her faith as a lay Christian. Elisabeth Leseur deserves to be better known as an important lay figure in the history of Christian Spirituality.[1] The specific challenges she confronted were many. First, her marriage at the age of twenty-three to Félix Leseur profoundly threatened her faith, and she struggled to regain that faith and develop it into a robust committed dedication to God. She found herself married to an unbeliever in an age of unbelief in France, and she adopted an apostolic strategy of unconditional loving presence. Despite this difference of religious belief, the Leseurs show evidence of deeply loving each other throughout their marriage.

Second, her approach to spirituality from the beginning of her adult conversion was always thoroughly lay in character. She developed a rule of life that maintained a set of priorities related to her responsibilities within her marriage and family. The couple remained childless, which seemed to bother Elisabeth more than Félix. Elisabeth responded to this lack by maintaining deep involvement with their extended families, including giving special attention to her niece and nephews, as well as by developing her own intellectual gifts through a disciplined program of study. Her studies included languages, literature, philosophy, and Christianity.

Third, she experienced many forms of suffering in her life. She endured many illnesses, beginning with an intestinal abscess that developed toward the end of their honeymoon and that never completely healed. That illness was followed by a carriage accident

1

(1895) in which she was struck on her side by the horse's hoofs. From 1908 on she had recurrent problems with her liver, forcing her to spend a great deal of time resting during each episode. In 1911 she developed breast cancer, from which she died in 1914. She learned how to turn this physical suffering as well as her spiritual isolation into a form of prayer and participation in redemption, making a pact with God offering her sufferings for the conversion of her husband. In addition to her physical and spiritual sufferings, Elisabeth constantly confronted deaths and life-threatening illnesses within her family. Her father died just after her honeymoon, when she was too ill to attend his funeral. Her youngest sister, Marie, died as a child from typhoid fever, and her younger, adult sister Juliette died from tuberculosis in 1905. Her nephew, Roger, died in childhood as well. Her belief in the communion of saints helped give meaning to these experiences of suffering and loss.

Fourth, she had an expansive view of the world from extensive travel and reading. The Leseurs counted among their friends, musicians, artists, writers, philosophers, politicians, doctors, and lawyers—believers and unbelievers alike. She recognized a special call to minister to the needs of this segment of society.

Fifth, she participated in the developing lay movements of her time, deeply affected by the social teachings of Leo XIII and the evangelizing efforts of the embryonic Catholic Action movement. She also embraced the budding developments in Catholic theology and spirituality—the beginnings of historical criticism and better understandings of the scriptures, the early liturgical movement as promoted by Dom Guéranger, and the return to the importance of the Eucharist as fostered by Pius X. She was deeply engaged in trying to harmonize faith and reason, faith and the new democracy, faith and culture. In many ways she was clearly an exceptional prototype of a happily married lay woman, educated in her faith, immersed in society, and carrying out in a secular context the specific forms of the lay apostolate that Vatican II would envision half a century later.

INTRODUCTION

The Leseurs

Introduced by family friends, Elisabeth and Félix were immediately attracted to one another.[2] It was certainly love at first sight. They both loved music, culture, literature, opera, and travel. Félix was just finishing his medical degree and expected to serve in the colonies. Elisabeth assumed that they came from similar family backgrounds—their fathers were both lawyers and both families were Catholic. Elisabeth believed that "Félix was everything she desired in a husband."[3] He had been educated by the Oratorians, and Père Bordes, an Oratorian and one of Félix's teachers, presided at their wedding. On the eve of their wedding Elisabeth discovered that Félix was no longer a practicing Catholic and had become a complete agnostic.

He promised to respect and support her practice of the faith, even accompany her to Mass at times, but after a short period Félix discovered he was anything but neutral and increasingly tried to influence her toward unbelief. He became a journalist and worked for two of the most anticlerical journals in France. In 1892 he replaced his good friend, Maurice Ordinaire, as director of the *République Française*, founded by Léon Gambetta,[4] when Ordinaire was offered a cabinet post by the undersecretary of state for the colonies. Ordinaire was first a deputy and senator of Doubs, then vice-president of the Senate and a close friend of Félix. The Ordinaires lived near Jougne, where the Leseurs eventually purchased a summer home in 1902. A year after joining the *République Française*, Félix moved to *Siècle* in order to write editorials on colonial questions. He hoped thereby to launch his colonial career. When his friend, Théophile Delcassé (1852–1923) became minister of the colonies, he offered Félix a posting that would have taken the Leseurs to Africa in 1894. Fearful about Elisabeth's delicate health, her family intervened and in 1894 invited Félix to become part of their prestigious insurance company, thus ending Félix's ambitions for Foreign Service.[5]

This brief description of Félix's friends and activities gives some indications of the social and political circles in which the Leseurs entertained, worked, and socialized. Félix was immersed in the anticlerical, rationalist thought of his day and wanted

3

Elisabeth to join him. He had a library that included Protestant writers, rationalists, and modernists. Elisabeth's habits of recollection and her practice of the faith began to weaken in the whirl of travel, social life, entertaining, and Félix's constant activity.[6] He describes himself as returning after their evening meal to the office or to public or cultural functions and coming home in the early morning hours. Elisabeth began to study Latin, which Félix could not criticize because it was not only the language of the church but of the classics as well. Sometime in 1898, when Elisabeth mentioned she had nothing to read, Félix suggested she read Ernest Renan's (1823–92) *Origines du Christianisme*. Instead, she chose Renan's *La vie de Jésus* from his library.

This book marked the turning point in her spiritual crisis. Elisabeth was not at all persuaded by Renan's account and quickly dissected his argument. In order to justify her critique she turned to the Gospels and was deeply affected spiritually by reading them daily.[7] She engaged in a program of reading, study, and prayer, and she began writing in her journal one year later, after the Leseurs returned from their trips to Spain and Germany. Eventually, she assembled a library of two hundred volumes of philosophy, morality, spiritual writing, apologetics, and religious biography. Although Elisabeth certainly participated in all of the popular forms of religion characteristic of nineteenth-century French Catholicism, her strong mind and the intellectual environment of their social circle compelled her to find answers to her pressing religious and social questions through reading.

In 1903 the Leseurs accepted an invitation from friends to join them on a pilgrimage to Rome. There, at the tomb of St. Peter, Elisabeth describes a religious experience that marked the beginning of a "new life" for her, confirming her in her renewed commitment to Christian life. Finding herself isolated in her religious practice and deep faith, Elisabeth confides her resolutions, rule of life, significant insights into herself, and her vocation in a private journal, *Journal et pensées pour chaque jour*.[8] She had no one to talk to about her unfolding spiritual life until she met Père Joseph Hébert, OP, in 1903, when a co-worker of Félix's asked her to be his sponsor for baptism.[9] Subsequently, Elisabeth sought spiritual direction from Hébert in the context of the sacrament of penance twice monthly when the Leseurs were in Paris (September to May) and when Elisabeth was well enough to leave her home.

Elisabeth, recognizing that faith is God's gift, prayed constantly for the conversion of her husband. She suffered deeply from the inability to share a life of faith, so meaningful and important to her, with her husband, with whom she shared everything else. The pact she made with God offering her suffering for his conversion convinced her that Félix would not only eventually return to Catholic practice but would also become a priest. Gradually, Félix became more respectful of his wife's religious practices and witnessed the consolation she experienced in prayer at Lourdes and when she received communion at home during her final illness. Félix also met some other religious people, Elisabeth's epistolary soul-friend, Soeur Goby,[10] and several priests whom Elisabeth assisted in fund-raising events and in pastoral ministry. His attitudes toward religion softened, but he had not returned to the faith before his wife's death. Elisabeth's sister Amélie urged her to preserve her journal instead of destroying it, as she had already instructed her sister to do. At that point Elisabeth decided to agree with her sister and thought the journal might help Félix understand her better after her death and be of some comfort to him through that spiritual understanding. Indeed, the bereft and grieving Félix returned to the Catholic Church in 1915 through reading Elisabeth's journal and feeling her presence guiding him from beyond the grave. Four years later he entered the Dominican community, becoming a priest, making Elisabeth's apostolate of prayer and suffering known and promoting her cause for canonization throughout his priestly life.

Elisabeth's spiritual evolution seemed to unfold in four distinct phases. From her marriage until 1897, Félix appeared to weaken her religious observance and seriously undermine her faith. In the first phase of her adult development from 1897 to 1898, Elisabeth underwent a spiritual crisis and recommitment to Christian faith. In the second phase, from 1898 to 1899, Elisabeth returned to her faith, strengthened by the crisis she had resolved interiorly. From 1899 to 1903, her third phase, Elisabeth progressed spiritually through her own solitary prayer, study, meditation, and writing. In the fourth phase, from 1903 to 1914, Elisabeth continued to grow spiritually through exchanges first with Père Hébert and subsequently with Soeur Goby.

Elisabeth Leseur's Spirituality

Marriage and Family

Elisabeth carefully integrated her family life and her spirituality. Tutored in devout humanism with Francis de Sales as her guide, she fully accepted his teaching that a life of devotion is fully compatible with marriage.[11] Since her conversion occurred nine years into her marriage, she assumed that this call to a deeper, more intimate relationship with God was to be lived as Félix's wife. Despite their inability as a couple to share faith as they shared everything else, every reference to her husband suggests a loving and mutually respectful relationship. She felt Félix loved her deeply and supported her by his presence, companionship, and expressions of affection. For instance, she wrote: "Some joyful days because of a present from Félix, and more because of the words that accompanied it—words so full of love that made me very happy. I do not deserve to be so loved, but I rejoice fully in it."[12] She felt Félix's love and support during her sister's death and her niece's first communion six weeks later,[13] and they enjoyed one another's company when they traveled together, visited friends, and summered in the countryside with Elisabeth's extended family. Despite their childlessness, Elisabeth consistently described a healthy and mutually loving marital relationship. In her letters she remarked frequently about how busy her husband was with no trace of resentment on her part. From his side, Félix was devoted to her and remained constant in his love and affection for her through her multiple illnesses. The devastation he describes when she died was evidence of the depth of his love and his emotional reliance on her.

She both took for granted the gender expectations of her role—managing the household, including the supervision of the servants, planning the necessary round of dinner parties, and responding to the charitable needs of the poor—and questioned restrictions on this role. (Her views on women will be explored separately.) She involved herself with her extended family—her mother, her sisters and their children. The children stayed for long periods of time at the Leseur's country home near the Swiss border, where they all spent quality time together. Elisabeth took an active role in encouraging the faith life of her niece and nephews by preparing them for first communion and writing spiritual treatises for both of them on this occasion.[14] The children loved their Aunt Bébeth and wrote postcards and notes to her as young adults; they seemed anxious to share their lives with her.[15] They were impressed by her hour of daily meditation when they were with her in Jougne, noting that they were not to disturb her during that time. Elisabeth's correspondence to family members and friends discloses a regular round of meal-sharing and visits with family and friends. These were simply the givens of the upper-class family life that Elisabeth embraced as part of her spiritual journey. This involvement with family as well as concerns related to both society and church characterize lay spirituality.[16]

Pattern of Devotional Life and Ascetical Practices

Elisabeth devised a flexible rule of life that organized her devotional and ascetical practices.[17] These she outlined in the second part of her journal, titled "Notebook of Resolutions," which spanned the years 1906–12. Despite the specific structure, she modified it by the two principles of flexibility and charity. She did not want her devotional life to interfere with either the comfort or needs of those she loved. She strictly followed her program when she was home alone and did not need to consider the rest of the household, and she was entirely flexible where others were concerned.[18]

She maintained a daily pattern of morning and evening prayer including meditation. She went to confession and communion every two weeks. She would have liked to communicate more often if she could have done so "without inconveniencing or displeasing anyone."[19] She made a one-day spiritual retreat monthly. This meant as much solitude as possible, more time in meditation, an examination of conscience, reflection on her life, and preparation for death. Annually, she tried to make a few days of retreat. Her letters indicate that by 1911, she felt fortunate to go to Mass and communicate three times a week.

She also organized her outer life as part of her spiritual program. She considered family and social responsibilities first—Félix lovingly headed the list. She carefully monitored what she said to him about spiritual matters, and by 1906 she had resolved to say as little as possible. Since she was relatively healthy, she adopted work she felt she could do, was actively involved with the poor, and sought to treat her servants as warmly as possible without crossing the boundary of familiarity. Finally, she developed an asceticism based on silence, self-giving, and austerity. Love determined all. What was the loving way to be, the loving thing to say, the loving thing not to do or say?

She defined each of these virtues in her own situation. Silence meant not imposing her illness, pain, or even graces on others. She actively sought to conceal her suffering and to avoid a natural tendency toward self-absorption when ill. She spoke about her interior experience only if she thought she could help another who sought spiritual guidance or emotional support from her. By self-giving she meant a radiant and active charity—real love expressed in every relationship and activity in her life. Finally, personal austerity meant that she avoided anything harmful to herself physically. "I need to preserve and try to improve my health, since it can be an instrument in the service of God and of neighbor. But in this illness…the precautions I must take, the discomforts it brings and the deprivations it imposes…there is sufficient opportunity for self-denial."[20] Any other choice related to personal austerity had to have a positive effect on some one else. For instance, she continually tried to be gracious, lively, and good company in social situations while at the same time concealing the pain caused by religious hostility on many of these occasions. Her ascetical choices were carefully ordered to charity. If they did not serve love or increase her intimacy with God, she did not do them.

Primary Influences on Elisabeth Leseur's Spirituality

There are complex and multiple influences on the spirituality of any single Christian. First, there is the melange that constitutes the historical period in which a person lives. For Elisabeth, this included the popular forms of French Catholicism that constituted the context in which she experienced sacramental life in the church and available resources for developing her own interior life. Second, there are the public examples of other notable Christians either immediately preceding a person's life or contemporary with a person's life. Third, there are spiritual writers both historical and contemporary who reflect, challenge, or nourish someone like Elisabeth, who had almost unlimited access to books and time to read them. Fourth, there are the particular circumstances that constitute the "givens" of a person's life to which each person creatively responds in the artful fashioning of a unique way of living.

Popular Religion

Several analyses of nineteenth-century spirituality agree on some of the main trends in popular Catholic piety in the second half of the nineteenth century. In 1854 the dogma of the Immaculate Conception was formerly defined and promulgated. In France this official impetus for Marian devotion was preceded by Catherine Labouré's vision of Mary in 1830 with the prayer invoking "Mary conceived without sin" and the striking of the Miraculous Medal, depicting the woman of the Apocalypse. It was followed in 1858 by Mary's appearance to Bernadette Soubirous at Lourdes, where Mary identified herself as the Immaculate Conception. Thomas Kselman describes a rather circular relationship in the way the church used these apparitions and the healings that accompanied them as affirming, almost proving, the dogmatic definition. By approving these apparitions and orchestrating the healing cults that grew up around them, the church supported the prophetic hope for healing and for a restoration of the religious faith in France.[21] In addition, as these pilgrimage sites developed, the devotions practiced included confession, Eucharist, the Rosary, or other popular devotions specific to the site.

Kselman aptly characterizes popular nineteenth-century French piety with its amazing array of devotions as manifesting three themes: the sentimentalization of Catholic piety; the guilt of the modern age and the need for redemption; and the virtues of poverty, simplicity, and humility. The sentimentalization of piety tended to increase the affective intimacy between the devotee and the object of devotion. This was part of a more general and sophisticated trend toward a religion of love rather than fear that was still quite strong in preaching and in the religious culture in general.[22] This trend could also represent the emphasis on the irrational and affective over reason in the face of nineteenth-century rationalism. Metaphors of family life were especially important. And in the nineteenth century the family was becoming a new locus of affective intimacy and friendship. The autobiography of Thérèse of Lisieux is a stunning example of this theme as well as the one that follows.[23]

The guilt of the modern age and its need for redemption underlay a dramatic increase in devotions throughout the nineteenth century that focused on the sins of the modern world and the role of prayer and suffering to make reparation for these offenses. There were at least three sources for this renewed emphasis. First, the French clergy consistently attempted to frighten their congregations into moral behavior through preaching and confessional practices that relied on fear of eternal punishment for moral transgressions, usually related to sexuality and blasphemy. Second, the social and political unrest in France, which destroyed the monarchy and finally developed into a republic, gradually separated church and state from one another. Thus, it became socially possible to express publicly one's agnosticism or atheism. Anxiety about the salvation of these skeptics and unbelievers required that those who continued to believe make up for this loss of religion in a formerly Catholic culture through prayer and reparation. Third, life-threatening illness and other forms of suffering remained a fact of human life. There is a psychic need that supports an appeal to the crucified Christ (or Mary, who suffers with him) that others might live.[24] Kselman suggests that the shift specific to nineteenth-century France was from concern about individual salvation to concern about the salvation of others. One could earn salvation or conversion for another through prayer and suffering. This, of course, included the ever present and growing devotion to the Sacred Heart, which developed its modern form through the visions of Saint Margaret Mary Alacoque at Paray-le-Monial from 1673 to 1675 and which reached its peak in the national vow in 1873 that initiated the building of the Basilica of Sacré-Coeur on Montmartre.[25] Sacré-Coeur was completed only on the eve of World War I. Of particular note in relationship to Elisabeth Leseur, Leo XIII consecrated the entire human race to the Sacred Heart in 1899, one year after Elisabeth's resolution of her own spiritual crisis.[26]

Finally, an emphasis on the virtues of poverty, simplicity, and humility was an antidote to the growing wealth, a higher standard of living for some, and the hubris of secular proposals for public life that threatened religious values. Virtually all of the visionaries of the nineteenth century were poor and rural. Their pastoral poverty contrasted with the growing urban wealth among some. In these visionaries the church began to celebrate the moral superiority of the poor. Their simplicity contrasted with rationalism and their illiteracy with the education of scholars. Humility ensured that neither visions nor prophecy would lead to pride. Their humility was linked to obedience and ensured humble submission to church authority.

In addition to these trends in popular Catholic religiosity, church elites in the nineteenth century began to influence devotional life through a renewed emphasis on liturgy; frequent reception of the Eucharist; a retrieval of the importance of scripture and the beginnings of historical criticism; and the more compassionate moral theology of Alphonsus Liguori, which gradually replaced the previous rigorist practices in the sacrament of penance. These were all strong influences on Elisabeth. She read Alphonsus in Italian.[27] Msgr. Louis Gaston de Ségur's promotion of frequent reception of communion was very widely known in Paris. Fénélon's *Letter on Frequent Communion* was republished by Dupanloup in 1855, selling 100,000 copies, and Pius X encouraged daily communion for religious orders and in 1915 allowed any Catholic in the state of grace to receive communion. As mentioned above, Elisabeth had a deep appreciation for the liturgical seasons, a theology of Eucharist, and meditated on the New Testament. She read the works of Dom Prosper Guéranger (1805–75), abbot of Solesmes, an authority on liturgy. She would have attended Eucharist with a hand missal.[28] Elisabeth also regularly read Dominican Marie-Joseph Lagrange's (1855–1938) *Révue Biblique* and comments on how much she appreciates it.[29] There is less emphasis in Elisabeth's writings on popular devotions than on a combination of interior recollection, meditation, and a sacramental practice that conflates the Real Presence of Jesus in the Eucharist with the Sacred Heart. She possessed a solid theological and philosophical understanding of Christianity. It is true that Elisabeth went to Lourdes in 1912, accompanied by Félix, primarily in gratitude for her nephew Maurice's recovery from a serious injury to his hand, but for herself as well. She went to the Chapel of the Visitation at Paray-le-Monial while her husband had legal business there. Her friend Soeur Goby prayed for her there at another time and also at the shrine of the Curé of Ars, Saint John Vianney (1786–1859). She also had a single volume of meditations for "souls devoted to the Sacred Heart," which she used and distributed. This strata of popular devotions appears to be the taken-for-granted background rather than the primary focus of Elisabeth's spirituality.

Lay Exemplars

Although Elisabeth's ecclesial milieu could scarcely be characterized as an age of the laity, she was aware of a number of prominent lay Catholics in France who had made unique contributions to the life of the church. Most notable among them were Frédéric Ozanam and Pauline Jaricot. Ozanam (1813–53), descended from a Jewish family, was a lawyer, author, and professor at the Sorbonne. He responded to the challenge of social radicals to Catholics who had ignored the plight of the poor by founding the Society of St. Vincent de Paul in 1833, a lay organization that "personally served the poor, the sick and the unemployed without distinction of race and creed";[30] the Society was organized at the parish and diocesan level.[31] Ozanam participated from the beginning in the development of a social Catholicism in France that looked beyond private charity to public reforms intended to address the situation of the impoverished masses. A specialist in Dante and Francis of Assisi, he joined his intellectual life with practical social action. Pauline Jaricot (1799–1862) was no less innovative, although her status as a single lay woman caused her great suffering. She founded the Society for the Propagation of the Faith,[32] which began as an association for the missions in 1820. Another group of lay men joined forces with her to solicit financial aid for the missions. Pauline made a private vow of perpetual virginity at the age of seventeen. She also founded the Union of Prayer in Reparation to the Sacred Heart, an organization for working girls. In 1826 she established Loretta House, a home for the same group.

Elisabeth also names Joseph de Maistre, Charles Montalembert, George Goyau, and other scholars, writers, diplomats, politicians, and philosophers who represented admirable efforts of lay Catholics to live their faith in the public arena as they came to terms with the shifting relationships of church and state in postrevolutionary France.

Spiritual Writers

Elisabeth mentions the spiritual writers she appreciated and who seemed to help her the most in the course of her letters and journal entries. Her husband also annotated her library, indicating which volumes she constantly read and reread, underlined, and which she talked about or distributed. Elisabeth lent her books to friends and acquaintances she thought would benefit from them. She simply replaced them if they were not returned. She considered this enlightenment of others through sharing resources one form of her intellectual apostolate.[33]

Elisabeth writes about reading the lives of Bridget of Sweden, Teresa of Avila, and Catherine of Siena. She claimed Teresa and Catherine as patron saints. Félix notes that she liked the *Dialogue of Catherine of Siena* very much. In addition to these mystics who encourage interiority, contemplative prayer, suffering, apostolic activity, and strength in women, there are strong Salesian influences on Elisabeth. Few other women would have possessed fifteen volumes of the works of Saint Francis de Sales. Contemporary writers whom she mentions include Msgr. Charles Gay (1815–92), Père Auguste Gratry, and the English Oratorian Frederick William Faber.

Elisabeth Leseur appears to have been a woman on a search, like so many lay women today. She was intellectual, deeply affectionate, and spiritual. From a loving and close-knit family, she sought love and affection in her marriage and maintained affectionate bonds with both families throughout her life. She extended this love and affection to her social circle of friends and acquaintances. She longed for the kind of friendship Francis de Sales describes in the *Introduction to the Devout Life* as almost a necessity for Christians who live their lives in a secular environment. This spiritual friendship she found only late her in her life when she met Soeur Goby. She had to find a way to God that included both head and heart, affective nourishment and intimacy, as well as a defensible, thoughtful history and philosophy she could draw on to justify her religious practice to herself and to unbelievers. She had to find a way to relate the spiritual dimension of human persons to reason. She wanted to find a way to discover the spiritual core of unbelievers who were genuinely good people but who had no faith. She had to do this as an upper-class, married woman in Paris.

Elisabeth echoes several major themes of Francis de Sales and Jane Frances DeChantal. She is convinced God is a loving God and that human happiness consists in experiencing that love in prayer and in embodying that love in life and action. Her childhood journal already shows the beginnings of this affective intimacy with God. According to historian and biographer Geneviève Duhamelet, more than twenty pages of this journal speak of death and heaven. She burst out with this exclamation to her parents: "That the good God will welcome you one day in his beautiful heaven, you are worthy of that. This is the wish of a little girl who loves you tenderly." And again, she reports being surprised in the midst of her meditation by a servant who cared for her. "My meditation today was on heaven; Oh, I had been transported in reading about that; I had stood up straight, crying, 'My God! Heaven!' Mamie came in at that moment and asked me if I was performing a play. I said to her no, but I thought that she wasn't sure. Oh! Heaven! Heaven! The house of the good God; and I would like to be there; what happiness it must be to see God!"[34] As an eleven year old, she reveals something of her ecstatic nature but also a Salesian sensibility of the goodness of a loving God and the realization that death is not to be feared because it means being with God. Her understanding of the Eucharist is similar in that she experiences God in her heart. As an adult, Elisabeth found in Francis de Sales a way to pursue this intimacy with God as a married woman. His focus on the cultivation of the virtues includes *douceur*, humility, simplicity, and poverty. Wendy Wright gives a number of meanings for *douceur*, a word almost impossible to translate into English:

> "Sweetness," "gentleness," "graciousness," "meekness," and "suavity." None of these translations do it full justice. *Douceur is* a quality of person that corresponds to the light burden offered by the Matthean Jesus to those otherwise heavy-laden. It connotes an almost maternal quality of serving that is swathed in tender concern. Salesian *douceur* also suggests a sense of being grace-filled, graceful in the broadest use of the term. This gracefulness extends from external demeanor—polite manners and convivial disposition—to the very quality of a person's heart—the way in which a person is interiorly ordered and disposed. Here one is reminded of the tradition of the *l'honnête homme* popular in the seventeenth century which stressed the harmony, beauty, and grace of the whole person and which De Sales saw as reflecting the beauty and harmony of God.[35]

This reflection of God dwelling in her, embodied in the gracefulness of her attentive, empathetic presence, became Elisabeth's apostolic strategy. She also aspires to simplicity of life and detachment from wealth, on which De Sales gives advice in "The Poverty of Spirit to Be Observed in the Midst of Riches" and

"How to Practice Genuine Poverty although Really Rich."[36] Elisabeth discreetly responded to the needs of those she knew with generosity and consistency. She gradually persuaded Félix to stop giving her expensive gifts by explaining that monetary gifts she could use for the poor would give her more pleasure. At the same time she deliberately dressed as attractively as possible to further her apostolic goals—attracting others to her joyful, radiant interior secret as well as honoring Félix's social standing, which required her to dress appropriately for numerous social events.

From Salesian spirituality she adopts De Sales's approach to austerity or mortification. One was to acquire the virtues through hidden mortification—using the circumstances of daily life to cultivate humility, patience, gentleness, and so on. Elisabeth exhibits this moderation of self-denial in the service of developing personal qualities that contributed to a peaceful and loving environment for those around her. She never aspires to the heroic or masochistic practices of self-inflicted physical pain or excessive fasting. Quite the opposite, her physical vulnerabilities to illness provide all the material she needs. Taking care of her health without making a project of it is her form of asceticism. Her asceticism is largely internal, monitoring her internal responses and resisting the depression and lethargy that are normal accompaniments of serious illness. This kind of hidden practice of virtue and prudent asceticism is also echoed in the writings of Teresa of Avila. Self-denial is ordered to love, as it is for De Sales. Finally, the gentle bishop of Geneva used his *douceur*, his gentleness, and his loving approach to the people in his region to win them back to the faith and to develop peaceful relationships with Protestants in this Calvinist stronghold. De Sales understood that hearts are won through love and gentleness, not through violence or hatred. Elisabeth found here the strategy she was looking for in her social life with intolerant and often bigoted atheists and agnostics. She learned in this environment not to debate but simply to be a radiant, God-filled presence.

As a lay woman, Elisabeth found able spiritual guidance in Francis de Sales. She also found much to support her in contemporary spiritual writers. French spirituality in the nineteenth century had a strongly moralistic tone that only gradually changed when the influence of Alphonsus Liguori began to soak into French consciousness and several other writers began to emphasize the centrality of love in the Christian life. Elisabeth's preparation for first communion consisted in a nearly two-year program supervised by her mother and her tutors. She was given a copybook and encouraged to write in it. The entries reveal the voice of a bright, lively girl who felt very loved within her family. This journal is more like a typical diary except for her struggles with her faults, as she sees them, accounts of positive experiences with confession, and a day-by-day account of her first-communion retreat.[37] The retreat focused on death, judgment, and the loving reception of the sacrament. Elisabeth was clearly interested in being good and choosing the path to heaven. She was required to write little essays after attending religious education in her parish church taught by Abbé Seguin, her parish priest.[38] In addition to meditating on this instruction, she was also supposed to monitor her behavior and dispositions through examination of conscience and to improve herself. Her mother's role was to accompany her to instructions and then to supervise her ongoing reflection.

When she begins her adult journal in 1898, she follows a similar procedure, except there are far fewer entries about daily life. She uses this personal journal to monitor her responses, to formulate a way of life, to record resolutions, and to remember the more significant insights and religious experiences that unfold. At this point in her life she has no one with whom to share her interior life. The journal becomes a way of recording, reflecting, remembering, and mirroring the important movements along the way, especially as she works out what this new life will mean for her and how it will affect her. It is not a record of mystical experiences or of visions. About these she is mostly silent. When she does note experiences of God's presence or of consolations, they typically accompany sacramental practice—the focus is eucharistic. It is Jesus present in her then. After 1911, when she cannot go out to Mass, she mentally prays in her room while imagining she is present in her friend Soeur Goby's chapel when her community is at prayer. She has a strong sense of Eucharist and holy communion—as sacrament, for making intentions, and as spiritual communion when ill. Part of the appeal of Elisabeth's spirituality is precisely its lack of emphasis on extraordinary mystical experiences. At the same time she exerted an extraordinary influence toward good on those around her.

Elisabeth writes of the influence of Msgr. Charles Gay. His *De la vie et des vertus chrétiennes considérées dans l'état religieux* was given in conferences to nuns, but he thought it might also be useful to priests and to devout laity. Based on seventeenth-century spirituality, it was strongly Christocentric, drawing on Saint Paul's teaching that each Christian participates in the body of Christ and on the Johannine theme of the vine and the branches. He wrote in his preface:

> What I have tried to do above everything else is to make Christ present in every part of this work;...the whole book should be simply and solely Jesus Christ. The person of Jesus should never be separated from His teaching. If that teaching is life, it is because it comes from Him who is the life: the blessed words that He speaks, the commands that He lays down, the counsels He suggests, the attractions He displays, the advances He makes, the helps He provides and the pledges He gives—all these are simply bringing life to His beloved human creatures, that life which is real, close, fulfilled, endless union with Him who is true life....The sum of our perfection and of our holiness—is our living union with Jesus.[39]

Gay differed from Pierre de Bérulle, the great seventeenth-century spiritual writer, by giving more importance to the human starting point for holiness. One needed to understand human nature and build on it. He proposes a harmony between the natural and the supernatural. Faith uplifts and perfects reason, it does not extinguish it. Christian life is nothing more than Christ living in us the life of the Trinity. Gay is less interested in the "states" and "dispositions" of Christ than in the Thomistic doctrine that grace builds on nature. Virtuous life is made possible by this indwelling of God.[40] Gay's emphasis on human development and on the role of fostering virtues useful in relational human life is one of the influences on

Elisabeth's program of meditating on a specific virtue each month as part of her retreat practice.

Two other nineteenth-century Oratorians were favorites of Elisabeth: Auguste Gratry (1805–72) and Frederick William Faber (1814–63). Gratry appealed to head as well as heart, while Faber was known for his emotionalism. Gratry taught moral theology at the Sorbonne, subsequently being elected to the Académie Française. He contributed to a renaissance in Christian philosophy with works that were both apologetic and polemic. He is criticized for placing excessive weight on emotion in the discovery of truth. In reflecting on the knowledge of God, he appealed to "a sense of the infinite" that is superior to intellect. Elisabeth considered him a kindred spirit. She clearly assimilated his sense of the supernatural and his assumptions about prayer. He wrote in *Les sources*, for instance: "Those who pray help everyone. They help their brothers and sisters often by the salutary and powerful magnetism of a soul who believes, who knows, and who wills. They are able to do all things as Saint Paul says through their prayers, supplications, and their graced actions for all."[41]

Frederick Faber, known for his effusiveness and emotional tone, clearly promoted a vision of a loving and merciful God. He was a prolific writer and a popular, successful preacher, drawing from the Italian and French schools of spirituality. He was an insightful spiritual director and had a reputation for shining a light into the dark places of human nature. Faber was also accused of being so lenient that he was "sending people to heaven on a featherbed."[42] Pierre Pourrat, an expert on the history of spirituality, characterized him as "ultramontane" in the true sense. He was deeply respectful of the pope and promoted an attitude of duty and love toward the papacy. Despite his expansive and florid style, Faber drew on many sources and presented his teaching in an original way. He placed a great deal of emphasis on "the soul's individuality," the psychosomatic unity of the individual, "the necessity of spiritual reading," and "friendliness to all men, especially to those not of the faith."[43] This last theme would have held particular appeal to Elisabeth as she sought to respond to the many unbelievers around her. She also appreciated his book on redemption, *Le Précieux Sang or le prix de notre salut*, which she read sometime after her surgery for breast cancer.

Church and Society

Duhamelet characterizes Elisabeth Leseur as ahead of her times in her thoughts about social concerns.[44] Perhaps this is an instance in which Elisabeth's own social location confronted her with systemic problems and her unique life circumstances drove her to find ways of understanding and responding to many of the serious social problems of her times. These included how Catholics participated in the changed political situation of the nineteenth century. Elisabeth lived during the Third Republic, but she looked back to the example and thoughts of committed Catholics during the Second Republic for guidance. Most wealthy Catholics allied themselves with hopes for a restored monarchy. Elisabeth did not. She recognized that democracy was going to stay, and she thought there was no incompatibility between democracy and Catholicism. She was also deeply influenced by the social teachings of Leo XIII, whom she greatly admired and whose wisdom she appreciated. She wrote in 1903: "I think a great deal about Leo XIII, recalling his beautiful face that is so present to me in spirit. If Catholics had listened to him better, many things would have been able to have been avoided."[45]

By the time Elisabeth Leseur recommitted herself to Christian practice in 1898, the church had reversed its position in relationship to social issues and church-state relationships. Leo XIII, in conjunction with White Father Charles Lavigerie (who hosted the Leseurs in Carthage when they visited Algiers) and others, advocated that monarchists give up their resistance to the Third Republic and for the sake of the common good of both church and society work within the legally constituted government and political institutions. In many ways this was a pragmatic solution, since Leo XIII wanted to maintain a positive alliance with France against Italy, which had taken control of the papal territories, and to encourage loyalists to recognize that the republic was unlikely to fail. The pope worked out these recommendations in *Au milieu des sollicitudes* in 1892. He recognized that a purely Catholic conservative party was unlikely to work. According to Adrien Dansette, the pope hoped for "the creation of a large conservative party of which Catholics would be the right wing and the moderate republicans the left and which would have the support of a majority of people in the country, thus creating an effective barrier against the irreligion of the radicals."[46] This represented a dramatic change for both clergy and well-placed laity in France.

At the same time, Elisabeth recognized that the Third Republic maintained an unjustifiable nonviolent persecution of Catholicism from 1877 until her death. She deplored the arbitrary expulsion of dedicated religious from French territory. The fact that the Third Republic had no real social program of its own besides attacking church institutions made Elisabeth's participation in Social Catholicism all the more urgent because this movement did attempt to address pressing social issues in a faith-based way.

Georges Goyau made the term Social Catholicism popular in France from 1887 on. At the time, with only a few exceptions, influential Catholics lacked any kind of social understanding of the responsibilities that came with middle-class privilege. The young Goyau "criticized the pharisaic attitude of the middle class who enjoined resignation in the name of the gospel on the lower classes, but failed to insist on justice from the upper classes."[47] Elisabeth wrote her sister Amélie about Goyau:

> I read the books of Goyau that really interest me. I will lend them to you. At least there are Catholics who are not hopeless and who do not believe in the restorative power of politics but who preach the action of words and example. These are hard words, entirely appropriate for the sort of people known as conservative, a good word that deserves to be better applied. He says with reason that when one preaches the gospel to these people and demonstrates to them that society (their society) is anti-Christian, one seems to be revolutionary, and the "good old times" for which they long are simply the time of their privileges and not that, even more

21

distant time, when all classes were imbued with Christianity.[48]

Adrien Dansette describes the historical development of social Catholicism in France as being governed by two dominant influences: one aristocratic and the other democratic.[49] The aristocratic influence relied on the authority of the upper classes and their ability to create and support institutions. Democratic influences drew from an alliance with the lower-middle classes and intellectuals. Albert de Mun, one of the leaders of right-wing Social Catholicism promoted the Oeuvres des Cercles, workers' groups organized by the aristocracy for the people. These mixed groups did give the privileged classes a better sense of the problems of the working classes and fostered a sense of the responsibility in the upper classes for workers. However, someone like Léon Harmel, who began as a right-wing member of the movement, was a factory owner and man of action who became increasingly democratic. He initiated reforms in his own factory that included a total set of services from cradle to grave.[50] He also promoted self-governing workers' associations.

Leo XIII's great 1891 social encyclical, *Rerum novarum*, contributed to a number of important issues in this already developing but as yet embryonic social consciousness. For the first time in a papal encyclical, "the faithful were solemnly warned that Christian principles applied to the conditions of the working class life and that they could not remain indifferent to the abuses of capitalism. Nor was it enough to provide...insufficient palliatives."[51] By 1892 Albert de Mun came to terms with accepting the Republic, following papal leadership. In the Chamber of Deputies he promoted a program based on *Rerum novarum* that all Catholics could unite behind. This program:

> 1. Included the formation of a professional organization intended to provide the working class with a voice in politics, to fix salaries, provide insurance funds for accident, sickness, and unemployment, and to establish a pension fund and arbitration machinery.

2. Included provision for the administration of property belonging to the corporations and looked forward to legislation limiting the hours of work, particularly of women and children, rendering certain forms of family property free from liability to distraint and encouraging profit sharing.[52]

Elisabeth Leseur seems to have drawn from both strands of Social Catholicism. When she writes a treatise on the Christian life for her nephew, she explicitly cites as exemplars Charles de Montalembert (1810–70) and Joseph de Maistre. Montalembert, politician, journalist, and orator, valiantly strove to bring about a rapprochement between the church and liberal society. He was relatively unaware of issues related to social justice, but he fought valiantly in parliament for the passage of the Falloux Law, which permitted the church to resume operating secondary schools and to establish independent theological faculties in Paris. He suffered a number of political setbacks at the hands of the ultramontanists and felt that Pius IX repudiated his positions in *Quanta cura* and the *Syllabus of Errors* (1864). Montalembert died loyal to the church during Vatican I, even though he disagreed with defining papal infallibility. He was a complex historical figure, deeply committed both to the church and to democratic political institutions. De Maistre (1754–1821), a survivor of the revolution and Leseur's second example of a Christian in public life, proposed a philosophy of providence working through tradition more than through individuals. Leseur encourages her nephew to join with other young men to promote "social peace and true charity and to work slowly and patiently at the necessary reconstructions" advocated by de Maistre.[53] Elisabeth envisions Christians working in partnership with God to bring about in new social forms the necessary support for achieving human destiny in and through the church. This text is addressed to a twelve year old, encouraging him to envision university life and some kind of public calling.

The Women's Movement

In a parallel first-communion essay written in 1905 for Marie Duron, her niece, Elisabeth Leseur expresses strong opinions about the role of women. These also occur in prior entries in her journal. Leseur firmly believes in education for women and wants a better education for Marie than she herself received. In her journal in 1899 she speaks of the advantage of women studying philosophy to develop a capacity for thinking clearly, to develop "a habit of reasoning," and to "remove the narrow ideas" they "pass on religiously to their sons"[54] She is keenly aware of the restrictions French society places on women's role and influence, yet she embraces the task of developing her own intelligence further through consistent study as a means to "understand one's times and not despair of the future." She argues for the philosophical equality of women and men on the basis of their reason, action, and love. She encourages women to reclaim their right to responsible action.[55] Finally, she fully embraces religious freedom and religious tolerance. These are not typical attitudes of the upper-bourgeoisie Catholic laity, most of whom still resisted the progress of democracy under the Third Republic.

Six years after these first journal entries and her reconversion to Catholicism, she continues to search for a way to unite faith and reason. She begins her argument with the rational nature of human persons, embracing the Tridentine teaching that God may be known through the light of natural reason. She then adopts Thomist assumptions that grace builds on nature and that faith is the basis for spiritual life. Christians share rational life with non-Christians, but grace (supernatural light) transforms the Christian through offering intuitive insight into the mysteries of suffering and death and the beauty and usefulness of activity in the world. Appreciating and embracing this faith requires "active acceptance, a lively assimilation of truths that surpass the mind." It is in this context that she places a woman's intellectual life as a Christian duty. She wants her niece "to be very well-educated, or even learned." From the perspective of faith, she wants her to be open-minded to the ideas of others and to discover "that which is true or fruitful among incoherent and varying ideas."[56] She takes the apologetic position of Justin Martyr that some truth can be found within most systems of thought. She suggests her niece will grow and develop humanly and spiritually through a serious education. She wants her to have an intellectual knowledge of the gospel and of church teachings, as well as of literary and scientific knowledge. She encourages a higher standard of education for women than was common in her day so that Marie can better fulfill her role as wife and mother, and also take her place in society.

Although the specifics of this social role beyond the home remain vague, Elisabeth clearly reflects raised expectations for women resulting from early stages of French feminism. Women's suffrage was debated from the 1880s on, and a new divorce law was passed in 1884, allowing a woman to initiate a divorce. However, the more pressing goal for French feminists "was equal rights for women within the family under law."[57] A second pressing issue was the attempt to secularize girls' secondary schools. The purpose seemed to be to undermine the faith of young women rather than to improve their educational prospects. The government did not intend to achieve full equality in education for both boys and girls. The single feminist volume in her library was written by Msgr. Félix Dupanloup.[58] Although this writer was not interested in improving the content of girls' education in the beginning, in another book he firmly supported raising the standard of girls' education because he thought "a solid education which improved their level of general culture would at the same time serve to give them a firmer grasp of their religious faith."[59] Private Catholic initiatives in response to the separation of church and state in 1905 included Mlle. Desrez's opening the École normale catholique in 1906 and the founding of the École normale libre at Neuilly in 1908, where girls were prepared for the exams of the higher educational system in a Catholic atmosphere.[60]

Elisabeth herself had been educated at home by tutors and later became one of the first pupils of her women tutors when they opened their own school. The curriculum included French, piano, and literature, among other subjects. Elisabeth, however, undertook a solid program of study after she married, learning Latin, Russian, Italian, and English, as well as studying philosophy. She was gifted in languages and read significant literature in each of the languages she mastered. She read extensively and recommended that women do some intellectual work every day.

James McMillan argues that the philanthropic work of middle- and upper-class women who sought to address pressing social concerns was one avenue that led women to feminism.[61] Women came to play an increasingly important role in various forms of Catholic Action. Elisabeth Leseur participated in three typical forms of these projects. She founded a home for young working women in Vésinet.[62] She worked with other Catholic women in the parishes in the northern suburbs of Paris near St. Denis, visiting women confined to their homes through illness or with their children. And she prepared children for first communion among this same population. Finally, when she was too ill to leave her home to do this work, she served as the secretary for La Ligue des Femmes Française. This was one of two major organizations of Catholic women who joined with the bishops in Catholic Action, a program of apostolic and charitable work supervised by and extending the pastoral work of the clergy. This movement, fostered by confraternities, sodalities, and other church-based organizations, preceded the retrieval in Vatican II of a stronger role of the laity in all aspects of the church. Gerard Cholvy and Yves-Marie Hilaire describe the rapid growth of these chapters of the two women's leagues. These women reanimated existing efforts within parishes and initiated new ones. For example, a listing of foundations by these women's groups by 1910 included 124 libraries, 121 clubs for young men, 7 holiday camps for children, 24 day nurseries, 42 housekeeping schools, 18 study circles, 14 endowments, 45 sewing rooms, 43 secretarial schools, and 11 aid societies. Committees organized the teaching of catechism, and both women's groups had their own newspapers, which spread their work and ideas even further.[63] The women held regular conferences and spread the cult of Joan of Arc among women. La Ligue des Femmes Française was particularly successful in Doubs, the region of the Leseurs' summer home, "in a parish where twenty women assist at Mass, and when the league is organized, two hundred will come."[64]

Cholvy and Hilaire assert that both major Catholic women's groups, as well as those espousing the Catholic Social movement, tried to contribute to the programs of both Leo XIII and Pius X in "going to the people" with real dedication while avoiding anything that appeared to be condescending. Elisabeth's writings reflect this agenda. According to Cholvy and Hilaire:

> It was a question of raising up profoundly believing women in each parish, cultured, good managers of their households, devoted to others and apostles among the families they visited so systematically. This adult pedagogy helped close the gap so harmful to marital harmony because of the difference between male and female education. In this period of rising feminism and on the eve of the Great War, during which women assumed heavy responsibilities, a new type of Catholic appeared.[65]

Elisabeth was among these, looking toward a better future for women and for a return to Catholic belief in France. Her feminism was an outgrowth of her social concerns and her desire to be an apostle. While more radical feminists had direct political and economic goals, Elisabeth sought social change in the service of the spiritual or "moral regeneration of society."[66]

The Communion of Saints

The theological theme that most informs Elisabeth Leseur's spiritual understanding and practice is a comprehensive intuition into the mystery of the communion of saints. Emilien Lamirande states that she "made the dogma of the communion of saints the great reality of her life, finding in it the Christian meaning of her friendships, her bereavements, her responsibilities, and her worries about those dear to her."[67] She returns to this theme in all of her major writings. She describes how she understands this doctrine in her journal, in her letters on suffering, in her first-communion treatises to her niece and nephew, and even in her letter to Jeanne Alcan, published under the title "Advice to an Unbeliever."

For Elisabeth, the communion of saints was both a philosophical and a faith reality. In Adrien Dansette's evaluation entitled "Catholic Revival among the Elite" he describes a new climate at the end of the nineteenth century, just prior to World War I, in which "cases of acceptance of the Church's teaching and of return to the faith were too frequent to be regarded as exceptional."[68] He gives a number of specific examples of prominent returnees, especially writers, from 1905 on. Relevant to Elisabeth's history was the philosophical influence of Henri Bergson (1859–1941).[69] Bergson helped her develop a spiritual vision of the hidden supernatural life of each person, participating in a great exchange of spiritual goods in the communion of saints. Félix reports that Elisabeth died with Jacques Maritain's volume on Bergson on her bedside table.[70] It was Bergson who released the Maritains from their metaphysical anguish, enabling them to overcome their Sorbonne-induced skepticism. Catholic literary figures of this period stressed a Catholic view of the human person and society in their writings. These literary figures included Paul Claudel, Charles Péguy, Louis Le Cardonnel, Lucy Félix-Fauré Goyau,[71] Francis Jammes, Léon Bloy, René Bazin, and Henri Bordeaux. Elisabeth, as mentioned above, was deeply influenced in her thinking by Georges Goyau. According to Dansette, Goyau believed these writings "were dominated by the idea of the communion of saints and it was this that gave them their enthusiasm."[72]

The doctrine of the communion of saints has historically carried a twofold interpretation. During any epoch one or another of these strands has been dominant. Its earliest meaning seems to have been a "communion in holy things." This meant participation in the intimate sharing of life with Jesus and the followers of Jesus through the sacraments of initiation and a life of discipleship. One shared in the sacred mysteries, the eucharistic meal that constitutes the community of believers. The second meaning is related to the cult of the saints: a communion among holy persons, living and dead, especially the martyrs. By Elisabeth Leseur's time the doctrine implied an underlying social solidarity in grace that in turn implied the ability of individual Christians to effect good for the whole body of the church. A contemporary of Elisabeth's wrote this interpretation in 1904:

> Through the sacrament of initiation the baptized become members of the body of the Church: a body whose head is Christ, whose members are all the righteous, dead, living, and to come, from the beginning of the world until its final consummation. In addition, the holy angels themselves, to whatever hierarchy they belong, form part of this society. By entering into the Catholic Church, the new Christians thus find themselves in communion with all the saints of earth and heaven.[73]

Elisabeth's writings both assume and explicitly express this interrelated community among the living and the dead, as well as those yet to be brought into its web of relationship. This notion of a final consummation, yet to come, fuels her hope that the future lies in God's hands and that she will be reunited with her beloved friends and family with God in heaven. Elisabeth clearly expresses a sense of these temporal dimensions of the mystery. All the living participate in this Christic life. The living include those who enjoy eternal life as well as those presently on earth. Among those on earth, a supernatural, spiritual communion exists among believers independent of physical proximity through partaking of the Eucharist—effecting literally a communion in the Risen Christ among everyone anywhere in the world who shares in faith or in the sacrament. This supernatural communion extends beyond the moment of reception of communion to a union of hearts and minds in personal prayer. Thus praying for one another's intentions, uniting together in offering sacrifices or being lovingly present to another in love, and engaging in the spiritual or corporal works of mercy are all activities expressive of this communion.

In his treatment of the communion of saints, Thomas Aquinas combines these themes of participation in the good things of the church and the interchange between the persons themselves. *The Catechism of the Council of Trent* adopted this approach. Emphasizing the relations that exist between the members of this communion, Félix Leseur reported that Elisabeth had a much underlined copy of this catechism among her books. Aquinas's concluding section about the church on earth stated:

29

We should realize that not only is the power of Christ's passion communicated to us but that the merit of this life and of all the goodness achieved by the saints is also common to all those in charity, because all are one, according to Ps.118.63. "I partake, Lord, in the good things of all who fear you." It follows that whoever is in charity partakes in all the good that is done in the entire world. But those for whom that good was especially intended have a special part in it. For one person can make satisfaction for another....Through this communion, therefore, we obtain two things: first, participation in all the merits of Jesus Christ; then the communication of one person's good to another.[74]

According to this theology, the members of the communion of saints on earth can effect the spiritual good of others through intentional practices that draw on the grace of Christ. They can obtain spiritual benefits in the future lives of those on earth for whom they pray or offer their sufferings in the present. They can do this only through their membership in the spiritual body of Christ. Thus, they share in the power of their head.

It is in this context that Elisabeth prays and offers her sufferings for her husband's conversion. Her vision here is deeply relational. From the time of her first communion she had a vivid sense of heaven as God's presence, and she looked forward to a reunion of the living and the beloved dead with God in heaven. Reflecting on her sister's death, she describes to Soeur Goby this sense of continuity in loving relationships and their reunion in God: "How good it is to love and to know that these important loving relationships come from God and will return to him, and that after having grown through sorrow, they will end in joy and in the most radiant union!"[75] Thus, heaven meant shared life with God and reunion with all of her beloveds. In relationship to her husband, she could not bear to imagine heaven without Félix. She longed for a fuller communion of shared life in God than they were ever able to enjoy during their marriage. It was this she wanted so passionately and for which she made her secret pact with God.[76]

Personal Vocation

A corollary of Elisabeth's deep belief in the communion of saints was her sense of her personal vocation. She records her thinking about vocation in the section of her journal titled "Daily Thoughts":

> God, in giving us life, gives each of us a mission to accomplish and a role to fulfill in his eternal plan. The most important thing, then, is to recognize this particular mission, to discern the divine will in our life, and then to work to make of our entire life and death a means of salvation for ourselves and our brothers and sisters.[77]

From almost the first page of her journal, after her spiritual conversion, she instinctively knew whom she was to serve. Her second journal entry describes her particular call as a Christian beyond her marriage and responsibilities to her extended family. "I want to love with a special love those whose birth, religion, or ideas separate them from me; it is those especially whom I want to understand and who need me to give of what God has given me."[78] In several entries that follow she shares her understanding of this call. She must try to understand others. To do so she engages in respectful and thoughtful dialogue, listening carefully to those who confide in her, seek her advice, or reveal something to her of their spiritual reality. She reads incessantly in an attempt to understand the social, cultural, and religious questions of her times. She collects a library, not only for herself but for the benefit of others. Conversion begins with a change of mind and heart. She attempts to reach hearts through her unconditional, radiating love. She reaches minds through education, shared reading, and earnest search for truth. In her journal she describes this as an intellectual apostolate. She is an apologist for faith through a strategy of unconditional love and engaged, respectful dialogue.

She realizes that her own transformation is paramount. God can work through her with her cooperation. She recognizes that her ministry is not directed at grand projects or addressed to the anonymous masses but rather to one individual at a time. She excels in an interpersonal ministry of spiritual accompaniment, an absolute respect for the integrity of another, of the other's "soul."

She becomes in her own way a gentle guide and a spiritual teacher through these conversations and through the letters that followed after the conversations. These letters often contain further reflection, a desire to express something more clearly with an exquisite delicacy to the particular person she addresses. Her correspondents kept these letters, treasuring them and rereading them.

Her ministry to unbelievers is particularly remarkable. Henri Brémond judges that Elisabeth's most important contribution to Christian spirituality is her religious tolerance; her respect for each person's spiritual path; and her love of Jews, unbelievers, and atheists.[79] Brémond places Elisabeth's approach in contrast to another attitude reported by Père Hébert to Félix. Père Hébert had shared Elisabeth's writings with a very distinguished man. Hébert was shocked, almost scandalized, by this man's response. He criticized Elisabeth for not having any hatred![80] Elisabeth suffered enough religious intolerance and hatred to banish it from her own behavior and feelings.

Elisabeth refused to relate to the people she knew through polarizing labels of any kind. She expresses in some of these letters her awareness of prejudice toward Jews and commiserates with her Jewish friends. She recognizes the danger of religious fanaticism in its violence and dehumanizing disrespect of the other.[81] Her religious concern for unbelievers betrays little anxiety about their salvation. She is convinced that those who live good lives and devote themselves to doing good are spiritual and participate in some way in the communion of saints through their basic concern for human good. There exists a human solidarity in good or evil prior to explicit faith in God. She appears to be convinced, as Pius IX taught in 1863, "We are aware, as you are, that those who labor under invincible ignorance with regard to our holy religion and who scrupulously obey the natural law and its dictates, which are written in men's hearts by God, and are resolved to show their obedience to God by decent living may with the help of the divine light and grace attain eternal life."[82]

Elisabeth appreciates that faith is God's gift and that unbelievers, agnostics, and even lapsed Catholics have not necessarily rejected God or faith. Faith is a grace, and she describes their situation: "There is a veil between them and God, a veil that allows only a few rays of love and beauty through. Only God, with a divine gesture, may part this veil, and then the true life shall begin for them"[83] The same entry connects this theological view with the communion of saints:

> And I...believe in the power of prayers that I unceasingly offer for them. I believe in [prayer] because God exists, and because he is the Father. I believe in this mysterious reality that we call the communion of saints. I know that no cry, no desire, no yearning of our inmost depths is lost, but all go to God and through him to those who inspired us to pray. I know that only God effects our intimate transformation, and that we can only point out to him those we love, saying, "God, make them live."[84]

This sense that in the economy of grace nothing is lost—no effort, no prayer, no suffering—consoled her to the very end. She struggled with darkness, with a lack of sensible consolation, and with her husband's lack of faith in her lifetime. As the above passage so clearly states, only God transforms, only God can withdraw the veil. The intercessor trusts that God will eventually bring her desires to fruition, but she neither expects nor demands that they occur on any time line other than God's. This attitude bespeaks her respect for the unique way God and an individual human person communicate with each other in the depths of the human spirit. This relationship often remains unavailable to any observer. Elisabeth trusts in God's providence and in God's loving desire to share life in some way with all humanity.

Suffering

As Elisabeth's physical and emotional sufferings began to accumulate, she grew to understand that her vocation was essentially a contemplative one, since God had deprived her of activity.

She became an intercessor through her prayer and suffering, She embraced her suffering as part of her vocation. Unlike other mystics before her, she did not seek to increase her physical sufferings in any way. There is little masochism here. She seems, rather, to use ascetical means to resist the limitation and tendency to self-absorption that often accompanies chronic illness. She tries to live her life as fully as possible within the limitations imposed by her various illnesses.[85]

In many ways Elisabeth makes a virtue out of necessity. She experienced significant suffering on many levels over a long period of time. She learned to put physical suffering in perspective. She infused her involuntary suffering with a surplus of meaning through her belief in the communion of saints, through which she understood that her sufferings could benefit others in genuine and profound ways known only to God. Elisabeth believed that suffering accepted and offered to God accomplished greater good for others than intercessory prayer or charitable actions. She believed that God's hidden action could work more effectively through suffering, both in transforming the one who suffered in this way and in gracing others through the great exchange in the communion of saints. Thus, her deeply mystical sense of the communion of saints undergirds her approach to the meaning with which she endows her suffering.

In her letters to Soeur Goby she comments many times on these assumptions. She describes the suffering people experience when they witness the suffering of those they love and seem powerless to help them. "Suffering is so powerful and obtains so much; an hour spent in pain united to the Cross can do more than hours consecrated to the poor, to action, and according to this very beautiful saying: 'Suffering is also a sacrament.'"[86] Although she believes in the efficacy of suffering, nevertheless she prays for the complete healing of Soeur Goby's mother. She supports her friend by empathetically witnessing her distress over her mother's suffering. She asserts a positive value to it, but she does not encourage her to relinquish the desire for her mother's recovery.

In a letter written a month later Elisabeth reflects further on this kind of suffering. There is an educative aspect when those we love suffer. Experiencing only our own sufferings does not allow us fully to know suffering. She draws on the example of Jesus, who shares in the sufferings of those he loves. She advises:

> Let us raise our eyes toward him, when sorrow or anxiety overwhelm us: and let us place our burden gently in his blessed hands and it will seem less heavy to us. Then let us take our miseries, our anxieties, our private heartbreaks and put them in his heart, so that from that heart they may go to God, then shower down on souls by that same royal road of love and become for others spiritual graces and joys.

She continues:

> The stoics used to say: "Suffering is nothing," and they were not telling the truth. But, more enlightened, we Christians say: "Suffering is everything." Suffering asks for and gets everything; because of suffering God consents to accomplishing all things; suffering helps the gentle Jesus to save the world. At times, when I feel overwhelmed by the immensity of my desires for those I love, by the importance of what I have to obtain for them, I turn toward suffering. I ask suffering to serve as the intermediary between God and them....Suffering is the complete form of prayer, the only infallible form of action. So, my beloved sister, may suffering accomplish what we desire, may it obtain the realization of our desires, may it benefit these dear people and praise God![87]

This passage suggests several important strategies Elisabeth adopts to discover some value and meaning in suffering. Most important is the relationship with God she discovers in suffering. She turns her suffering over to God; she places it in the Heart of Jesus who places it in God's heart. She does not bear suffering alone. She resists the isolation that often accompanies suffering. She suffers in communion, in the presence of God. She is not alone in her suffering because God is with her in it.

Second, she is aware of a long-standing spiritual teaching that suffering is educative. There is something to be learned from suffering. At one stage of the spiritual life, suffering creates a condition that opens a person radically to grace. Unable to bear suffering stoutly alone, as the stoics might encourage, this inability drives one toward God and opens one to God's grace as it manifests itself within this experience.

Third, by this time she has already discovered a fundamental spiritual truth that at an even more basic stage of the spiritual life facing various forms of suffering results in a gradual increase in one's capacity to suffer, to discover what John Dunne calls "the indestructible part of the self."[88] In this experience of surviving frustration, lack of gratification, or physical pain, the self is weaned from its initial narcissism and becomes less dependent on immediate gratification. A certain amount of suffering strengthens the self, or at least enables it to discover that it may be stronger than first imagined.

Fourth, she understands that within the full itinerary of the spiritual journey, certain forms of unrelieved suffering accomplish the profound spiritual transformation called the "dark night" by John of the Cross. Mystics have frequently used pain as something of a "wedge in consciousness" that creates a split between ego and non-ego, and that can thus support a breakthrough into full mystic consciousness.[89] Elisabeth refers to this kind of dark night in her letters on suffering. She suffers an eclipse of God and of consolation in her struggle with breast cancer. Physical pain overwhelms her, weakens her physically and morally, and deprives her of joy. Yet she resists a feeling of being abandoned by God. She rallies her hope, and she infuses her suffering with potential meaning for the future. She writes:

> For several weeks God has seen fit not to treat me too gently physically and morally. After having been treated by God like a spoiled child, it's only fair that I be led along a rougher road, and for almost two years that's the way it has been. My dear sister, how well I understand now what the ascetic authors say about this straight and painful path that must be walked in order to reach the

First Light. I'm catching quite a glimpse of the "dark night" of Saint John of the Cross! When God drew me to him, by some wonderful means without any human intermediary, he *lavished* me with such graces and flooded me with such ineffable joys that I have been completely conquered forever. But until now he was the perpetual giver, doing everything for me who had never done anything for him, who had, on the contrary, worked against him. That was all well and good. It was just that the time came for personal work, for labor, for effort; the time for self-giving, for self-denial, for sacrifices; the time when I would finally be able to offer something to the one who had given me so much. I had already suffered when my sister died and because of my health, but to suffer in the joy of the spirit is nothing. That's why the trials of the soul, the most intimate and subtle heartaches had to come to purify, and transform. This divine work continues, and I daily offer my sorrows or my efforts to my unique Friend, to the one who alone knows me in my depths.[90]

One of the ways she does this is through her correspondence with Soeur Goby, whom she experiences as able to share her religious world view, to support her by her prayers and sufferings, and to be her soul-mate and human companion through this experience. She writes:

How open I can be with you my friend, so easily and simply. The atmosphere in which I live is hardly favorable, from a religious point of view, to this kind of self-disclosure. I run into people in distress, suffering hearts, and hostile or indifferent minds every day. And from this contact arises considerable suffering and at the same time an interior consolation from trying to do a little good.[91]

She finds relief for the first time from her spiritual isolation, about which she comments throughout her journal.

In these letters to Soeur Goby, Elisabeth also reveals the depth of her compassion. One of the fruits of her various forms of suffering is compassion. When she encourages her correspondent to embrace the particular form of suffering entailed when witnessing the suffering of someone she loves deeply, it is clear that Elisabeth knows what she is talking about. She is aware of her own helplessness in the face of the death of family members, especially Juliette's death. The intensity of Elisabeth's emotional responses has not been numbed by her own suffering and illnesses. She continues to feel deeply and to suffer emotionally as a result. She witnesses her friend's suffering; she is also aware of how much Félix suffers when he witnesses the particularly acute and intense periods of physical suffering in the course of Elisabeth's illness.

Elisabeth believes that entering into suffering with God can be used to obtain the specific graces sought for others through conscious suffering. She thinks that suffering is the most efficacious way to achieve them. Yet there is paradox in her approach. She believes and trusts that this is, indeed, the case. But she also knows that she can only accept and offer her suffering, and hope that God will do what she wishes. In other passages she places all into God's hands. In fact, she does not see her husband converted before her death. Despite this disappointment, she trusts God: "Only God can pull back the veil."

But why suffer rather than try to change the situation or escape suffering? Elisabeth seems to suggest that suffering is more efficacious than the active life or the works of mercy. While she idealizes Soeur Goby's spiritual and physical care of the ill and dying, there is often some escape from emotional and spiritual pain through agency. The "I" can still "do" something about which "I" can feel pleased or proud and thus avoid feelings of futility and helplessness. Elisabeth simply thinks suffering embraced and accepted (not sought or increased) is potentially less self-centered, more open to God, and perhaps more valued by God because the person chooses to love God for God's own sake. It is a purer form of love.

Elisabeth did understand social evil, as is evident from her participation in reform movements. She realized that the deeper work of societal transformation is a gradual and graced process, not the result of purely political change. Elisabeth, however, was most concerned with conversion of heart and embrace of faith among her friends and family, especially Félix. This change requires the cooperation and participation of the other. It is God's work, but it requires a free response. Elisabeth believed her suffering could be fruitful through the sharing of spiritual goods and grace in the communion of saints.

Elisabeth's sources for her approach to suffering, beyond her belief in the communion of saints and some aspects of contemporary devotion to the Sacred Heart, are found in Teresa of Avila, Catherine of Siena, and John of the Cross. All three consistently write about suffering, recommend asceticism, and embrace suffering in various ways. All three of these mystics describe an educative role of suffering and of pain. In addition, all three consider the capacity to accept and enter into the sufferings that are part of every human life as a sign of increasing spiritual and moral maturity. In addition, they also emphasize this acceptance of suffering as a privileged way of entering into the mystery of intimate relationship with the crucified Savior.

Physical pain or emotional suffering helped these mystics to focus attention, to fix their minds and hearts on the mystery of the crucified Christ. Pain and suffering became a way of encountering the mystery of God's compassionate love in solidarity with suffering humanity. Teresa of Avila, for instance, describes an increased ability to suffer for the sake of others as a mark of the approaching spiritual marriage. Book V of *The Interior Castle* has many examples of this emphasis. Teresa seems to be describing a person more focused on the divine beloved, someone strengthened and made courageous through the mystical transformation underway. In addition, the mystics who experience such suffering are less absorbed in the experience of suffering and more focused on prayer, love of neighbor, or in Teresa's own case, the work of establishing reformed convents. This enlarged capacity of the self to endure suffering without self-absorption or fear is a mark of authentic mystical experience and spiritual maturity.

In her spiritual teaching Catherine of Siena was less interested in mystical experience than in the fruits of authentic spiritual transformation and love for God. Catherine, influenced rather strongly by a theology of atonement that required suffering and sacrifice commensurate with the offense, actually prays to be punished for her own sins and to suffer on behalf of the church and others. In her *Dialogue*, Truth teaches her that human persons do not have the power to atone for evil, only Christ does. Catherine is made to understand that "all the sufferings given during life are not given as punishment: they are meant to amend and cure the child who has failed. In fact, atonement is made by the soul's desire, with true repentance and displeasure of sin"[92] The educative role is clear in this passage; however, there is more.

What really matters is not the suffering but the dispositions of the one who suffers. In a religious context in which self-inflicted pain was standard ascetical practice, willful asceticism is relativized in favor of a more subtle shift away from physical practices to interior attitudes. Catherine of Siena advised others not to follow her example in self-mortification but in love. This love was never imaginary but was actual love of one's neighbor. Love for God always proved its authenticity in compassion and love for actual human persons. It is only a surplus of love that participates in atonement for others. Truth teaches her:

> As you see, satisfaction is made by the soul's desire, when it is united to me, infinite Goodness, more or less, according to the perfection of the love in the person who offers prayer and desire....Feed, then, the fire of your desire, and let no time pass without appealing to me for them by humble and continuous prayer.[93]

Elisabeth Leseur found in such passages from *The Dialogue* clear guidance for fruitful ways of using the suffering that was simply part of her life. Other passages in this text fill out more of the picture of a love that is tested and made fruitful in suffering. A path of suffering love leads to discernment; to intimacy with God; to knowledge of truth, light, and love. "The wider love grows, the wider sorrow and suffering grow: sorrow increases with love."[94] Further, Catherine teaches that once one has matured in this agapic love, there is overflow in many ways on behalf of the neighbor. "Once one has improved oneself by the union of love he has made with me...he extends his desire to the salvation of the whole world....He helps his neighbors according to the various gifts I have given him to administer, either by teaching or sincerely advising, and by the example of a good, holy, honorable life."[95]

Elisabeth seems to have appropriated this approach to suffering. She consistently focuses on loving intention, trust in God, and laboring with God in the salvation of others, rather than on the suffering itself. However, as her breast cancer progresses, she does endure some terrible periods of exhausting and overwhelming physical pain. It is only toward the end of her life that she begins to see suffering as the primary focus of her spirituality. Until then, she engaged in many practices that enabled her to live a relatively normal life rather than identify with the role of invalid.

Her letters to Jeanne Alcan, who suffered from episodes of depression, give some indication of her conscious attempts to resist her own periods of depression resulting from her various physical illnesses and, perhaps, her childlessness. She advises her friend to summon what energy she can and to maintain a normal rhythm of work and relationship; in other words, do what one needs to do. She is empathetic and suggests that depressions may be periodic—that they do end eventually. She also advises her to focus her mental energy—to do some objective mental work each day.[96] She also recognizes the healing, uplifting quality of nature, especially the mountains that were so suffused with God's presence for her. She preferred the sunnier climates of the Mediterranean countries to the darker skies of Northern Europe, and even of Paris during its more dreary seasons.

Elisabeth describes some of these same strategies in her journal. Its pages reveal a woman fiercely determined to monitor her every reaction in order to avoid being a negative, irritable presence in the company of others. She uses her journal and at times her letters as an opportunity to clearly express what she is actually feeling and suffering. She engages in an expressive exercise but does not visit all these feelings on others. She makes behavioral and dispositional examinations of conscience and chooses how she wants to be with others.

Few even in her inner circle knew how seriously ill she was from 1911 until her death. Even during the sunnier years, from

1898 to the onset of her cancer, she suffered intensely over her younger sister's death in 1905. Her feelings were deep. Yet she found ways to moderate her interactions with others. Her physical and emotional sufferings seem to have led her to live from the deeper level of God's reality in her whether or not she could actually experience it. Those around her experienced this peacefulness and radiance, commenting on her serenity, liveliness, and lovingness.

Many feminist writers have struggled with dolorism, a false spirituality that required women to suffer situations of oppression as God's will.[97] Enduring illness and social oppression became a mark of holiness of life. The emphasis on humility worked against agency and resistance. Patricia Wismer suggests a complex approach to women's suffering that requires the acknowledgment both that suffering is part of the web of life, an inevitable and persistent human experience, and that unnecessary social and physical suffering is to be resisted in one's own behalf and in behalf of others.[98] Dorothy Soelle agrees. Some forms of suffering, called radical suffering by feminists, is disintegrative of human life. It can destroy both body and soul. However, suffering can also be integrative, suffused with meaning, productive of transformation. When the fruit of suffering is present, transformative grace is at work.

Soelle's later writings question an absolute resistance to feminine suffering based exclusively on feminist social analysis.[99] She argues that this approach can deprive postmodern people of a mystical approach to such suffering. While she encourages active resistance to the kinds of suffering that maintain systems of oppression and disintegrate the victims, she describes a mystical resolution of suffering through the solidarity of compassion and through a person's choosing to love God for God's own sake alone, even in the face of suffering. She points to the constancy in the mystic way of the far-near God, the dereliction and the absence of God that is part of the mystic way. But she refuses to embrace this mystical approach to suffering without also including an affirmative mysticism of appreciation and ecstasy. Elisabeth Leseur's spirituality of suffering love and the communion of saints can be appropriated anew in and through this feminist criticism, mysticism, and contemporary understandings of pain control.

Friendship Within the Communion of Saints

In many ways Elisabeth Leseur's contribution to lay spirituality remarkably coincides with the vision of the laity that was eventually affirmed in Vatican II. Her life demonstrated the one holiness of life to which all Christians are called. Her marriage and social locations were paths of sanctification for her, for her family, and for acquaintances. She developed a vocational vision of the role of lay persons in family, society, and church. This vocation was richly dialogical. She engaged in her own dialogue with church and society; with belief and unbelief; and with the joys, grief, and suffering of her own times. She considered herself to be privileged by the breadth of experiences that entered her life through travel and through multiple forms of conversations that she had with a wide cross-section of society from rich to poor. She was deeply immersed in her world as she knew it. Despite her natural introversion and contemplative bent, she remained engaged with the world and resisted every tendency to withdraw into the protective cocoon her wealth and social position might have afforded her.

When she embraced her vocation to love those different from herself with a special love, she disciplined herself in both a style of dialogue and a way of understanding differences. She studied philosophy so she could think more clearly and objectively, and so that she could look for the truth, the good, and the possibilities of compatibility in another's thought and way of life. Her deep respect for each human person's uniqueness, convictions, and conscience enabled her to learn from those who differed from her and to allow others to learn from her. She conceptualized all of this as an intellectual apostolate. She exercised it in conversations in many settings and through her writing. Although her journal is her best known work, she never intended to publish it. She did, however, compose a series of small treatises, each addressed to a particular person whom she wished to influence through the written word.

She privately published her account of Juliette's saintly death for family and friends. And she wrote letters to many different people. In these personal letters she displays the range and variety of her friendships. Some of them reveal a depth of spiritual friendship that often rises to the level of spiritual direction in this context of friendship.

Foremost among these friendships is her relationship with Soeur Marie Goby, a Hospitaller Sister of St. Martha of Beaune, whom she met in 1910. The Leseurs had stopped at the historic Hôtel Dieu when they were in the vicinity. Beaune was on the route to their summer home in Jougne. There, Elisabeth met Marie Ballard, a ten-year-old tubercular patient of Soeur Goby's. Marie's little bed had been placed in the courtyard of the hospital so she could enjoy the sunshine. Elisabeth asked her if there was anything she could do for her. Marie asked her to send picture postcards. Excited by her interchange with this "grand lady," Marie talked about Elisabeth's visit and promise. Soeur Goby told Marie gently that such people don't always do what they promise. To her surprise, the postcards began to arrive. Soeur Goby helped Marie write thank-you notes and wrote one herself. Later she inquired if Elisabeth might send Marie a doll. Elisabeth did so, and Marie promptly named the doll Juliette.

Thus began an epistolary friendship between two age peers, one a nursing sister and the other a married woman. Elisabeth and her husband visited Soeur Goby once at Beaune and once at Dijon, where Soeur Goby was having treatments for an eye problem. The third planned visit never happened. Elisabeth wrote seventy-eight letters to her. Soeur Goby wrote less frequently, about forty-five letters. Elisabeth found in Marie Goby a soul-friend. They immediately established a deep rapport with one another, beginning with their care for and concern for the poor. Elisabeth admired Soeur Goby's nursing ministry and expressed interest in particular patients for whom she cared. They prayed for one another and shared insights about their spiritual reading and their particular forms of spiritual and emotional suffering. Soeur Goby was threatened with the loss of her eyesight and returned to her nearby local village to care for her frail mother. After several months of caring for her mother, Soeur Goby became deeply conflicted about whether she should stay with her mother instead of returning to the hospital and convent. During these two crises Elisabeth offers gentle and wise spiritual direction to her friend. Félix published Elisabeth's letters to Soeur Goby under the title *Lettres sur la souffrance*, which were never translated into English until this volume. The correspondence shows a mutual relationship that meant a great deal to both women. Elisabeth shows a deep appreciation for Soeur Goby's vocation and ministry. Soeur Goby developed a relationship with both Elisabeth and Félix. After Elisabeth died, Félix sought support and comfort from Soeur Goby.

Elisabeth also wrote letters to family members, especially her mother and her sister Amélie. These letters to family members are full of affection but also contain commentary on current political and cultural events. Another set of letters is addressed to the painter Charles Duvent, a friend of both Félix and Elisabeth. He seems to be another believer within a much larger circle of atheists and agnostics. This correspondence was collected and preserved when Félix introduced Elisabeth's cause for canonization.

Félix published a third group of letters under the title *Lettres à des incroyants*. They are addressed primarily to three correspondents: Jeanne Alcan, wife of Emile Alcan, both non-practicing Jews; Aimée Fiévet, a teacher who lost her faith and was deeply influenced by Félix Pécaut, the liberal, Protestant director of the Ecole Primaire Supérieure de Fontenay; and to Yvonne and Félix Le Dantec. Yvonne was a lifelong friend of the Arrighi family, growing up with the Arrighi children. Yvonne, several years younger than Elisabeth, was like a younger sister to her. She, like Elisabeth, married an atheist. Most of the collected letters are to Yvonne, but every so often Elisabeth wrote to Yvonne's husband, engaging in dialogue about his thoughts and the effects of his books on others. With each of these correspondents Elisabeth's approach is different. Jeanne was a good friend, and Elisabeth shares the ups and downs of her life freely with her. Jeanne has no religion but does have spiritual sensitivities that Elisabeth supports and cultivates. She engages in vigorous dialogue with Aimée Fiévet, an intellectual and teacher. In her letters to Yvonne she often slips in remarks to be passed on to Félix le Dantec and occasionally addresses him directly. All the letters presume the mutual affection, esteem, and friendship that extended social intercourse beyond their face-to-face visits, dinners, and public events.

These friendships display an amazing diversity. Most were with upper-class, well-educated, and cultured people. Elisabeth appears to see herself primarily as friend and companion to each of her correspondents. She relates first to them as friends, friends she hopes to have now and later beyond death in the lasting communion of saints. She is friend not only on the affective level of shared tribulation and challenge but also their soul-friend. Most families suffered the loss of children and siblings to tuberculosis, typhoid, and other diseases now treatable with antibiotics. Death and bereavement was a constant challenge. As their soul-friend, Elisabeth seeks to make a spiritual connection, if such is possible. Speaking about spiritual matters, even writing short treatises if she thinks her correspondent can benefit, is a matter for discernment. Otherwise, she remains silent about such things but seeks to reach the basic goodness of the other through her compassion, love, and intelligence, gently opening the way to mystery, and it is to be hoped, belief.

The Writings

Elisabeth Leseur wrote on an almost daily basis in her normal round of activities. Prior to her death she had privately printed only *Une Ame*, a memoir of her sister Juliette's illness and saintly death. She had written the two essays on the lay Christian vocation for her niece and nephew, mentioned above. She had also written short pieces for particular friends or family members. She wrote essays on Christian hope and on peace for her sister Juliette. These she gave as a gift to Marie Duron, their niece, as well. She wrote from time to time in her journal. She also kept a notebook of her distilled thoughts on the spiritual life in one of the notebooks that contained part of her journal. Finally, in addition to the two volumes of letters to the four correspondents mentioned above, she maintained a voluminous correspondence with family members and friends. Extant letters submitted for the process of her canonization are estimated to be about two thousand.[100] In her concern for her mother's spiritual well-being when she was struggling with crippling arthritis, she wrote a letter inviting her mother to live a more interior life since her external activities had become impaired.

After Elisabeth's death and his conversion to Catholicism, Félix became a man with a mission to make his wife's writings known. He had been so powerfully affected by reading Elisabeth's journal that he determined to publish it. It was difficult for him to find a publisher during World War I, but finally Gigord Press took the risk and released an initial printing of 1,500 copies in 1917. The first run sold out almost immediately, and *Journal et pensées pour chaque jour* sold 140,000 copies by 1954, according to the documents submitted for Elisabeth's canonization. The *Journal* was translated into English (1919), Italian (1919), Portuguese (1920), Spanish (1923), Dutch (1925), Polish (1924), Chinese (1933), and Czech (1936).

Having received many letters in response to the appearance of Elisabeth's *Journal*, Félix published Elisabeth's letters to Soeur Goby under the title *Lettres sur la souffrance* in 1918. This correspondence began December 19, 1910, and ended March 12, 1914. Père Hébert, Elisabeth's spiritual director and confessor, supplied an introduction to the volume. Félix wrote his own lengthy introduction, in which he included many excerpts from the letters he had received from readers of Elisabeth's *Journal* and described many circumstances about the two friends drawn from his own knowledge and extracts from Soeur Goby's letters to Elisabeth. By the time this correspondence was published, Félix had decided to become a Dominican priest, as his wife had predicted both in a conversation with him in 1912 and with Soeur Goby about the same time. This volume was translated into Spanish (1924), Italian (1920), and Portuguese (1921).

Félix brought out a third volume of his wife's writings in 1919. This was entitled *La vie spirituelle*. He gathered together all of the shorter essays described above, including the memoir of Juliette's death. All of the pieces related to living a spiritual life as a lay person. Elisabeth's letter to Jeanne Alcan advising her how to live a spiritual life as a nonbeliever was first published in this collection.

Félix included Elisabeth's "Retreat for Each Month," in which she described and listed one virtue on which she reflected for each month of the year. Félix also included "A Litany to Obtain a Conversion" (namely, his own), which Elisabeth had copied into her notebook. He also included an annotated bibliography of her library. This third volume was translated into English (1919), German (1922), Catalan (1922), Spanish (1926), Italian (1920), and Portuguese (1922). One year later, in 1920, Gigord published extracts of each of the four most important essays: the retreat, the advice to her niece and to her nephew, and the letter of advice to an unbelieving friend.

The success of these pieces impelled Félix to assemble a collection of letters to their close unbelieving friends, which was translated into Italian in 1924. Père Reginald Garrigou-Lagrange, OP (1877–1964), provided the preface to this volume.[101]

After his ordination, Félix as Père Albert-Marie Leseur continued to promote his wife's cause for canonization. He published a biography, *La vie d'Elisabeth Leseur*, in 1931, and her childhood journal, *Journal d'enfant d'Elisabeth Leseur*, in 1934. This was Elisabeth's first-communion journal and was translated into Italian in 1935. The Archdiocese of Paris opened Elisabeth Leseur's process for beatification and canonization in 1936. The devastation of World War II intervened, and the testimony of witnesses and the examination of Elisabeth's writings was presented in the *Transumption* in 1954. In 1994 the French Dominicans attempted to reopen the cause, but the necessary formal documentation and production of a *Positio* have not been completed.

Note on the Translation

The *Lettres sur la souffrance* were translated by Religious of the Sacred Heart of Mary Sisters Rita Arthur and Moire McQuillan, and Sister of Charity Therese Grace Murray. They initiated a fluid, contemporary translation of these letters, one which I refined and harmonized. We tried to find contemporary equivalents of language used at the turn of the century in order to make Elisabeth Leseur's voice and spiritual wisdom more accessible to new readers.

INTRODUCTION

I continued this process in my new translation of the *Journal et pensées pour chaque jour,* the pieces on Christian vocation, and additional selections from *Lettres à des incroyants.* Selections from the *Lettres sur la souffrance* and *Lettres à des incroyants* have never been available to English readers. I have retained some key words such as *soul* or *sweetness* in contexts where the meaning absolutely required it. However, I translate *soul* with a number of other synonyms, such as "persons," or "others," to better represent the wholeness of human persons. Likewise, *doux* is translated in many instances as "loving," "tender," "consoling," "gentle," and so forth when the context warrants it, since "sweetness" becomes too repetitiously saccharine today. I have translated language about people inclusive of both genders but did not eliminate the male pronouns referring to God; to do so would have overly convoluted the sentence structure and obscured Elisabeth's language about God. I frequently translated "Our Lord" as "God" when it referred to God rather than Jesus.

JOURNAL AND *DAILY* *THOUGHTS*

Translator's Introduction

Elisabeth Leseur composed her spiritual journal in a distinctive process and for her own purposes from September 11, 1899, to April 4, 1906, and from October 19, 1911, to January 9, 1914. Part 1 of her journal begins one year after she resolved a crisis of faith that ended after she read Renan's *Life of Christ*. Reconstructing her faith life through reading, praying, and reflection, she records the highlights of her reflections and some of the movements of her interior life. Her notations are markings for herself about her most important thoughts and experiences. Following some of the procedures taught at the time of her first communion, she uses her journal to examine her conscience and to make resolutions about the future. Until shortly before her death in 1914, she intended that these bound copybooks be destroyed when she died.[1] She rarely recounts events of daily life unless they illustrate or reveal the unfolding sense of her personal vocation. These details are found in her voluminous correspondence and in her husband's writings. The journal entries emphasize her losses and their effects on her, her spiritual isolation, her spiritual philosophy, the writers who echo her deepest convictions. These two parts of her journal were written in two black, leather-bound copybooks. In the front of the second book Elisabeth recorded her daily thoughts during the same years she wrote the first part of her journal. During this period of time she wrote her journal in one book and wrote her distilled thoughts and aphorisms about the spiritual life in the other. When she resumed writing her journal in 1911, she filled in the second copybook after the "Daily Thoughts." During the intervening years she kept a third notebook, from October 1906 to July 18, 1912.

Although many of these entries are dated, she gave it the title "Notebook of Resolutions." This notebook contained her rule of life. She detailed the pattern of her spiritual life, her regular practices, the flexibility with which she adapted her practices to her own health and the needs of her family. This section allows the reader to learn from Elisabeth how to live the spiritual life within a lay context. This notebook reveals how consistently she reflected on her moods, internal attitudes, and external behavior. She remained vigilant about how she wanted to live and affect others despite the challenges posed by her various illnesses, losses, spiritual isolation, and disappointments. Like life itself, she constantly repeats a handful of themes that she regularly confronts. Writing was one spiritual practice that enabled Elisabeth to reflect on and respond to the graces she received. When Félix Leseur assembled these writings for publication in 1917, he included a separate document, Elisabeth's "Spiritual Testament," to complete the volume.

The original French edition of the *Journal et pensées de chaque jour of Madam Elisabeth Leseur* was published in 1917 in Paris by J. De Gigord. This translation is based on a 1927 reprint of that edition and follows the order established in the French text. The first three sections of the journal have been included with only very small omissions, and the final section, "Daily Thoughts," has been included in its entirety. The original edition and its subsequent translations included a lengthy introduction, "In Memoriam," by Félix Leseur, in which he tells the story of his experiences with Elisabeth's journal after her death. An English translation of Félix's narrative may be found in *My Spirit Rejoices* (Manchester, NH: Sophia Institute Press, 1996).

The Journal of Elisabeth Leseur

Prayer for the Virtue of Hope

My God, who allows us human hopes, but who alone gives truly Christian hope, grant, I ask you, through your grace, this virtue to me, to those I love, and to all Christians. Let it enlighten and transform our lives, our suffering, and even our death, and let it sustain in us, through the disappointments and sadness of each day, an inner strength and unalterable serenity.[2]

The Journal: Part 1 (1899–1906)

"I give you a new commandment, that you love one another. Just as I have loved you, you also should love one another" (John 13:34).

September 11, 1899

For a year I have thought and prayed a great deal; I have tried unceasingly to enlighten myself, and in this constant effort my mind has matured, my convictions have become more profound, and my love of souls has increased, too. What is greater than the human soul, or finer than conviction? We must create in ourselves a "new spirit" (Ps 51:10), the spirit of intelligence and strength; we must renew ourselves and live our interior life intensely. We must pray and act. Every day must bring us nearer to the greatest good and intelligence—that is, nearer to God.

September 19, 1899

I want to love with a special love those whose birth, religion, or ideas separate them from me; it is those especially whom I want to understand and who need me to give of what God has given me.

September 20, 1899

I began to study philosophy, which I really like. It clarifies many things and orders the mind. I do not understand why it is not considered the crown of women's education. Women so often lack right judgment, a habit of reasoning, and sustained thought. Philosophy could give them all that, and remove so many prejudices and narrow ideas that they pass on religiously to their sons to the great detriment of our country.

September 21, 1899

How wonderful was the beginning of the Christian church recorded in the Acts of the Apostles!…"Having the goodwill of all the people" (Acts 2:44–47), that is, with the little ones, the humble, those who believed as they did, and those who did not yet share their faith. The despised and hated soon found a way of "having the goodwill of all the people."

How many Christians today can say the same? How many burn with an evangelical flame that purifies and enlightens all who come near? Let us return to the holy source, to the gospel, the word of God. Let us draw from it lessons of moral strength, heroic patience, deep love for all creatures. Let Christians never "break the bruised reed" or "quench the burning wick" (Isa 42:3). That reed is perhaps the suffering of a brother or sister; and the humble flax extinguished by our icy breath may be some noble spirit that we could have restored and lifted up. Let us be attentive; nothing is so delicate and so sacred as the human soul, nothing so quickly bruised. Let all our words and deeds be full of life, penetrating other spirits, communicating light and strength, and so reveal God to them.

September 25, 1899

No one knows what goes on in the depths of our souls. To sense God near, to meditate, to pray, to gather our thoughts so as to reflect on them more deeply, that is to live the inner life, and this interior life is the greatest joy. Such inspiring thoughts and ardent desires and generous resolutions, however, should be translated into action, for we are in the midst of life and a great task awaits us. This is the time for painful effort. We must tear ourselves apart, give up thought for reality, face action, know that we will either not be understood at all or completely misunderstood, and that we will perhaps suffer at human hands for having willed the good of humanity. We must already have drawn from God an incomparable strength, and armed our hearts with patience and love, in order to undertake day by day and hour by hour the work that belongs to all Christians: the moral and material salvation of our brothers and sisters.

February 14, 1900

The task that the world at present offers us, the moral renewal, the transformation and education of souls, is so immense that it may well confound us. What can be done in the face of evil and indifference by someone as obscure as I? Nothing of myself, no doubt, but all through and with God. I believe that in the good there is a great expansive force; I believe that no humble, unknown act or thought, seen by God alone, is lost, and that all, in fact, contribute to the good of others. I believe, according to the saying...that "when we do good we know not how much good we do." What we have to do is to work on ourselves, to accomplish our own inner transformation, to fulfill our obligations and do all the good that we can, each day and each hour. Above all, we must ask God to fill us with an intense charity. Charity is the love of God that renews and transforms us and our lives, and becomes the hidden source of our actions, our love of all creatures, our powerful and vital love of souls, our love of all who suffer and grieve. Such love can save the world. Why complain when we can act? Why hate, since hate destroys, when that divine love enlivens and transforms our hearts?

March 28, 1900

This winter's exhausting activity, which in spite of everything is so empty, is beginning to end. During that time the only good moments were those given to God, to the poor, and to work. I am going to give myself to these more eagerly than ever. From one point of view, my ideas have changed. I believe much more in individual effort and in the good that I can do by ministering not to the masses but to particular people. The effect one can have is thereby much deeper and long-lasting. Did not he who remains our model in all spiritual things do the same? And it did not prevent him from transforming the world. Following him, let us turn lovingly to every person, however poor or sinful, and let us try to be "all things to all people" (1 Cor 9:22). Let us think less of humanity and more of men and women; or rather, let us remember that humanity is only made of human beings and that each one of them needs the strength that God gives, and it belongs to us to spread this light as far as we can. What a mission for weak and sinful creatures! I tell myself again and again that the apostles were hardly better than we when they began their mission, and that the strength of the Holy Spirit was necessary to transform them and make them into new men and women. Let us ask God zealously for this coming of the Holy Spirit, who is at once strength and gentleness, love and peace. Let us ask God for the complete transformation of our inner being and life that will enable us to labor for our brothers and sisters.

March 29, 1900

A great conversation last night with [our guests]. So many people of this generation lack any guiding principle, and yet we really need to be led by an ideal greater than ourselves. How beautiful is congruence in a human life, when every act, whether great or small, springs from one fundamental thought, when every-thing—heart, mind and will—has but one purpose, when God's love possesses the soul and transforms it, when that harmony is the result of long interior work, sometimes painful but always fruitful, making of one "something achieved," something spiritual, a unique book, continuously read and continuously new, immi-nently beautiful, resplendent with truth, of exquisite grace and charm, from which we can endlessly draw, never exhausting it! O blessed gift of God, why do people forget you when through you alone they can learn charity anew?

May 29, 1900

After five weeks of travel in Spain, I resume my ordinary life but, I think, under different conditions. During this trip I have thought and prayed a great deal and have seen clearly into myself and into my life. I have consecrated my life to God; I have given myself to him with my whole heart; I have prayed fervently for those whom I love, for him whom I love more than all others. Now I want to be no longer useless; I have seen my greatest obligations clearly, and I want to fulfill them. To do each day all the good that can be done humbly, so that only God may see it; always to seek out all the misery and grief surrounding me in order to relieve it, to cultivate a lively affection for everyone; and to do all this for God alone—that is the goal of all human life. My own life, which until now has often been so empty, will be transformed, I hope, by the strength of close union with God. There are around me many that I love deeply, and I have a task to fulfill in relationship to them. Many of them do not know God or know him only imperfectly. It is not in arguing or lecturing that I can make them know who God is for us. But in struggling with myself, in becoming with his help more Christian and more courageous, I will witness to him whose disciple I am. By the serenity and strength that I intend to acquire I will show that Christian life is great and beautiful and full of joy. By cultivating the best qualities of my mind I will proclaim that God is the highest intelligence, and that those who serve him can draw without end from that blessed source of intellectual and moral light. In order to give, one must receive; to serve my brothers and sisters before God for one day, or for even a small part of one, I must first purify and strengthen myself for many days.

July 30, 1900

We have been spending a week with our friends…on the banks of the Meuse in complete relaxation. We came back along the Rhine and saw Aachen, Bonn, Frankfurt, and Mainz. From Mainz we went by boat to Koblenz, from there to Luxembourg, and returned by way of Metz. This last town left a painful impression on us; it is both French and German: French in its appearance and population, German in its innumerable soldiers and barracks. After thirty years the *parfum français* still rises from the soil of Lorraine. Deeply moved, we saw the battlefields planted with crosses. During all this travel in Germany one thought never left me: that we are still a great people from a moral and intellectual standpoint, *le grand peuple*, and that it is up to us to remain so always. The collective energy of everyone is necessary for that, as well as a profound sense of duty; we must strive to perform all the tasks providence has given us, to banish egotism and hatred from our lives, and make the name of the French synonymous with justice, light, and moral energy. We must become truly strong, not only by military force—that is too little—but by the courageous nobility of character, from the humblest to the greatest. Chastity, determination, and the dignity of life should be faithfully taught and developed in all. Women, whose immense role and influence the French do not yet fully grasp, and who do not always grasp it themselves, should from now on realize their task and consecrate their lives to it. To shirk responsibility and sacrifice is cowardly. It is an obligation to bear children (and it is often a sacrifice); it is an obligation to care for those less fortunate in wealth or education; it is an obligation to develop unceasingly one's intelligence, to strengthen one's character, to become reflective and determined; it is an obligation to view life with joy and to face it with energy. Finally, it is an obligation to understand one's times and not despair of the future.

All this women can do. As much as men, they are beings who think, act, and love; they can proudly reclaim their right to responsible action. But for that they must draw their strength from the source of all strength, and to develop their intelligence they must bring it into contact with the wisdom of God. But this also is true for men. They are also powerless without God; and the great and strong nations are those who make God the foundation of their social and national organization—only this foundation must truly be God and a true religious sensibility, not merely the exploitation of this greatest of all feelings. God must live in our hearts and lives, and there must be complete religious freedom. The expression *to believe* implies the adherence of one's whole being and is incompatible with religious intolerance. My obligation as a Frenchwoman will always be as sacred to me as a Christian, or rather, one obligation includes and implies the other. I only trust that I will always understand both in their broadest and noblest sense.

September 12, 1900

After going back and forth between Paris and the country and entertaining strangers, I am again peaceful. I am reading Latin authors—after Horace, Juvenal—and I shall continue at this. I am very interested in exploring a time and a society that I know so imperfectly. For two days I have been able to read and meditate quietly, and that has quieted my agitation and done me good. I do not abandon the New Testament, and the more I read the Gospels and Epistles, the more I find an attraction, a strength, a life that is incomparable. God is indeed there; from this reading I am calmed and strengthened each day, and my will is fortified and my heart warmed. God, the true teacher, through this book of books, educates my inmost being. [This reading] helps me understand life, smile at responsibility, and choose clearly.

November 28, 1900

Inasmuch as I advance, sustained by God, in the way that he has indicated for me, my "duty" is increasingly clear to me. It is important not to lose myself in unrealizable plans and projects, not to live in the future, but patiently to turn thought into action, good will into determination.

[I have had] much conversation and discussion with some dear friends who do not believe. More than others I love these whom divine light does not illuminate, or rather whom it illuminates in a way we do not understand. There is a veil between them and God, a veil that allows only a few rays of love and beauty through. Only God, with a divine gesture, may part this veil, and then the true life shall begin for them. And I, who am worth so little, believe in the power of prayers that I unceasingly offer for them. I believe in [prayer] because God exists, and because he is the Father. I believe in this mysterious reality that we call the communion of saints. I know that no cry, no desire, no yearning of our inmost depths is lost, but all go to God and through him to those who inspired us to pray. I know that only God effects our intimate transformation, and that we can only point out to him those we love, saying, "God, make them live."

[I have] reflected a great deal on social questions, which even the least of us might help resolve. These are essentially the questions of Christianity, since they are concerned with all people's place in the world and their material, intellectual, and moral improvement. These questions, which will last as long as the world, can advance only through Christianity; that is my strong conviction. Christianity alone addresses the individual, that which is most interior; it alone penetrates to our depths and is able to renew us. All Christians are obliged to be concerned about this crisis through which we are passing. This will perhaps change us profoundly. New needs require new apostles. The people—the masses, the majority of the country, those workers, peasants, and humble laborers of every kind—need to be shown the true source of all freedom, justice, and real transformation. If we do not make God known to them, we shall have failed in our most important obligation. But this is a work that demands self-forgetfulness, a disinterestedness, a steady determination for which we need God and for which we must completely transform ourselves.

January 17, 1901

...What serious thoughts came with the beginning of this century, the ending of which I shall not see—gratitude for God's gifts, a stronger turning to him, a zealous desire to increase his kingdom within me! And how many prayers, spoken or implied, have gone out from my depths that God alone knows, asking for light and for true life, the inner life for all those I love, for him whom I love most of all. Perhaps neither my dear Félix nor my family nor those others for whom I can do so little, know how much I love them. In eternity, in the very center of love, we will claim the fullness of joy in our loving relationships. But, O my God, how can we love if we do not love through you?

March 11, 1901

Some joyful days because of a present from Félix, and more because of the words that accompanied it—words so full love that made me very happy. I do not deserve to be so loved, but I rejoice fully in it. Apart from the love that is the very foundation of my life, I am always meeting with wonderful affection, for thus has God blessed me. Now I must make sure that it is not an egotistical happiness that results, but that these affections are transformed into devotion and charity, that they impel me to act with God for others.

I found Father Gratry's *Sources* very interesting, and have now read another of his books in which I often find my own thoughts.[3] These arise from within to the surface and then return to that place, from which they will soon emerge again, transformed by God into action and words full of life.

April 22, 1901

"I have said these things to you so that my joy may be in you, and that your joy may be complete" (John 15:11)—"I give you a new commandment, that you love one another. Just as I have loved you, you also should love one another" (John 13:34). Jesus, after the Last Supper, in the peace and sadness of the evening, you spoke ineffable words that have come to us through the centuries. The world has often forgotten them and forgets them still, but the least of your children can sense them pulsing in her ear and in her heart. After the meal, there resounded like a blessed refrain the last words of Christ, an appeal for love among people and for love of people for God: "Love one another." This is the law, the highest testament of him who is love. He who has ceased to love is not a Christian, not a disciple of Christ. There is no exception to this. Those who are separated from us by birth, education—all are entitled to our love, all should be brothers and sisters to us. Do they not all stand before God, beloved by God? Has not each a soul like our own, which should be only the more precious to us for being far from the Light? Let us open our hearts to welcome all humanity. At the touch of God, let us resound with every generous thought, every human affection; let us learn to find in each soul the point at which it is still in touch with God.

June 10, 1901

On April 8, Maman and Juliette left for Italy. On May 9 Pierre Leseur made his first communion.[4] The day before, Roger [Arrighi] became violently feverish and shortly thereafter became very ill.[5] His parents and I nursed him. On Sunday, May 12, Maman returned, and on Monday, May 13, at eight in the evening, [Roger] died. Those hours spent beside him, at times so heartrending, were also sometimes very tender. He left us quietly for eternity, and the veil between the two worlds seemed thin indeed. Dear one, you who are in the midst of light and of love, pray for us.

Renewal of effort and work on myself, and prayer with more determination and serenity, which I pray God may sustain in me.

For several days I have longed for calm and solitude, and felt a strong desire to get out in nature, to be like Saint Francis in the midst of flowers and birds, and there to pray, work, and meditate in solitude, or at least (for Félix always belongs to my solitude) with a few loved ones who sometimes leave me alone with God. My God, will you give me one day the joy of this solitude for two, united in the same prayer, the same faith, and the same love? But for now I must banish these thoughts. God wants other things from me, and when I wish to meditate I only have an internal solitude.

August 28, 1901

[We] stayed in Savoy from July 14 to 31, in a pleasant and peaceful landscape. An exquisitely tranquil life, full and rich interiorly. Beautiful mountains, carpets of green, great fields of oats, churches nestling in every corner—these made up our lovely environment. What a wonderful life one could lead there with those one loves.

...O my God, it is true that you alone can make certain things understood; all the arguments in the world are nothing compared to your own voice in the depths of the soul. You alone can penetrate the depths and reach that mysterious place where great transformations occur.

That thought is reassuring. Without it I would sometimes suffer terribly from being unable to express what I feel, from being unable to be transparent about what God alone has done in me— all the love and joy he has showered on me. May his Spirit act in these others who are so dear to me, in him who is dearer to me than all others, and may the light shine upon them, bringing with it true life.

A few days in Holland, from which I came back ill. Interesting country, full of fine things. A rather depressing landscape. I love the countries of light, of those beautiful, gentle colors, where all looks so harmonious: Greece, Italy, the East.

Now to return to daily life. I want to study Latin this winter, to be usefully but quietly occupied, and to live from day to day doing the work of the moment, which I believe is the best way, to accomplish each task well.

September 10, 1901

Consoling and joyous meditation on those words of Christ, "I came to bring fire to the earth, and how I wish it were already kindled!" (Luke 12:49). That fire is charity, the total, exclusive, and zealous love of God and, through him, of all humanity. But who will be holy enough to make others understand what this charity is, and how this fire is to be kindled? Each one of us can work at this great task, and I have seen clearly what I can do in my own milieu. Above all, to work on myself, to try and develop all the instincts God has given me; to strengthen my determination by regular work; to elevate my soul unceasingly by sacrifice and the acceptance of my usual sufferings, and by a constant and loving affection for all who approach me. To do the smallest things with the conviction that they always bring the beauty and truth for which I long. To love exclusively and to fulfill my obligations, however obscure or painful, whether intellectual or material; to miss no opportunity for action or devotion, especially if no one will notice. Never willingly to omit or neglect these [practices] except when it brings me praise or feeds that subtle pride that so quickly arises.

To go always to the little ones, the suffering, those for whom life is hard, but not to scorn those carefree ones who live for themselves. They more than the others, perhaps, need to be loved...to show God to them. Resolutely to devote my mind, my will, my heart, my whole being to God, to the advancement of God's kingdom. To raise, strengthen, and spread a little of the warmth that God has put into my heart, the "fire" that kindles me, which I regret being unable to kindle in others.

When I have done this, God will do the rest. We pray, suffer, and labor unaware of the consequence of our action and prayers. God makes them serve his plan; gradually, they take effect, winning one soul, then another. They hasten the coming of God's kingdom and by [all] they give birth to, they will exert a lasting influence.

One resolution I have made and put into practice, notwithstanding physical and moral weakness, is to be "joyful" in the Christian sense of the word, as joyful as I can be toward life, toward others, and even toward myself. God, help me, and "your kingdom come!"

October 9, 1901

Days of great interior happiness, rich in firm resolutions. I am going to fill my life with work and love and the fulfillment of my obligations.

November 20, 1901

I love interior solitude with God alone; it strengthens me, and gives me light and energy again. But sometimes isolation, which is different from solitude, wears me down. I long for spiritual companionship, to bare my soul to those who are dear to me, to speak of God and immortality and the interior life and charity. But the human soul is so subtle and delicate that it must feel the same notes resonating in another of those divine instruments before it can make its own sound. The perfect union of two souls—what beautiful music that would make! With him I love best in the world, let me one day make this music, O my God!

I have planned my days so that as much as possible they may represent, as it were, the whole of my life in miniature. Prayer, my precious morning meditation, work seriously performed, some work or care for the poor, and my family and household responsibilities. Right now, visits to Juliette replace those to the poor. As soon as I can, I want to devote myself to some fine and useful work.

November 28, 1901

Talked to [Emile Alcan] and his wife yesterday about the unjust and un-Christian treatment of Jews in certain circles. My God, will you not give to poor human beings a spirit of intelligence and wisdom, which is the gift of your eternal Spirit? Will you not awaken soon in them the spirit of charity that you came to bring to the world, and which you said contained "the law and the prophets?" I wish I could organize a holy crusade against hate and promote justice and love among men and women. At any rate, in this garden God has given me to cultivate, I want to plead by my attitude, my words, and my actions before everyone I meet the great cause of charity. Will I not thus be defending the cause of God? My God, help us; send a ray of light and love into our midst.

December 18, 1901

I love the study of Latin. It opens up a whole horizon of reading and intellectual pleasure for the future. In the eyes of many, a woman's life is constricted between her twentieth and her fiftieth years. And how much energy is wasted in the twenty or thirty years that, for too many women, are an empty time in their lives! Serious work, intellectual activity, action all the more fruitful because it is based on judgment developed by experience and on a strong will—these should fill the mature years and give them a special serenity and beauty.

But that needs a long preparation. One must have acquired in youth the habit of work, organized one's life, and achieved self-control, so that, at least on the surface, no physical suffering, none of the heartrending experiences of old age can disturb one's being. One must have lit in oneself so bright a flame of affection and kindness that all who are beginning as we are ending can come to find there light and fire.

The suffering sent by God that I offer to him is the fact that among all the friends surrounding me, I have no one to whom I can totally open my heart...who might understand and help me.

But perhaps to hear one's ideas and beliefs always criticized, to have them misunderstood, to experience prejudice and ignorance is to some extent to suffer persecution for justice's sake. Could all this evoke some compassion from God? Because it is a deep and secret suffering, one that only God sees, and for which he sometimes makes the most loving compensation. When I want to pour out my soul, I go to him, and whether at church or in the silence of my room, he brings me increased strength and fills me with an unutterable joy. After all, perhaps God alone can penetrate to the infinite depth and sensitivity of the human soul.

February 3, 1902

A very bad time for more than a month—bodily fatigue, household troubles, and worse than that, a kind of sadness and moral apathy, a lack of the fervor and inner joy that God sometimes gives me so abundantly. And yet not for a single moment has my will ceased to belong to him; duty has cost me dearly, but it has not ceased to be duty. A new year has begun. I want to make it fuller than previous ones. Many things to reform: pride; the tendency to procrastinate getting to work, to let days slip away; allowing myself to be invaded by external agitation. And yet I have an immense need for tranquility and interior life. God alone knows what difficulty I sometimes have in overcoming physical and moral distress in order to arrive at complete self-possession, at that Christian serenity that nothing can disturb.

Increasingly, to try, by example and kindness and by developing and elevating my intelligence, to spread more light among those I encounter along my way.

To show that what good I have is from God, and the rest is alas! from me.

To examine and decide, after reflection and prayer, to what work I shall consecrate my life this year, apart from my immediate responsibilities.

Holy Saturday, March 29, 1902

A week of meditation and prayer and union with God.

My God, help me to fulfill the work, to break the last bonds, to complete that interior process that you alone have accomplished in me, in whom the mysterious working of your providence is always visible, for which I never cease blessing and loving you. I have a great task before me, and nothing to help me to fulfill it. Perhaps one day I shall have the great joy of seeing my faith, which is my whole life, understood and shared by those in my circle, and by him whom I love so much. As it is, all my desires, enthusiasm, and tenderness must remain enclosed and poured out only to God. Whatever suffering this entails, I offer for those who are so dear to me. Nothing is lost, not one suffering, not one tear.

I am reading Father Gratry's *Knowledge of God*—it is strong and beautiful.[6] The eternal Word, that "enlightens everyone, was coming into the world" (John 1:9), lifted a corner of the veil that conceals the one true light for Plato. He knew the only way the soul may know God and describes wonderfully that place where we experience God. This is an inspiring book; it truly reaches that "root" of the soul of which Plato speaks.

September 3, 1902

More than five months without writing, but much has happened. Our stay at Jougne was a very loving and happy time for the family.[7] [Our house was] enlivened by the shouts and laughter of children; then came the short trip to Siena, which I ended painfully exhausted physically and morally. [On our] return, we heard the startling news of Adolphe's death;[8] then [we enjoyed] another peaceful and lovely two weeks. Coming back to Paris I felt such interior emptiness, sadness, and suffering that nothing but prayer and God's help can enable me to change these into joy for others and strength for myself. At the same time, I have never ceased to feel the active presence of God. When I look back and see the wonderful work that God has accomplished in me, I realize what obligations this grace entails; I hope, with all my heart, that some day soon he will give the same grace to the dear one who is so close to me and whom I love so deeply.

I want to live an entirely new life. No one must know the struggles, regrets, and griefs that, like every other person, I endure; I must organize my life in such a way that all its various and sometimes complicated duties have their place. Since I do not have a consistent life in broad, clear lines but must partly conceal my inmost being in order to encounter ideas and feelings opposed to mine, I want at least to unite with this first duty my desire to work for God and for others. It is a delicate task, for which I need the help of a strength beyond my own. Help me, my God, and, without my knowing it, use me for a little good. According to an image I like, let me be a rough vessel emanating light and warmth. You are that light; come, and enlighten through me, those who are incredibly dear to me. What a joy it will be when they shall know and love all that you have made me know and love—I who am so insignificant and weak. What a joy when I shall be able to reveal to them this new creation you have truly accomplished in me, when I shall live with them—with him—O my God, this deep, intimate, and blessed life that makes new creatures of us and that transforms everything!

October 18, 1902

I feel that all my knowledge, assisted by that inner light and grace, the effects of which are so apparent in my life, must be a knowledge of reconciliation. I must simply and strongly profess a faith that God has gradually created in me. But I must do this in a way that never harms or offends conviction or its absence in others. I must relinquish, unknown to anyone, my tastes and preferences, everything but the principles by which I live. I must fulfill my obligations—works of charity, devotion to others and to the poor—in a way that can offend no one nor interfere with my household. I must never give up intellectual work but must do it consistently. I must even become a little "worldly," in spite of my love for simplicity of life and solitude, in order to please Félix and those around me. In fact, this is my responsibility to do my different duties without anyone's suspecting how hard it is for me to reconcile all this. [I want] to forget myself, to develop my God-given gifts of reason and intelligence, to banish even the most subtle forms of pride I know so well, to love unselfishly, to accept with God's grace my daily responsibilities, however insignificant. Although I often fall, God's help, for which I pray daily, will not fail me. Anyway, to live is to struggle, to suffer, and to love.

May 12, 1903

How much has happened in a few months in my interior life! What a gentle and smooth process this long transformation, orchestrated by God, has been. Only now, looking back from where Jesus has led me, can I see the progress, and praise what he has done. In Rome, where we stayed three weeks, I had some very good times. At St. Peter's one morning, in close and joyful communion with him who desires my whole soul, I made a solemn consecration of myself to God and to the work of charity and light from then on.

On our return, [we had to face our nephew] Maurice's painful illness—many miserable hours. He is better—may God be blessed![9]

In regard to [my niece and nephews,] I have a mission to fulfill: to be their friend and guide, to use all the intelligence and devotion I can to instill character into them and make them strong Christians.

July 23, 1903

I must review these graced memories and deepen them in my awareness. First, the continual life-giving action of God during these last years, and then the wonderful and natural conclusion. Unforgettable hours in March, in the chapel that is now closed; then at St. Augustine's, in complete union with God, and the sober feeling that a new life was beginning; then that moving baptism, also prepared by God, mingled with all those special memories. Then the journey to Rome, which seemed willed by God to bring all to completion.

Two mornings there I will never forget. The first, Sunday, April 19, when we received a ticket for an audience with the Holy Father....We waited an hour sitting in the second row, opposite the papal chair, in the midst of the serious and thoughtful crowd. Greeted by acclamation, Pope [Leo XIII] appeared, in a chair carried by men clothed in striking red velvet. He climbed the steps of the throne and seated himself. I was able to observe closely that thin, transparent face, full of intelligence and goodness. His eyes were unusual, full of life, suggesting thoughtfulness and a strong will. His soul radiated from those eyes. He spoke for a few moments, telling us how much he loved France, and that this great nation ought not to lose the traditions that made it strong and beautiful. He ended by giving his apostolic benediction to us. Deeply moved, I bowed before this old man, this father, the trustee of the Eternal Word, and silently I presented all my loved ones for his blessing—the living and the dead, as well as the new life opening before me. Then we passed in front of him, and I kissed that large, white hand that is lifted only to bless. After a last farewell the Holy Father mounted his chair, accompanied by more acclamations, and disappeared. Just as the chair turned, he leaned toward us and made an emotion-filled gesture. I looked at his beautiful face for the last time and said "good-bye" from the bottom of my heart, knowing I would not see him again. I was not wrong, for last Monday, July 20, after a long agony, Leo XIII died. That great light went out, or rather, went to shine above our darkness, joining the one eternal Light.

The second unforgettable memory was my morning at St. Peter's the following Wednesday, April 22. I left for St. Peter's alone. After going to confession to a French-speaking priest, I received communion in the Chapel of the Blessed Sacrament. Those moments were completely and spiritually happy. I felt the living presence of Christ, of God himself, conveying undescribable love. This blessed one spoke to me, and the infinite compassion of the Savior passed quickly into me. Never will this action of God be obliterated. The triumphant Christ, the eternal Word, he who as a human person suffered and loved, the one living God possessed my soul for all eternity in that unforgettable moment. I felt renewed to my very depths, ready for a new life, for responsibility, for the work intended by providence. I offered myself and the future without reserve.

I then stayed for Mass in another chapel, in profound joy and peace. I prayed again, and then I knelt close to the [reliquary of Saint Peter], in a last, intimate and formal consecration.

On my return I found myself in an atmosphere of irony, criticism, and indifference. But it was of no consequence; the flame of Christ was still burning within me.

How many memories from that journey press in upon me! The visit to the Church of St. Paul of the Three Fountains on the day of our arrival, the tranquility and poetry of that place where I wanted to stay and pray longer. The next day, Palm Sunday, the first visit to St. Peter's, during High Mass, and one moment of joyful recollection alone; the colorfulness of the palms, yellow and green. All Holy Week; Friday, the end of the day in St. Peter's; Easter Sunday at St. John Lateran and St. Peter's in the morning; afterward, a Mass held at the Trinita de'Monti. Then the visit to the catacombs and churches and all Christian Rome; and [sites] of ancient Rome that are also so fascinating in another way. And then the departure, with loving memories of this city unique among cities, where every bit of land recalls something, where the stones themselves seem alive. This city is truly royal, first by power and then by love, and which, victorious, was defeated by that strange conqueror who said, "Love one another" (John 13:34). A conqueror so powerful that for twenty centuries he has been and will continue to be adored.

Since our return, many trials for me, as if God would accomplish my purification through suffering: Maurice's illness, terrible anxiety about Juliette's health and that of others, physical fatigue and suffering; and then the feeling, more acute and painful than ever, of the great spiritual divide between myself and Félix and many of those around me. How hard it is to see all that one loves and lives be misunderstood or attacked by prejudice and hatred, even to feel others' complete indifference toward the things I most value in life! Through this, God imposes on me continual effort and the deepest suffering, all the better for being known only to him, and a sort of turning inward, to my depths where he lives. If only my dear ones, especially my most beloved, knew the depth of my love for them, and what joy it would be for me to open wide my soul to them! For the moment it cannot be. O God, once more I beg you to come to him, to come to them, that they may live the interior life deeply as well as an outer life renewed by Christianity. The harvest is plentiful; my God, may they be laborers in it; may their life and mine be works of beauty and love, and may we labor together for the coming of your kingdom.

August 11, 1903

A good, long conversation with the Abbé Viollet.[10] He has a warm, keen heart, such as I would like to see in every priest, in every Christian. He understands what is of lasting value in Catholicism and that wonderful spiritual domain that so few know how to explore. Without suspecting it, he has renewed my energy and encouraged me to work more than ever for the material and moral welfare of everyone, and above all for those who are so mistaken and yet so interesting. To know how to understand them will be part of the task, to love them deeply will be another, but to love them for themselves alone and for God, without any expectation of return or consolation, simply because they are persons and because Christ, in looking upon them one day, uttered this loving remark, "I have compassion for the crowd" (Mark 8:2). Let us also know how to have mercy.

August 24, 1903

Thanks to God, progress in self-mastery in spite of my poor health, many preoccupations about Maman and Juliette, and much sadness poured out to God alone. To acquire more and more the complete serenity that comes from God, and to learn how to sacrifice all I had desired, and to endure the lack of all human support and strong Christian accompaniment. Père Hébert's absence deprives me of rare but good conversations, as well as of any strong human voice to console me. I turn to the great heart of Christ, who is my best friend and who knows how to comfort and strengthen. With his aid I will be able to help so many around me, for whose sake I must only forget my weakness, my suffering, and my longing for consolation.

November 3, 1903

More than two difficult months of almost continual physical suffering and terrible anxiety on account of Juliette; the distressing belief that my illness will last as long as I do, always interfering with my life. Complete surrender, but without joy or any inner consolation. The resolution to use my misfortunes for the good of others. To fill my life with prayer, work, and charity. To maintain serenity through everything. To love more than ever those who are the dear companions of my life. A great trial in being unable to do the works I am interested in now.

January 20, 1904

A new year begins, which I entrust to God.

A fuller life, a deep constant sense of the presence of God. Regrets only for all the pressing duties and difficulties that interfere with my activities and prevent me from being more completely involved with the religious and social work that I love so much. To offer God this sacrifice and await the time when I can do more. This morning at Charonne I made the acquaintance of the little girls who were making their first communion. In them I will sow the seed and leave the harvest to the Savior.

March 9, 1904

Great suffering, on Juliette's account and because of my usual trials; a fragmented life, often more fully occupied than I would like. But intense prayer, and an inner life full of God, in spite of weaknesses and faults. To try as much as possible not to miss my daily meditation, in spite of activities and responsibilities. In that meditation and close contact with God I find greater strength to perform the tiresome and repetitive daily tasks, to act. Everything that has first been prepared with the Master and Friend is better carried out, and the soul remains at peace in the midst of every disturbance and sorrow.

Increasingly, go to others, approaching them with respect and delicacy, touching them with love. To try always to understand everything and everyone. Not to argue, but instead, through presence and example, to dispel prejudice, to reveal God, and to make him felt without speaking; to strengthen one's mind, to enlarge one's heart more and more; to love tirelessly in spite of disappointment and indifference. Above all, to attract the humble and the little ones so as to lead them to God, who loves them so much. Deep, unalterable respect for others; never to do them violence, however gentle one tries to be, but to open wide one's heart to show the light and the truth that lives there, to let that creative truth enlighten and transform without any merit of ours but simply by the fact of its presence in us.

Nothing eccentric, mean, or confusing in one's attitude. Straightforwardness, simplicity, and, when necessary, the quiet affirmation of one's convictions. But never any display in that statement. Nothing extreme or partisan. Never show the hurts caused by hostility, declarations, or misunderstandings; to offer them for those who cause this suffering.

To increase one's determination; to do everything to acquire knowledge. To strengthen one's thoughts, one's will, and even one's feelings, and yet preserve all their gentleness and depth. To Jesus, my savior, I offer all these resolutions, having been to confession and having prepared to receive him this week. May he help me follow truly Christian ways, to be completely Catholic, and to work for the coming of his kingdom.

May 3, 1904

Has my life known any unhappier time than this?...The cruel, ongoing trial of Juliette's illness and the fear of the future, the painful knowledge of our mother's grief, my usual bad health and painful oppression of mind and body—all this now makes my life a sacrifice I offer to God silently for Juliette, for those I love, and for all others. It is a great, double sacrifice I offer: my life and my spiritual isolation, so different from what I desire. To be always with dear ones or friends to whom I can never open my heart even for an instant, to whom I can never reveal anything of my inner being, is an intense sorrow. Jesus Christ must have known it, he who had so much to give and who endured rebuffs and contradictions compared to which mine are nothing.

And yet through all these trials and despite the lack of interior joy, there is a deep place that all these waves of sorrow cannot touch. There my inner life is hidden; there I can feel how completely one with God I am, and I regain strength and serenity in the heart of Christ. My God, give health and happiness to those I love and give us all true light and charity.

External events would also be distressing if I did not have firm confidence in the future of Christ's church and great hope for the future of our country. How shattering to see the ignorant masses deceived and driven to evil and hate! My God, give us "children of light" (John 12:36; 1 Thess 5:5). Let apostles arise with burning hearts to go to the little ones wholeheartedly and bring them truth and love. You alone can save and transform. Give me, weak and little as I am, some of your divine strength, and come to me so that I can do much good.

I am going to try again to act with renewed strength; at any rate, I know, thanks to the wonderful communion of saints, that I can certainly act through my present suffering, and God will do with it what he wills.

July 4, 1904

Painful time of illness. Always the same uncertain future. Yesterday, a spell of weakness and tears, which I regret. Today the resolution, with God's help, to be weak no more; to become joyful again; to master the body through the soul, which belongs more than ever to God, in suffering more than in joy.

My God, give health and happiness to those I love; give them faith and love, true life, and I ask for nothing more.

A day of great joy: a present of a lovely little writing desk from Félix, accompanied by words that touched me deeply. His love is the greatest happiness of my life. To hold firmly each day to my resolutions: daily meditation, regular and thorough work, and peaceful action. Not to give in to the lethargy of mind and body that come inevitably with poor health; to maintain my energy and to force myself to be neither sad nor discouraged. In eight days we depart for Jougne. It is sad to leave Maman and Juliette; joy to have Félix near me and to occupy myself with the children. I place these months in God's hands, as well as the winter I see coming.

August 31, 1904

We returned last night from Jougne, after a difficult beginning because of the illnesses of Juliette and my mother-in-law. We had three good weeks in which I fully appreciated that country and the full, sweet life [we can live] there. To have the children near me, to be involved with them, to raise them in the best sense of that term and to impress on them things that will never be forgotten; to take an interest in everyone and to make our home into a vital, life-giving place—all this has filled my days, and I will always remember this happy time. Our departure and return were sad, aggravated by fatigue. With all my heart I thank God for the graces he gave us during these six weeks, and I ask pardon for my weaknesses and faults.

I have made several resolutions, which I place in the heart of Jesus. To begin a work that will make him better known and loved. To give myself regularly and wholeheartedly to the two tasks in which I am engaged. To make our home more Christian. To fill my days with prayer, meditation, work, and a stronger and more lively charity.

September 13, 1904

I am going to take advantage of a rare, peaceful day in my increasingly troubled and fragmented life to make a serious examination of conscience and meditation. First, I want to write a little in this journal; it will do me good, for I feel great spiritual isolation, humanly speaking, and a word of faith or of charity from human lips would warm my heart.

It is God's will that, until my most intense wish is granted, I should walk the path of suffering that he has pointed out and that he has made quite rough for me lately. And yet more than ever, he is close to me and supporting me. From a human point of view, no light is visible. Sadness in the present, anxiety for the future, frequent impediments in everything through my illness, the deprivation of all that could have transformed my life: good and fruitful work, reading—and this because of more immediate and humble duties. Absence of the consolation that contact with people of intelligence, faith, and truly Christian love always brings; physical discomfort—all these at present make me dull and sad. Today in recollection and humble prayer I will seek the divine aid I need so much and plan out my life for this winter as it presents itself to me. First, I must firmly relinquish the concrete visible good I would have liked to do; my duty to the ill in my family comes before all, and since I believe in the communion of saints, I will ask God to apply to those I love and to others the fruit of this inaction. I must learn to use spare moments to write and work. I must not neglect my daily meditation for that is so necessary to me, and I will do it when and how I can.

To return to greater serenity, inner and outer; to struggle against absorption in my beloveds' suffering; to avoid speaking of my miseries, which is harmful to inner concentration. To be harder on myself and more indulgent toward others. Not to dwell upon the small assaults my feelings constantly suffer, but to offer them courageously to God. Not to give in to discouragement and a type of moral indifference that results from sadness and physical problems. But to keep alive spiritual joy and the determination to act, without any desire to know the results.

October 18, 1904

...Resolution always to be pleasant, without trying too obviously. If I wish to avoid all useless controversy and fruitless waste of energy, I must, nevertheless, know how to make myself all things to all people and take an interest in things that sometimes seem immature and sadden me by their contrast with my own attitude. Often people are like great children, but Jesus has said that what is done for children is done for him (Matt 25:40). So let us be kind to those who show the immaturity and incredible superficiality of so many around us, and insofar as it is useful, let us learn how to become little with all types of "little ones" (Matt 10:42), even the small of spirit. Let us try to speak a language they can understand, and with them stammer eternal truths. Has not God done the same with us, and has he not placed in us only as much light as we can bear?

October 24, 1904

One of those unforgettable days. I went from Moulins to Paray-le-Monial alone.[11] It would have been even happier if there had been two of us, and one day I shall have that joy. After buying a few souvenirs, I went and prayed in the church for a while. It is a twelfth-century church with a beautiful exterior—finer, I think, than the interior. Then I went to the little Chapel of the Visitation, where so many prayers have been left that the place is impregnated with them. I stayed there a long time, and I placed in the Heart of Christ the petition that was the main reason for my visit: Juliette's recovery. I confided to him many other desires, and I prayed for our country and for the church. I brought home with me some of the blessed peace that is only found before the tabernacle, because there lives, ready to answer us, the most holy One who walked the earth, who alone can understand us because he has known human distress and yet possesses, by the eternal Word, all divine knowledge. The day was spiritually complete because an enormous grief awaited my return—a suffering all the more acute because it struck him whom I love above all. I offered it to God for him, for Juliette, for all I love, and peace returned.

December 3, 1904

The moments spent with Juliette are among the best of my life. This dear woman moves and inspires me more than I can say. I love her soul, and I think she understands mine. This is a great consolation because, of those who surround me, apart from Maman, my sisters, and my dear Félix, no one knows my inner self. And the whole of my inner life will be understood by my beloved only later, when God will have brought him into the light.

On Wednesday I had a striking example of what God's grace can do, and I saw how abundantly it is given in the sacraments. I had spent the morning in a state of extreme prostration and sadness; during the day I went to confession, and I was at peace again; I seemed to be—and indeed I was—renewed by a strength other than my own. The sense of forgiveness and spiritual renewal in the sacrament of penance is wonderful. And yesterday morning I received communion with the same peace and the same abandonment to God. I felt Jesus truly living in me, and now I want to become different, be totally Christian, with all that that word means of self-forgetfulness, strength, serenity, and love. That others may see in me your apostle, may you alone, my God, know my faults and weaknesses, as you alone can forgive them.

February 11, 1905

A succession of emotions, the same heartrending trouble, a grievous blow from someone whom I do not think I ever deliberately harmed—that is the balance sheet of the new year. Not enough deep recollection, partly due to circumstances, partly due to lack of resolve. Today there is exterior tranquility; I turn inward and I feel myself nearer to God. Next week I will receive communion again and draw divine grace from that contact with our Savior. I will destroy egotism in myself, all "touchiness" and pride, and I will try to be gentle and kind even toward those who cause me pain and affliction. Besides, I too have wronged them; I have not been sufficiently good and openhearted toward them. If they misunderstand me, so much the better—I shall have less pride, and it will be for God alone and with his love that I will try do good among them. Not to give in to moments of fatigue or sadness, to the temptation to lessen my efforts; to remain courageous in the face of any sacrifice, and in times such as this to invoke more than ever the spiritual strength that God gives. To apply myself soon to hard intellectual work, so useful for me, and to maintain equilibrium in my mind and in my life, which is filled with too many cares at present. To be unswervingly faithful to daily tasks, in big and little things, in work, in painful inaction, in illness and suffering, as much as in joy and health. May those who draw near me sense that I am firmly rooted in God and am peaceful and lively because of it The restless waves that sometimes beat against me are human things that come to me from outside; may others see in me only what is permanent and true; never may they hold back because I have discouraged them or because agitations and worldly complications have hidden the way of approach; may my spirit be as light as my smile conveys to all, and may your Word, O my God, inspire my words and make them fruitful.

February 18, 1905

My confession on Wednesday did me good and the sacrament of penance brought me consolation and peace. Yesterday I received communion with joy and renewed the offering of my life to Jesus, my Savior. May he give me the grace to be his apostle and to make known to others, by my example and my actions, the strength and life he gives and how he can transform a human being even as weak as I. The divine Spirit, who made apostles of burning zeal out of ignorant fishermen can make use of me to do a little good, and I fervently ask for this.

April 4, 1905

I suffer, I adore, and I pray.

O Jesus, in that garden where you saw the last night of your life descend upon your followers, and a still darker night upon your own soul, you suffered alone. Even those who loved you failed to understand you and your suffering. O my Savior, all men and women experience some form of that agony in the Garden; all Christians go through an undescribable crisis of suffering and desolation. And, like you, Christians are always alone in the Garden of Gethsemane, in spite of love and compassion sleeping nearby. No one can understand another's pain enough to pour soothing balm over it, and those who try sometimes cause only more pain. Remember, then, adored One, what that hour was like for you; have compassion on our weakness. You, who are the only consoler, the only heart that can truly understand, come soothe and strengthen us and help us to turn our sorrow into salvation, love, and a living proclamation of the gospel. O Lord, she whom I love is ill. You alone can save her. May that be your will! Have mercy on us!

April 13, 1905[12]

✟

July 4, 1905

It is three months since I uttered the cry of anguish that you heard, O my God, and did not grant the deepest prayer from my battered heart, or rather, you answered it differently and better. All that I so ardently desired for my beloved, all the joys, health, and love that I hoped for her and all the life that I prayed for, even her final happiness, all these you have given to her in taking her to yourself. I cannot believe that my constant ardent prayers, and those of others for her, and all the sacrifices offered and so much suffering accepted could all be useless. I do not believe that all her sufferings and grief, ended by a holy death, could be without fruit. If she was denied earthly happiness, if she knew bitter and sad separations, and if in the end she was taken from us, it is because a better life awaited her on the other side. The God of love prepared for her a joy beyond her suffering, and God wanted her to enjoy all good and beauty and to give her his light; God...purified her and so she could approach the holiness of God. My God, you wished, no doubt, to purify us also...and to transform us through suffering. I can only say to you with all my being, which is yours, the words I wrote on April 4: "My God, I suffer, I adore, and I pray."

I adore because I believe, because I have seen and tasted the depth of suffering, because my soul is forever rooted in you, my God, unless you abandon me. I adore because you are goodness, beauty, light, and life; because you are a father full of love and compassion; because you are my friend and my only consoler, O Jesus Christ!

But I suffer because she whom you took was my true friend and the gentle confidant of my faith and thoughts; because I spent some of the best hours of my life with her; because I loved her like a sister and like a beloved child at the same time; because we prayed, suffered, and loved together; and because her affection belonged to my life, my happiness, my heart.

Now, humanly speaking, my life is shattered, part of my heart has gone with my dear sister to live in you. Already my earthly happiness consisted only in the well-being of those I love, for gradually, all my human hopes had become, as I wrote to our sister, spiritual and Christian ones.

Félix's love and my dear ones' affection have been my share in human happiness, a share so great that I give thanks for it and accept my moral and physical trials. They seem small now compared to the grief that has struck us, which nothing can console. May we one day, at least, be reunited where there are no tears, no grief, and no separation.

Later, with God's help, I hope I shall write of Juliette's last days and peaceful death.[13] She received every consolation and grace until the last minute; she died on Thursday, April 13, six weeks before [her goddaughter's] first communion,…which she witnessed from heaven. The week of the retreat and the first communion was peaceful and centered. Marie was charming, deeply moved. I shall never forget that communion when we all prayed together. I offered myself to God for a new life and, upheld by [Juliette's] prayers, I want to become an apostle and to transform myself.

How can I describe what Félix was for all of us during April and also the first communion? "My beloved, since I have no better way of showing my love, let me write in our names a solemn blessing. May it bring you God's grace, and may you become a Christian and a saint. Juliette loved you deeply; she offered a part of her sufferings for you; may she obtain true happiness and life for you whom I love the most on earth."

And may she obtain for our poor Maman, whom I love more than I can say, the spiritual peace and consolation that come from God alone. May she be the loving protector of her children...and may she protect me, who am so weak, for whom her loving words and example did so much good.

With Louis Veuillot I say, "May God give me strength and leave me my grief."[14] May I work without weakening, and may my sufferings be transformed into charity and spiritual love for my loved ones, for the least, for the poor, and for all who do not know God.

My dear Juliette, may you still be my soul-friend. Pray for me and remember that you said to me one day, with such a loving expression and tone, that you could "no longer do without me." I do not ask to shorten by one hour the time that I must spend on earth. "All is brief that has an ending," whether it is days or years. I know with deep faith what awaits us at the end. But I ask you to sustain and accompany me in my pilgrimage, to pray that I be faithful and strong, and to welcome me at the hour of my death. My beloved, I believe the joy of reunion will surpass the pain of separation and waiting, and that then we shall live. You who see and know obtain for us a faint ray of this eternal light to guide and illumine us.

October 2, 1905

After a deeply restful time in Jougne, my return to Paris was very painful. To resume daily life without [my sister] who so filled it seemed a task almost beyond my ability. But was I not depending on my own strength instead of relying on Providence, who has never failed me? Once again providence helped me in the midst of my grief and frequent bodily pain; I was still able to remain in deep union with God's will. As Juliette would say, I want to "reform my life." That is, without any great external change or remarkable behavior to stabilize myself in greater serenity, true humility, and charity. I want to be truthful more and more, and it is sometimes more difficult than it seems. Even if my grief is inconsolable and has totally changed my life, I must not give in to depression and sadness. Since I am not entirely able to lead the life I would like, it is all the more necessary to make my actual life more fruitful for God and for those entrusted to me. After all, workers do not choose their task, and children yield to the loving desires of their parents. The only important thing is to accomplish my calling; the milieu and the means matter little. It is true that I have less human joy and comfort than if I lived in a Christian environment, but I know from experience that God makes up for what is lacking with great generosity. He gives us inwardly what outward circumstances deny. With him and by him I must become more loving, strong, and peaceful, live the inner life more, and yet give myself generously to those I love and to all whom providence has put on my path.

To speak little of my physical suffering and yet take care of myself adequately. To expect nothing from those whom I try to help, except, of course, those whom I know well. To accept silently the disappointments, the misunderstandings, and even the disdain that always come to those through whom others think they can attack God. To live in the remembrance of grace, in prayer and action, in hope and attentiveness. To be completely reasonably, spiritually Christian. To pray, to act, to work, to love.

October 7, 1905

Firmer resolution to maintain a deep inner stability and to accept the waves of difficulties, agitation, and confusions that, though caused by my health, do not touch the depths, as well as painful disappointments caused by some people. To love those who have betrayed my confidence and made me suffer, or at least to forgive them fully. Not to project onto others my own faults but to accept the humiliation of having given my confidence too quickly. For the future, without discouragement or bitterness, to be very prudent in regard to work and new connections, and in all things to observe the greatest moderation. To be loving to all, but not to let everyone enter into my heart too easily. To respond to an attraction only when I have solidly tested it, and yet to be kind to all. Never to compromise with ideas and principles, and yet to be completely tolerant of those who differ most from me in their point of view. To maintain, by prayer and daily effort, integrity of will and moral energy in spite of the oppression and failure caused by poor health. I think it was Bichat who said, "The soul creates its body. And when God dwells in the soul, how shall it not be stronger than the very evil that affects the body and sometimes overwhelms it?"[15]

October 17, 1905

...When I look back in spite of suffering and tears, I can only bless and adore. I begin this new period of life—long or short, peaceful or sorrowful, according to God's will with these words from my depths: I believe, I adore, I hope. I want to be Christian to the core and to be transformed by grace. This year I will accept and offer to God for others and for the church the difficulty of external distraction and distress, which aggravates pain. I will defend my home...from all who are unworthy, for that is a duty. I must not give in to my immense longing for seclusion and solitude in spite of my inconsolable grief and natural aversion to superficiality. To live a life of work and action, in an atmosphere of faith with Félix, surrounded by friends and family—that is my dream. But if that dream came true, it would be a taste of heaven already—and this earth is not heaven. And yet I must say in all humility how hard it is for me to make the necessary effort and how I suffer through my life, which is too fragmented for my taste and into which no glimmer of faith or consolation comes from outside. Perhaps that is why God has made himself everything to me—why he has taken care of all of my needs and accomplished everything in me....May God help me to accomplish my resolutions and give me his grace! May he do a little good through me!

All Saints, November 1, 1905

...This is a lovely feast, the feast of those who already live in God, those whom we have loved and who have attained happiness and light; it is the feast of eternity. And what a fine idea to make the feast of the dead follow so soon! During these two days a vast stream of prayer and love flows through the three worlds: between the church in heaven, the church on earth, and the church in which souls wait and atone. The communion of saints seems twice as close and fruitful. We feel that the dead and all those we love are close to us in God; and this living doctrine, by God's grace, gives life to many on earth and in purgatory. Not one of our tears, not one of our prayers is lost; they have a power that many people never suspect. I want to spend this month in prayer, remembrance, thoughts of heaven, as well as in charity and peaceful, courageous activity.

November 13, 1905

Seven months today since [Juliette] left us! And I suffer as on the first day, or even more, because indifferent people around me have forgotten that I still feel this loss and because my external life allows me less quiet and recollection. I have let my peace be disturbed by outside influences, and by anxiety about Maman's health, and for the future; but my deeper serenity is not affected, because more than ever I feel abandoned to God and willing to sacrifice all for him and for the good of those I love most. But too many things still upset this more exterior part of my soul and make it suffer. Worries, sad memories, an atmosphere of unbelief, indifference, or scorn, and the painful awareness of never being able to make either God or one's soul known to others—all this has battered me and knocked me to the ground, bruised like the gentle Savior. But all this brings me to a humble act of faith, love, and acceptance, and a new resolution to be more courageous, to steady myself in peace, and to submit to these offenses without revealing the suffering they cause me. With Félix I ought to be more even tempered, stronger; with Maman more gentle and attentive; with everyone kind and self-forgetful. My weakness is great. I have had new experience of it, but I must say with Saint Paul that "I can do all things through him who strengthens me" (Phil 4:13). My beloved Félix has many cares, Maman an immense grief; they need me, or even more, they need only God. Through my sufferings and sacrifices I can obtain spiritual transformation for them. Is this not the task: to sacrifice the self-centered self and offer up all that attacks and wounds this self? My God, assist her who, in spite of her faults, desires above everything to make you known and loved.

January 3, 1906

...I went to communion on Christmas Eve and on Christmas Day, and drew strength and peace from that blessed contact with the Savior. And yet now I suffer from great physical exhaustion, and longing for what I lack—candor, recollection, and Christian action—causes me pain. In spite of my resolutions I have allowed certain offenses and activities to disturb my peace. My God, I long for your peace and this joy that you sometimes give me—this beautiful light that enlightens and transforms all. To possess even a glimmer of it is already a small portion of heaven, and that is why you give it so infrequently as one loves you more deeply and progresses further along your way.

Through suffering and in silence I want to pray, love, and act. It is best for God alone to dispose of what we offer him; if we knew the result of our efforts, if we knew the mysterious influence of our sacrifice and prayer, pride, always near, would take over. In eternity we shall know these things. I shall know all that Juliette has been to me, and all that she obtained for me, and perhaps I shall have the joy that one of my sacrifices offered for her obtained a little peace and grace for her at the hour of her death. "O my beloved," for whom I have prayed and who, I hope, knows my spirit now—"pray for me, and ask only for the grace to love God more and more and to be a humble apostle of Jesus Christ."

January 31, 1906

I interrupt my meditation to write down an idea that just came to me.

For some time I have gradually been sharing too much of my interior life. This is not usual for me. My inner life was known only to God and to my spiritual director, as much as those things can ever be revealed. But due to grief and the love and attention surrounding me, I gave in to this sort of appeal and began to speak too freely of myself, my sorrow, and my illnesses, and even of the graces I have received. I have even spoken too much of you, my God, for it is true that in this world that does not know you, one should carefully weigh one's words concerning you. These reflections and the attitude of some who are dear to me have already given me a useful lesson in humility and reminded me of the need for silence. This is my reso-lution: silence in regard to my trials, silence about my interior life and what God has done unceasingly in me, silence about all spiritual things, about my hopes and my faith. I believe it is my responsibil-ity...to proclaim Jesus Christ only through my prayers, my suffer-ings, and my example. My interior companion must be guessed at rather than plainly seen; everything must speak of him without my saying his name; I must be an influence without ever being a profes-sion of faith. Anything that even in the most subtle or indirect way leads to pride and egotism must be eliminated from my heart and conversation. Is there not a little self-absorption in the slightest dis-play of oneself? I do not want to be a spiritual gossip except when charity requires it. I want to keep this great silence about spiritual matters—this encounter with God alone that preserves one's inner strength. Nothing must be dissipated; one must direct one's energy entirely to God, so that it may shine all the more.

February 21, 1906

I have kept my resolution about silence fairly well, but I have too easily yielded to an exhausting mixture of irritation and lethargy caused by poor health. What a great thing the soul is, and how distinct from and independent of the body! In depression and physical pain our poor mental abilities share the fatigue of the body. The soul remains free and continues to live a life of its own; sustained by a force that comes from above, it animates the body and keeps it in its place. How much we need God! And how quickly we should be conquered without his grace!

New resolution of silence, work, and peaceful action. Resolution to do what God wants, not desiring work that is not mine. Resolution to pray and offer my trials more than ever to obtain for those I love the grace that is my incessant desire and the goal of my life.

February 27, 1906

Tomorrow Lent begins. I have just made a short meditation and my resolutions for this graced time. I want to practice recol-lection, penance, and charity. Recollection, which can exist in the midst of busyness and exterior obligations from which, less than any other woman, I can excuse myself. The soul can be a cell as white and empty of worldly influence as the cell of a monk. The crucifix and some books—that is to say, God and work is what fills the solitude of nuns and monks; this is what can make a woman who is completely flooded with noise and activity, solitary.

Second, penance. Apart from penances prescribed by the church, I must perform my own, unlike others. I will accept and offer to God social events and entertaining, the contact with indifferent people, those worldly activities that are more painful to me than ever during this month when I would prefer to return to my memories [of Juliette]. I will do this in a way that only God, I hope, will know how much it costs. And in the trials of my life or the distress of ill health, I shall have plenty of opportunity to deny myself.

Finally, charity. Increasingly, to make myself all things to all people, to forget myself for others, to be always tolerant and cheerful, to show more love to those around me, to go more to little ones and to the humble. Even in times of debility and physical exhaustion I must not be as lazy as I have been recently. I must prudently resume my work, but with more energy and perseverance.

And always silence, unless speaking can do some good. Not to speak about myself. To be more pleasant than I have been for a while. To smile and share in the joys and pleasures of others when I am physically very tired is more advantageous than when in good health, for the effort is greater. May others see in me only that which can console or do them some good, and may you alone, God, know the silent struggles within me. May Lent be a time of preparation and sanctification. May I perhaps become, O my God, your instrument and your apostle for those I love and for those you love.

April 4, 1906

I will go to communion tomorrow; and during this week, until my communion on Holy Thursday, I want to make my retreat.

I do not know if I shall be able to hear many sermons but have made these resolutions: to make a good daily meditation on what my ministry should be; to practice penance and charity without being noticed; to end my retreat with my Holy Week and

Easter communions. This will be an entirely interior retreat because my second resolution is that no one shall know what I am doing or suffer for my spiritual benefit. I must, on the contrary, try to be more cheerful and serenely gentle, so that if anyone should guess that God has been here, such a discovery would not dishonor him. It is a year since I wrote for the last time in this journal, before April 13, "*Fiat* for us, alleluia, for [Juliette]." O my God, give her happiness, and allow us our suffering and our memories, and let us all love one another one day close to you.

August 11, 1906

Before God, I close this journal in which for seven years I have noted my spiritual development. That written expression was good for me while providence was performing "in me, without me" a work that I only understood later. Now that I am more mature, when I review the past and look toward the future with serenity, this future can no longer bring any true sorrow because God is my horizon everywhere. I make an act of great faith, spiritual hope, adoration, and of gratitude for all the graces you have given me. Your gift, my God, has been entirely free, and you have dealt with me like a "favorite child." On the threshold of my new life I offer you in loving oblation, my whole past existence—my childhood and youth; those fourteen years with their joys, sufferings, and faults; the trials you know about, which have made my life somewhat unusual, but less so than your graces, O my God. I offer also these past two years, sorrowful and yet transformed, this time of purification and suffering, ending with the greatest trial of my life; these last months in which you refined my soul, perfecting the instrument, in your own way so you may use it for the good of others and for those I love. As Juliette said, "I love you and abandon myself to you."

And now I offer you the new existence opening before me. Sustained by your grace, I want to become a new woman, a Christian, an apostle; and I make these resolutions in order to reach this goal and to fulfill the mission that I see so clearly. First, *silence:* never to speak of my interior life or of my trials except when necessary. To conceal with the same prudence any display of my piety; to let my communions, prayers, and meditations be known as little as possible, that I may remain humble, and so that I may not contribute to the spirit of obstinacy and ignorance that surround me.

Then, *work*. Material work and spiritual obligations. Study, the cultivation of my mind. An intellectual ministry that God seems to will for me and for which he has prepared me. To complete one thing before moving on to another. Never to be idle or to leave this garden uncultivated.

Charity. To accomplish the task closest at hand before going to one further away. To prioritize my action: responsibilities to my husband, first, then all who belong to us, our friends, and those who depend on me. Charitable or social work, after the responsibilities of family life; to continue with these, and in the presence of others to maintain my usual silence. To remain humble and yet act distinctly and firmly.

Resolutions in regard to myself and others:

For *myself*—To be very strict. To vigorously maintain the spiritual practices that form the basis of my whole exterior life—daily prayers, meditation, communion as frequently as possible. These are such a great consolation and source of life. To accept troubles, sadness, suffering, and to practice voluntary mortification, all in the spirit of penance and reparation, and for the well-being of others.

For *others*—Not to speak of myself and my interior life,[16] to keep silence about my good actions. To be simple, true, always humble. Always to maintain serenity and never to betray physical suffering, anguish, or sadness. To be friendly and interested in others and their ideas, to try to enter into and understand them. To be kind, with that true kindness that comes only from the heart. To devote myself, to spend myself, all without excitement or useless distraction.

And in view of a greater good and for a higher purpose, to be vigilant over my attitude and my dress; to make myself attractive for God's sake. To make my home charming that it may be a center of good and positive influence; to encourage diverse spirits and hearts to gather there and to try to raise and enlighten them.

In summary: To *reserve* for God alone the depths of my interior life. To *give* to others serenity, graciousness, kindness, helpful words and deeds. To make Christian truth loved through me, but to speak of it only when explicitly asked or when the need is very clear. To preach by prayer, sacrifice, and example. To be *austere* to myself, and as *attractive* as possible to others.

These are my resolutions, my God. I place them in the protection of my blessed sisters, of those I love who live in you. I confide them to my guardian angel, to the saints in whom I have special confidence—my gentle patrons, Saint Teresa, Saint Catherine of Siena, and others as well. I confide them above all to you, Mary, Mother and blessed protector. Through you I offer them to God, and I wish in the future to live only for my beloveds, for souls, in the peaceful expectation of eternity, when we shall at last have happiness and where, loving us, you shall be adored forever, O Jesus Christ, my Savior and my God!

Notebook of Resolutions (1906–1912)

"To gather up all things in him" (Eph 1:10).[17]

(October–November 1906)[18]

This rule, which I now write so that I can better examine myself before God, should not be interpreted too rigidly. The milieu in which I live, certain people's hostility, the variety and sometimes the complexity of my responsibilities, the influence I can have on those who love me and on the spirits who come to me with confidence, all demand from me great discernment. Although I must be careful not to neglect the smallest detail of my rule when I am the only one affected, it would be inappropriate to act in the same way when others are concerned. My resolutions, therefore, should be adapted to circumstances. The rule of charity should take precedent over anything intended to ensure the stability and intensity of my spiritual life.

I place this project...under the protection of Mary, my beloved Mother, and of my guardian angel, of my holy patron, and the saints I especially honor, and also of the beloved dead whom God has taken and will give back to me in eternity.

In an act of faith and love, after giving thanks for all that God has done for me, I offer and consecrate myself to God, asking only one grace: to love him more and more and to be his apostle to those I love as well as to others.

Each Day:

Morning and Evening Prayer.

Meditation. Meditation is necessary for me; it is daily nourishment, without which my spiritual life would weaken. Meditation prepares for daily work; to be alone with God helps later in the midst of people, and enables us to share among them some of our morning provision.

To assist sometimes at the Eucharist, especially on Fridays.

To go to confession and communion every two weeks if possible. To receive communion more frequently whenever it can be done without inconveniencing or displeasing anyone.

Holy communion is a blessing that I would enjoy more often if it were not my duty…to avoid clashing with or offending the biases of others. The strength God brings, the tenderness of his presence, the vitality communicated through that blessed contact can neither be described nor really explained. One can only say to those who marvel at this divine love, "taste and see" (Ps 34:8).

Blessed are you, O my God, for those hours…in which my weary heart has rested in yours, and drawn from it peace, charity, the knowledge of divine things, and through that, the knowledge of human nature, its weakness, and its many forms of suffering. Through your compassion, your ability to console, and your gentle, loving tenderness you have taught me, my Savior, how to be empathetic, calming, and loving. How could I not love others, especially those most weak and guilty—I who, weak and guilty too, receive the depth of your love and the fullness of your forgiveness?

Each Month:

Give one day to a little spiritual retreat; go to Mass and if possible to communion. On this day, as far as possible, to abstain from going out and from worldly contacts. More complete meditation. Examine my conscience and my life. Prepare for death on this day.

Each year:

Make a few days of retreat—as much as possible, at least, in a great interior recollection. A retreat is to the whole of life what meditation is to the day. One gathers new strength and, transformed and made holy, returns to the tasks and responsibilities that fill our lives. Generosity is easier when one has renewed one's interior provision.

I do not include here all those precepts [of the church] that each of us would observe unless especially dispensed from doing so. My resolutions only concern the evangelical counsels. Their goal is Christian holiness and seeking that which will help me to come closer to this ideal, which is still so distant.

After these resolutions concerning prayer life, I come to the resolutions related to my exterior life and my relationships with my neighbor.

First, my duty to my dear husband: deep love...constant care to be useful and gracious to him. Especially, to be reserved concerning matters of faith, which are still veiled to him. If a quiet statement should sometimes be necessary, or if I can fruitfully show him a little of what is in my heart, that must be a rare event, done after careful thought, gentleness, and serenity. To show him the fruit but not the sap, my life but not the faith that transforms it, the light in me but not the One who brings it, to reveal God without speaking his name. This is the only way, I think, I can hope for the conversion and holiness of my dear companion, my beloved Félix.

Responsibility to my two families. Especially to the young, to whom I will open wide my spirit and my home. Responsibility to be an example, to pray, to influence. Responsibility to those whom Providence has put on my path and seems intentionally to have given to my care. Never to anticipate a new task or responsibility, but as soon as one presents itself that seems clearly providential, to welcome it and accomplish it.

Responsibility of consolation and tenderness to my dear maman.

Responsibility in work. To take on only a little and only what I can really accomplish. To speak about it very little or not at all. To be involved with it only...when it will not inconvenience anyone around me and not interfere with my family responsibilities. To bring to all of it humility and charity, as well as a clear mind and an understanding of spiritual and social needs. In dealing with the poor, to avoid familiarity, arrogance, or any kind of excess.

THREE GENERAL RESOLUTIONS

Silence. To avoid as much as possible speaking of myself, my troubles, my illnesses, and especially of the graces received from God. Breaches of trust and tactless speech easily lead to pride or to an egotistical self-absorption—an absorption, moreover, that hinders rather than helps true recollection. To depart from this reserve only in those rare cases when the good of another truly seems to demand it or when a real need for helping another or of counsel presents itself. Even then, to speak of myself truthfully and simply, without affectation or a covert desire for praise, wishing to glorify God's work by diminishing myself, or rather by allowing others to see all my weaknesses and faults.

The Gift of Self. Not only in fulfilling my responsibilities to everyone, not only in charitable work, not only in prayer, but in my whole attitude and way of life. Great and holy ideas and deep convictions often influence others only through the attractiveness of those who embody them. "You will know them by their fruits" (Matt 7:16), our Savior said—by the fruits of devotion, charity, and radiant faith, and also by those blossoms that first attract notice and precede the fruit; those are called tender love, graciousness, social refinement, serenity, equanimity, friendliness, joy, and simplicity. A truly holy person—mistress, by divine grace, of her body and its challenges—without ever speaking, exudes the delicate perfume of these flowers. Such a person attracts others by her gentle influence and prepares them for God's approach, which she eventually obtains for them through her prayers.

Personal Asceticism. By asceticism I do not mean, of course, anything harmful to the body or to health. On the contrary, I need to preserve and try to improve my health, since it can be an instrument in the service of God and of neighbor. But in this illness that afflicts me, the precautions I must take, the discomforts it brings, and the deprivations it sometimes imposes (or at least may in the future) there is sufficient opportunity for self-denial. Apart from that there are many other opportunities for self-denial, without anyone noticing it or being inconvenienced. On the contrary, our personal self-denial will often actually benefit others. To do this...in a spirit of penance, of *reparation* to God and to the heart of Jesus, and to obtain the salvation of sinners.

INTELLECTUAL APOSTOLATE

This is perhaps what God especially intends for me. He has treated me like a "favorite child.",...God has done everything to prepare me for this form of ministry. In making known to me his intimate and personal activity within people, in making me live in the midst of total negation and indifference and that impenetrable ignorance of the things of God that so many unfortunate people experience. God has doubtless intended that I should understand the most widely differing points of view, that I should have compassion for, share with, and turn toward those who blaspheme and doubt with greater understanding and love. To be the good Samaritan to so many discontented hearts, uneasy minds, and troubled consciences; to have delicate respect for others and knowledge of them; to try to approach them gently; to pour healing oil upon them or strengthening wine according to their weakness or the seriousness of their wound; to show God to them only by letting him shine forth from within me where he lives; to be all things to all people and thus conquer hearts for Jesus Christ: this is the apostle's task, which I accept from you, O my God, in spite of my unworthiness.

But I know well what this word *apostle* means and all the obligations it creates. First, the necessity of an interior life that becomes stronger all the time, of drawing more than ever charity and gentle serenity from the Eucharist and from prayer, as well as making wholly spiritual intentions. Then, to cultivate my own mind systematically, to increase my knowledge of all those subjects that I am ready learn; to do nothing precipitously or superficially; to achieve, as much as possible, competence in the subjects I study. To transform and make this intellectual effort holy through a spiritual motive, doing it humbly without any self-centeredness, but exclusively to help others.

To bring to all conversation and discussion a tranquil spirit, a firmness, and a friendliness that will eliminate bitterness or irritation from the opponent's mind; never to give in where principles are concerned, but to have extraordinary tolerance for people. Above all, to try, after discovering the opening, to present the divine, unchanging Truth to each one in such a way as to make it understood and loved.

To bring great flexibility of mind and clarity of judgment to any purely intellectual matter. Each time the conversation leads me to speak of faith, I will do so simply but in a direct and firm way that will leave no doubt as to my convictions. Cleverness means nothing in such matters; I am struck with the fact that unbelievers have more in common with people of deep faith than with those of inconsistent and utilitarian views. These precious unbelievers pay more attention to those who are uncompromising regarding the faith than to those who by subtlety and accommodation hope to bring them to accept the faith. And yet a bold statement must be made with intelligent sympathy and the liveliest and most delicate charity.

To ask God to give me greater knowledge of human souls. To go to them through mind and heart; to strengthen my mind and rekindle my heart. To work and act serenely.

Every morning to offer to God, as I already do, all the indulgences I can gain during the day for those in purgatory, especially those who are dear to me; to offer my activity and my suffering for various intentions: for those I love, for others, for the church.

More frequent communion since circumstances now make it possible. The Holy Eucharist is indeed food for the soul; to say so is a commonplace, but how true! Apart from the conscious joy it sometimes brings, even without that joy, the inner self becomes stronger and more alive; the Eucharist transforms it, although one may not be aware of this mysterious process. This incorporation into us of the divine substance, this assimilation of [God] into our being, this eternal life penetrating our lives, this close contact with the most holy and loving person of all…works within us and, if our will belongs to God, deeply renews us. Anyone who has received communion for many months or years without being changed inwardly and outwardly has not brought to the holy table the openness and childlike simplicity that is blessed by our Savior. This renewal is independent of all conscious consolation and exterior joy; the loving sense of Jesus Christ's real presence is a grace sometimes given to us, but it does not necessarily contribute to our spiritual progress. It is one thing to love God and another thing actually to feel the joy of his presence.

To draw a curtain between my suffering and the outside world. Illness, sadness, the absence of a Christian environment, which I feel so much; the grief [over my sister's death], although it has lost some of its initial pain, is still and will always be a great sorrow in my life....In the future all these things must be a hidden treasure, concealed from the gaze of the indifferent. Except for those whose deep love enables them to see through appearances, no one must know of my suffering or how difficult it is to conceal it. I must be all things to all men and women, responding only to others' griefs, not saddening or troubling anyone with mine. To let my faith be seen only in the works inspired by it, and my sorrow only in my interior transformation. To know how to smile, empathize, share, but to keep my burdens from all but God. Not to be ungrateful, to rejoice simply, with gratitude, in the great loves and pleasures that Providence has accorded me. To ask God to use the interior reservoir of suffering within me for the benefit of others and of those I love. Always to welcome trials of any size, to accept them and offer them. Then, to keep silence and continue to act in all gentleness and serenity.

(December 2, 1906)

Resolutions for this Advent:

Prayer. More intimate, more profound. Frequent holy communion. Meditation.

Penance. In a spirit of reparation. Self-denial sought and offered up. Completely hidden, done for God alone.

Charity. More lively, more self-forgetful, more spiritual. May the exterior be more attractive, more gentle toward all, in proportion as there is more interior detachment.

(End of December 1906)

...Greater efforts than ever to remove from my heart and conceal from others the hurt caused by many people's hostility to, ignorance of, and contempt for my faith. To offer up these frequent and painful stings, which sometimes strike to the quick, for the benefit of those who inflict them, for others, in a spirit of reparation.

Never to betray the confidence that another has entrusted. Always observe the confidentiality of the confessional for all intimate and spiritual self-disclosures.

In work for others, be vigilant against all pride and egotism. Not to forget that I am only the simple intermediary between God and others, the dull instrument Providence uses, and that my role consists in perfecting this instrument, for which I still need grace.

(June 1907)

During the month of the Sacred Heart, to meditate every day on the beauty, love, and holiness of the Heart of Jesus. To offer in a spirit of reparation part of the suffering and deprivation I now endure, consecrating the rest to other intentions: the conversion and holiness of those who are dear to me, the salvation of others, the good of the church. In the absence of all conscious joy, to establish myself more firmly than ever, by God's grace, in complete serenity. Never to show by irritation or by outward exhaustion, which is more likely for me, the moral and physical fatigue caused by certain difficulties and long illness. To do everything to preserve and improve my health, and to make of this disagreeable concern, my practice of self-denial.

To learn from the Heart of Jesus the secret of love for others and deep knowledge of them: how to touch their wounds without making them sting, and how to dress them without reopening them; to give myself to them and yet maintain my privacy. To disclose Truth in its entirety and yet to make it known according to the degree of light that each can bear. The knowledge needed for this ministry only comes from Jesus Christ, by encountering him in the Eucharist and in prayer.

(*July-August 1907*)

Resolution during this vacation: to persevere steadily with my daily prayers and meditations, my communions at least weekly, to increase and strengthen, by divine grace, my spiritual life. To be all things to all people, and in all circumstances to remain gentle, serene, full of love for those around me. By example, by my words and actions, to try to make Jesus Christ known and loved; to do through him (or rather to ask that he work through me) for the good of those for whom I can be the instrument of Providence. Each day to work first for God and then for my neighbor. To pray, to act. To speak to each one in the language he or she can understand. To live in my interior depths and to proclaim myself before all, yet in all simplicity, a child of Christ and of his church, and to make my outer life harmonize with this high calling.

Always, to maintain exterior calm and evenness of mood.

Not to hope too much for the fulfillment of my desires, even those that are wholly spiritual; to remember that God is in charge; to await the hour willed by him for those I love; to hasten it not by action that may be indiscreet, but by prayer, by my suffering, and by a love, free of all pride and egotism, that does not expect results.

To infuse my words, actions, and even gestures with moderation, a peaceful gentleness, that will be a constant sign of my interior serenity. In this way to reveal God always working in me to calm me, to soothe me, and to strengthen me.

August 23, 1907

After a meditation on the gospel account of the transfiguration:

Consecration, total gift of myself to Jesus Christ. He took me with him, led me aside, and that is where I wish to stay—*away from* evil forever; *away from the world* and *human things* insofar as the obligation of charity and of family life do not require my outward self. Never again to give them my inner self.

Renewed consecration of my life to Jesus Christ. To live forever for him alone; to maintain my loves and friendships in him, more graced each day.

To love with a more lively and faithful love; to practice the threefold apostolate of prayer, of atoning penance, and of action through good works, words, writing, and example.

I take as a motto for my whole life those words of [Pope Leo XIII, quoting scripture]: "to gather up all things in him" (Eph 1:10).

First, to restore myself in Christ, by prayer, communion, and meditation; then, my whole life, by penance, charity, and humility. To restore in people's minds the ideals of responsibility and of family; to prepare them for the return of faith and for spiritual life; to ask for the divine summons by my fervent prayers, my sacrifices, and my trials. To make Jesus Christ loved and his church known; to share untiringly, without looking for results, all that has been given to me; to make a ministry of all my actions, words, and affections.

(October 1907)

A new life is imposed on me by God—a sedentary life, which is similar to a retreat given by Providence as I begin my mature years.[19]

Here are my resolutions for this period of my life.

First, deeper *recollection*—more authentic, infused with prayer, meditation, and the constant awareness of God; abiding recollection that will strengthen me. To be an *apostle* through *prayer*, that important and fruitful form of action, the only activity allowed me, the more secure because it is hidden, and works with God.

To *make amends* through suffering, sacrifice, and the self-denial that arises daily, or that I can choose. Since exterior activity is forbidden me, to try to act by words and example upon those who come to see me.

To be open to those who wish to confide in me, but not to open myself to them completely; always to keep the greatest intimacy for God alone.

To receive my daily visitors with serenity, trying to be all things to all people, in the manner that uniquely fits each one.

To be pleasant, but with all discretion and simplicity.

To work and read seriously that I may improve and lift my spirit.

Spiritually, to go to communion every Sunday, since that is the only day I can do so; to go to confession whenever I can.

To offer this deprivation of communion, of the consolations that have been so tender and good for me, especially during this last year, for my usual intentions.

To be strict with myself, even more than in the past; externally, to make myself attractive so as to draw other hearts to the One of whose goodness so many people are ignorant.

To love others for and through Jesus Christ, without any selfish motive and without anything that could feed pride or egotism.

To give myself generously and not to expect any return or satisfaction; not to desire affection, esteem, sympathy or, even less, praise.

To practice my simple ministry for God alone, in abundant charity that is disciplined, lively, and detached.

The two foundations of all Christian life: penance and humility.

The formula of all Christian life: contemplation, then action, then sacrifice.

Prayer is the better form of activity; through it we directly influence God, while outward action is only directed to our fellow human beings. We are certain of the result of our prayer but not of our actions—unless their spiritual intention transforms them into another form of prayer.

To pray, therefore, without ever tiring.

To love for those who hate, to suffer for those who rejoice, to give oneself for those who hesitate.

More than ever to practice Christian asceticism: in my actions, in my food, and in the fulfillment of my responsibilities. To do so without injuring my health, being reasonable as well as spiritual. And to conceal my sacrifices and freely chosen mortifications under a veil of smiles and cheerfulness. In my home, my dress, my manners, my hospitality, to show nothing but grace and gentle love.

God has deprived me of all pastoral care, and for nearly three weeks my health has deprived me of both Mass and communion. That is the greatest lack that I can offer in a spirit of penance and reparation, the prayer that will obtain, I hope, the graces so desired for others from our Savior.

To be silent and to live in interior recollection. To pray and to practice self-denial, for that is all God seems to want now. To ask nothing from outside in the way of human or spiritual consolation; to look to Jesus alone for everything.

Externally, to give to those who come to me a gentle welcome, serenity, a word that is appropriate for each [while maintaining] much reserve. To do my daily tasks without haste and to avoid subtle forms of pride: love of my good deeds, of the influence I exert, of inspiring others with beauty. To pursue "self" to its last awful hiding place.

Total union with God; abandonment and full consent to his will in present illness and inactivity. To pray and to suffer since activity is denied me; to give to my suffering and prayers a spiritual intention; may they become, in silence and humility, a better form of activity that thus by God's grace I may work unceasingly for the good of others as well as offering reparation to God.

To speak as little as possible of myself. Always to share in others' joy and sadness. Not to give in to this despondency and listlessness that continuous illness and a confined existence encourage. Therefore, to renew myself each day by prayer, meditation, and voluntary self-denial, which will help me endure the mortifications God sends.

To offer to God as the greatest and purest sacrifice the deprivation of pastoral care that I must endure, especially the most difficult of all, the lack of the Eucharist. O Lord, that is indeed abstinence, the severest penance, and the most painful trial of all. It is a suffering that many do not know or understand. Purify and transform me by this. Perfect your simple instrument! Give me the only grace I desire: to be your apostle with those who are close to me, with those you have placed on my path, and with others, distant and unknown, for whom my prayers and suffering will obtain salvation from you.

During days of illness and physical exhaustion, one must do everything with even greater calm and purpose and protect oneself from exterior disturbance by an even greater recollection. Not to allow myself the slightest movement of impatience, and to resist unceasingly every inner inclination to irritability. To punish and humble myself for it afterward.

To ask Jesus to allow to shine from me a little of the gentle love and kindness of his heart. To make myself all things to all people, and to forget myself for all. Every day to renew my too-soon-exhausted store of tranquil love, strength, and serenity from our Savior.

To grow in gentleness, and to make myself more hospitable to all when, as now, I most long for solitude, silence, and rest. Nevertheless, to arrange to have as much time for recollection as possible, so that I may receive the nourishment I need so much, which makes me stronger, more peaceful, and more filled with spiritual life.

A long period of illness, during which I could only live in the deepest intimacy with God, forcing myself to accept and offer my sufferings. May God let them atone for my faults and accept all my intentions for them.

Most painful deprivation of many spiritual helps. And yet great joy, for the Savior comes each week to visit me and brings me, with the gentleness of his presence, a strength beyond my own. There are so many painful things in the empty monotony and dissipation of those times when we are ill. God alone can turn this void, these little sacrifices and successive deprivations, into a work of redemption. Is there no consolation in being on our Savior's cross and, so close to him, obtaining the grace of salvation or conversion for others, for those whom we love so much?

(April and May 1908)

The last two months have been spiritually fruitful, I can now see. The apparent inertia, the inner destitution, the humiliating prostration of body and mind were all concealing the mysterious work of grace taking place in my depths. And now I can joyfully say that God has made me progress in the way of renunciation and self-denial, teaching me to do without even his loving consolations. I want to love you and you alone, O my Savior—not the great joys your child sometimes receives from you. Help me to detach myself more and more from that which does not last and to attach myself to you. Give me the grace of being—by prayer at least, and by suffering—your instrument for others, those who are dear to me, and those whom I do not know but who need my humble intercession.

And then, O God, give me the grace I long for, and make yourself known to and loved by him whom I love most. Give all your light and peace to Maman, and make those I love holy, especially those children whom I ask you to make into courageous apostles. I give myself to you and renew...the resolutions of these last months and of all my illness.

(October 2, 1908)

Renewed gift of myself and consecration of my life to God [in the church at Jougne]. Renewal of baptismal vows. Consecration to the Blessed Virgin. Resolution to practice, with God's grace, evangelical perfection according to my state in life, to lead an apostolic life of prayer, penance, and charity. To make reparation for myself and for everyone.

A holy day, which completes that innermost consecration begun at the tomb of the apostles, starting a new era in my spiritual life and binding me permanently to the way of the evangelical counsels, the only life I can live now.

(November 1908)

...Prayer is a very powerful force that, going through the Heart of Jesus right into the very heart of God, seizes, attracts, and in some way quickens grace in others. Suffering and the practice of charity are other equally powerful forms of prayer.

It is quite clear that God's will does not intend me for action. Until I receive new instructions, I should confine myself almost exclusively to prayer and strive to have more of the spirit of sacrifice. Perhaps God deprives me of outer activity in order to purify all inclination to pride, even the subtle pride over doing good. In prayer we do not see the result of our efforts, however reliable they may be; we are truly instruments in the hands of the divine Artist. We can remain humble even while experiencing the great joy of working for God's glory and the good of others. Let that, O God, be my portion and my task; in silence may I do only your will.

(January 1909)

I want the joy of sometimes choosing someone apart from those entrusted to me for whom I pray incessantly—some guilty or hostile person, preferably—and of spiritually adopting him or her. Then, in a special way, with faithful persistence, I will often offer for that person part of the day's activities or sufferings and will pray and practice self-denial as well. It would be a very humble, hidden apostolate, which God's grace can make most fruitful. Does it not fit perfectly with my vocation, which seems above all contemplative and tending toward prayer and sacrifice?

I have just chosen someone for adoption, never to be abandoned, without neglecting the others—the needs of all my brothers and sisters and of those who do not believe—whom I already bring to God in prayer.

(July-August 1909)

Resolutions for this vacation:

Humility, charity to all, silence. Less self-preoccupation, to make myself less the center, not to speak of myself.

Interiorly, close union with Jesus Christ: Communion three times a week, meditation, prayer. Great interior recollection. A little more asceticism to make up for the unavoidable outer diversions. But nothing obvious: good spirits and smiles covering effort and sacrifice.

To entrust my holidays, those I love, and myself to the heart of Jesus, which is more and more for me the heart of the Friend.

(January 1910)

The word from God for this year: to try to give our Lord Jesus Christ to others by the most humble and courageous practice of charity, by suffering and self-denial, and above all, by prayer. That is in a special way my vocation.

To resist pride through humility; egotism through self-forgetfulness and the gift of myself to those around me; sensuality through silence, self-denial, and the renunciation even of spiritual joys.

To resist my longing, which is sometimes so strong, for a different life, for calm, recollection, and silence. To keep within wise limits my growing aversion to the world and external stimulation. To accept the suffering caused so often by hostility, indifference, or the incomprehension of religious things. To desire strongly, humbly, only God's will and to live through him and for him in the world from which I would like to flee to the solitude that I cannot have.

Not to neglect the responsibilities of my life, all the while maintaining as its basis the spiritual practices I need so much, which are my strength and joy. To be gentle and smiling outside, keeping for God alone the life that is "hidden" in his Heart.

In what concerns God:
To suffer and to offer.
In what concerns others:
To give myself, to pour myself out.
In what concerns me:
To be silent and to forget myself.

(February 1910)

O my God, you who do not refuse me suffering. For some time you have accustomed me to love you in the deprivation of all sensible joys, in a suffering heart, and often enough, in an exhausted body. I accept all from your hand and unite myself to your will. Is it not just that having received all from you I should give you something in return, and that I should offer you the trials, prayers, sacrifices, and humble activity that is your daily design for me? Through it all I want to try, by your grace, to maintain joy of spirit.

O God, for some time you have given me the grace of suffering: spiritual trials, the renunciation of my desires and tastes, deeply felt spiritual isolation, and now the illness of my sister [Amélie]. How well you know how to choose the most appropriate suffering, the one that crucifies us and allows the least possibility of selfishness. In my illness there were still subtle temptations for me, and satisfactions that were legitimate and yet too worldly. In leaving me this physical misery, with its inconveniences and helplessness, you have again hidden this from others and sent me other trials that are very painful and known only to you.

From the bottom of my heart, I say to you, "Thank you." Blessed are you, O God, for all this pain, through which you allow me to atone for my faults, draw near to your heart, and also to obtain, I hope, many spiritual graces for many people, as well as for those I love.

My God, help me to carry the cross you have offered me, and let none of this precious grace of suffering be lost.

(October 1910)

...Carefully, avoid all discussion of religious subjects. Prayer, example, words, and deeds filled with charity and intelligence—these are the elements of fruitful engagement. Intellectual combat will never open the way to God, but a ray of charity sometimes illumines the path on which some poor, distressed heart is wandering and leads it to its destination.

Renewal of my consecration to Jesus Christ, act of complete abandonment to his will, offering myself for special intentions.

After my grace-filled return to the faith and the inexpressible joy of union with God, after he has given me everything, the time comes to give him something in return. A second period begins after that, more serious, more difficult: a period of loss and interior stripping, of dryness even, and sometimes of real distress. We can then show our Savior the depth of our love; we atone for past faults and offer the purest reparation...; we can also offer reparation for others, make our interior suffering serve others and acquire more inner strength. From a spiritual perspective, we achieve maturity, and as Saint Francis de Sales says so well, God weans us from the milk of infants to give us the wine of the strong. From experiencing every suffering and darkness of spirit, we discover a great joy in finally doing something for God, to show that we truly love him—God, and not his consolations, which he lavished upon us not so long ago. The unfinished *alleluia* ends in a *fiat* that, in spite of all, is still joyful.

My God, I belong and always wish to belong to you, in suffering or in pain, in spiritual dryness or in joy, in illness or in health, in life or in death. I want only one thing: that your will be done in me and by me. More and more I seek, and desire to seek, only one end: to promote your greater glory through the accomplishment of your desires for me.

I offer myself to you in wholehearted interior sacrifice and ask you to dispose of me for your service as the most common, most useless instrument, in favor of those you love. Make me either passive or active, practicing in turn and as the hour requires the contemplation I love best and other good works according to your will.

Let me always be strict with myself, more gentle, loving, and helpful to others,[20] to make you loved through me, always hiding my efforts, prayers, and mortifications. Make me very humble and draw my heart to yours, my beloved Savior and God.

The Catholic liturgy has a great attraction for me; I love to live the great communal life of the church in the course of the year, uniting myself with its joys and sorrows, joining my poor prayers with its prayers, my weak voice with its strong voice. It is consoling to go through the liturgical cycle, living our Savior's life, from his incarnation to his death and ascension; through the words of the prophets, fathers, and saints of all ages to speak my faith and my love; to adore him in company with those who have adored him through the centuries; to offer myself with shepherds, disciples, and martyrs, with people from all times; to feel myself living in the great Catholic communion, after so many others, and before so many who will follow me, with my homage to the infant God, the suffering Christ, the risen Lord.

How sorry I feel for those who are ignorant of all these traditions and of Christian joys, who have rejected them with contempt or even with hate, because they have not really understood or experienced them in the past! How I regret that I cannot draw them to Jesus, and how fervently I resolve to pray, suffer, and act with more zeal and humility than ever for these poor misguided people!

When we feel powerless against hostility and indifference, when it is impossible to speak of God or the spiritual life, when many hearts bump against ours without really connecting, then we must enter peacefully into ourselves in the loving company that we never lack, and we must offer only prayers and the quiet example of our lives and the secret sacrifice that makes the most fruitful apostolate. All explanations, words, and efforts are not worth the weakest ray of the Holy Spirit in enlightening someone, but they may obtain all of God's light for those for whom we pray.

There are moments in life when we must look neither ahead nor behind nor to the side, but contemplate only the cross God offers us, from which will flow great graces for ourselves and others.

...Change of Residence: a new life begins,[21] which must be directed even more toward God. To be more recollected; yet to be all things to all people in giving myself generously to those around me, to the little ones, to the poor and afflicted, above all to souls.

And more than ever to maintain silence about my spiritual life, my pain, my health. Silence preserves humility. On the other hand, never to be silent when it is a question of others' pain, or generous praise of one's neighbor, or of doing good.

It is marvelous how God knows how to promote spiritual growth—how after seducing one by the tenderness and attraction of consolation, he strips one, imposes one renunciation after another, removes sensible joy, and leads one gradually to true love of God, a love that no longer considers joy or pain, good or ill health, death or life, and which no longer seeks conscious consolation that was one's light in the beginning of conversion.

Intense pain from an evening spent in hearing my faith and spiritual things mocked, attacked, and criticized. God helped me to maintain interior charity and exterior calm; to deny or betray nothing, and yet not to irritate by too rigid assertions. But how much effort and inner distress this involves, and how much I need God's grace to assist my weakness!

My God, will you give me one day...soon...the immense joy of full spiritual communion with my dear husband, of the same faith, and, for both of us a life turned toward you?

I will intensify my prayers for this intention; more than ever I will beg, suffer, and offer to God communions and sacrifices to obtain this desired grace.

A ray of light in the midst of the acrimony caused by conversations with my friends: a young Jewish woman, a convert, is entering the Carmelite convent to make reparation in the name of her brothers and sisters and of all of us who are sinners and to offer to God a sacrifice of love and supplication. Your kingdom come, in the world, in others, in all those you have entrusted to me or that are dear to me....May your kingdom be completely, deeply, and exclusively established within me; I renew my consecration to you. Make me your instrument and use me for the good of all persons and for your glory, my Savior and my God.

December 1910

God, I offer you my spiritual aridity and deprivations. I offer you the interior sadness, the injuries, the disappointments of my heart, so much anxiety for the spiritual well-being and the health of those precious to me, and all the many sufferings of life.

I offer you darkness of spirit, weakness of will, interior sorrow, and burdens.

I offer you my physical distress, this illness that has sadly limited my external life, the discomforts and exhaustion that my troubles bring right now.

I bind these things into a sheaf, Lord, and come humbly with the shepherds to lay it in the manger. Little Child, all love, all purity, all tenderness, give me purity of heart, tenderness, and charity. Accept my afflictions and use them for the good of others and for your glory.

May your blessed hands help me to carry [my burdens], and may your love and the union of our hearts relieve my isolation. May it end one day, when, by your grace, you will convert and make holy those dear persons whom I beg you to make Christians and apostles, O Jesus Christ, my Lord and my God.

December 31, 1910

The last day of a year that has been filled with deprivation. God filled the year with suffering, renunciation, sadness of every kind, and spiritually, with dryness, with the destitution of the manger, without the loving joys that make the divine dawning in us so radiant. But God taught me a stronger, deeper love, stripped of conscious happiness, and I offer the year that is over and the one to come with a grateful heart. I consecrate myself to God and accept in advance all that he wants of me, through me, or for me:

joy or sorrow, health or illness, poverty or riches, and life or death, according to what will be for the greatest good of others and the church. For myself I ask one thing: let me love you, without joy or comfort if need be, and use me for the spreading of your kingdom, Jesus my Savior.

It is a source of pain and difficult sacrifice to have to divide one's life so much and always to give to each one less than he or she expects. This sometimes leads others to feel not enough is being done for them, and they perhaps experience some sadness or regret, which becomes painful to her who is the involuntary cause of it. And then one's self-love dislikes the loss of esteem and appreciation as well as the feeling of being not up to the task. That perhaps is the hidden fruit of this trial: a little useful humiliation, less dangerous than empathy and admiration, interior pain that does not elicit any praise. To fulfill my obligations generously; to give to each one my energy, time, affection, a warm and hospitable welcome, even at the price of sacrifice and renunciation. To offer God my incapacity, and joyfully to endure being misunderstood a little, or rather, to endure being truly understood with my weaknesses, my laziness, my many imperfections. Without this drop of bitterness, the tenderness of the affection surrounding me might make me slide into laziness and complacency.

My God, I accept my dissipated life, so often not what I want—this sometimes fatiguing mixture of activities, tedious acquaintances, cares. Help me to fulfill all the obligations of life and yet preserve my spiritual life. Let the warmth of my hospitality, the serenity of my bearing, the friendliness of my words always hide from everyone my physical suffering and my spiritual efforts and sacrifices. Teach me to be all things to all people, to be more strict with myself. To practice greater mortification, especially in a spirit of reparation.

Meditated on the miracle of the multiplication of the loaves. Jesus Christ takes this lifeless, tiny, common thing, this bread, and by his blessing it becomes food and life for the entire crowd.

Why should I not be, in these same divine hands, the poor instrument for a similar work? Why should I not be given by God to others to sustain and revive? I am only weakness, but strength comes from God alone who uses me. I will let him distribute me to others, and I will serve them only as he wills. Loving, divine blessing, descend upon me! Multiply my prayers, sacrifices, and acts of charity! Let these fragments of your love in me become warmth and comfort for the spiritually malnourished, until the happy time when you, the one living bread, shall come yourself to revive and save them.

Worldly people do not realize that one can be very detached from all human things and live a deep spiritual life, and at the same time, take pleasure in the interests, activities, and joys of life. However, it is only when one has planted oneself in eternity that one can let one's humble little boat float on the surface of the waves and fully rejoice in the view from earthly shores. Storms do not frighten; the clear sky emboldens. The sun is always shining behind the clouds. The light, for all its beauty, does not conceal the eternal and splendid light that guides us to port and waits for us there.

The joys of life—affection, the beauty of nature, and the splendors of art—as much as or more than anyone I rejoice in you, for you are a reflection of the Beauty and Love that have taken possession of my heart. The sorrows of life—trials, illness, and painful infirmities, you dear companions who have been so faithful to me—I do not reject you. I love you because you are other aspects of the one true Love; because, united to the holy cross, you become good workers for the salvation and conversion of souls and for my own expiation; because, thanks to you, I can sometimes show my love to him who has done…everything for me.

May God be praised for all: joys and griefs. May God help me, through the spiritual joy that exists even in the midst of interior sorrow, to praise and glorify him until my last breath, until I enter eternity.

…My present challenge seems to be somewhat painful,[22] and I have the humiliation of knowing how badly I responded at first. I now want to accept and to carry this little cross joyfully, to carry it silently, with a smile in my heart and on my face, in union with the cross of Christ. This involuntary "hair shirt" will replace the one I would never be allowed to wear, and I will thus curb my pride, egotism, and laziness. My God, blessed are you; accept each day the embarrassment, inconvenience, and pain this causes me. May it become a prayer and an act of reparation.

March 17, 1911

...Special prayer. An intimate pact between me and God, my heart and the Heart of Jesus,[23] through the intercession of the Blessed Virgin and under the protection of Saint Joseph and Saint Teresa. Confident this time of being heard. Now, O God, I await the fulfillment of your promises, and I wish to receive faithfully what they bring me in your name. May God be blessed!

April 9, 1911[24]

May God's will be done.
May you be blessed for everything, O God,
and give me your pardon and your grace.
Bless my beloved ones, all of them;
grant them conversion and holiness.
May my nephews and my niece be Christians and apostles.
Give your grace to those I love,
light and spiritual life to everyone.
Bless and guide your church and make her priests holy,
my spiritual father among them.
And take me totally to yourself,
in life, in death, and for eternity.
Amen.

O God, I offer you this trial for my intentions, which you already know. May it bear fruit a hundredfold and let me place in your heart my sufferings, desires, and prayers, for you to do with them as I have asked.

O Mary, pray for me, for us, now and at the hour of our death. Amen.

June 8, 1911

Thanksgiving to God for the success of this surgery, for so many graces, for the comfort of such tenderness and precious affection.

Resolution to use my life—what God leaves me yet—in the service of our Lord; to put his interests and the spiritual good of others before everything; to live a more centered and vigorous spiritual life; to be all things to all people and to fill my life with prayer, suffering, and charity; to practice humility and silence and to accept with joy this new physical "disfigurement," which God will turn into beauty and spiritual light for those who are so dear to me.

...O God, you have laid your cross on me. Of all sufferings, you give me those that pierce my heart the most. Help me to carry this cross without bitterness, without falling, without self-centeredness. In spite of failings and humiliating weakness, I seem to be progressing in the way of renunciation and total abandonment. My God, let me renew my prayer: that there may be neither sin nor suffering for those I love, that your light shine on them, that you make them holy. I entrust them to your care, and I abandon myself to you. Placing my burden in your Heart—sufferings, desires, prayers, I will keep my heart for you, giving to others only my smiles. I want to carry the cross with you alone, letting nothing be seen of my interior misery but the light of Tabor (Mark 9:1–8), the light that once rekindled me and that has now been extinguished to give way to the darkness of the cross. On Calvary Jesus accomplished his work of redemption; it is in suffering that those chosen by him can likewise do theirs in desolation and humiliation.

(November 1911)

Resolution for this year, at the beginning of winter.

Be joyful and practice spiritual poverty. Joyful in spite of, or even because of, this prostration, discomfort, and lethargy into which my physical miseries sometimes plunge me. Serenity within, and always gentleness and smiles without, pleasant when I feel bad-tempered, hospitable when I long for solitude, patient and cheerful when I feel tired and on edge.

To be spiritually poor, detached from all that is purely human, and as much as possible to practice a little [physical] poverty in what concerns me alone. Poverty of spiritual joys, of the heart, of life's satisfactions, deprivation, abandonment. At the same time, more tenderness of heart, more warm and spiritual affections, more empathy for all, more compassion for those who suffer, more kindness and delicate attentiveness to my family. Not to reject, scorn, or neglect anyone. Not to allow the slightest sign of bitterness or irritability.

To suffer seems to be my true vocation and the interior call of God. Suffering enables me to do the work of reparation, to obtain, I hope, the great graces I desire so much for my family, for everyone. Suffering is the response to my abandonment of myself to God for my family, for others, and for the church. If I am heard, no sorrow will seem to have been too great, and I will sing a joyous song of thanksgiving here and for all eternity.

My Savior, I give myself to you and renew my intentions, my prayers, my complete consecration.

(Christmas 1911)

As Christmas approaches, I ask the dear Child Jesus for his most far-reaching blessings for everyone.

To be more spiritual, to put more of the spirit of prayer into my life, and through penance of the heart and of action to attain the interior joy that is its fruit.

(February 21, 1912)

Resolutions for this Lent:

Fasting—as much as I can, through the prescribed abstinences; my chosen self-denial in the matter of food, such as will not harm my health; other spiritual and bodily mortifications, accepted or chosen.

Prayer—through my precious communions, the sacrament of penance, attendance at Mass, visits to the Blessed Sacrament, the Way of the Cross, daily meditation—especially on the passion; through both silent and spoken prayer, the constant union of my soul with Jesus Christ, and interior recollection.

Almsgiving—through the gift of my money, my time, my heart, first for those closest to me, then for the neighbor who is further away—especially for the poor, the humble, the suffering, for others.

Greater asceticism for myself; on the outside, more light-heartedness, kindness, friendliness, joy, remembering that our Savior wants a cheerful face and a radiant joy in times of fasting and mortification. To hide from everyone my interior recollection, my prayers, my poor penances, my small attempts at charity.

Union with Jesus Christ, which we shall realize in heaven in joy and vision, is already possible for us on earth in suffering. That is why all those in love with Jesus, those who have heard the mysterious and irresistible call of Christ, love suffering, and far from rejecting it with an entirely human fear, ask for it, desire it as the sweet forerunner of the Master, as that which ushers us into his presence. Suffering reveals the cross to us, opens the divine heart to us, enables us to enter into this spiritual world that nothing human can reach, which we will know only in eternity, but from which a glimmer shines on us through the grace of suffering and the radiance of the cross.

You must love me, O my God, because I experience two clear marks of your love: extraordinary graces and rare trials. I praise you for this precious twofold gift. Help me produce a hundredfold for those I love, for all you love.

Saint Joseph: a life hidden in God, close to the heart of Jesus, beneath the gentle gaze of Mary, in silent contemplation and humble activity, accomplishing daily necessities with a generous heart, doing it joyfully, and with a completely spiritual intention.

May 18, 1912

> O my God, through the precious Blood of Jesus and His
>   five blessed Wounds,
> grant me today five graces:
> the conversion of a sinner;
> the conversion of a heretic, infidel, or Jew;
> salvation of someone dying in peril of everlasting death;
> a vocation to the priesthood or to religious life;
> and, for some new soul, the grace of entering into and
>   savoring the mystery of the Eucharist.

(The prayer that our Lord suggested to me after communion this morning, which I will try to say each day.)

To offer the morning with its prayers, thoughts, words, actions, pains, sufferings, and deprivations for those who are to die that day.

To offer the afternoon in the same way for the church or souls.

To offer the evening and night for all those I love, for their spiritual and temporal interests.

July 18, 1912

My God, I lay at your feet my burden of suffering, sadness, and renunciation; I offer all through the heart of Jesus; and I ask your love to transform these trials into joy and holiness for those I love, into graces others need, and into precious gifts for your church. Into this abyss of physical prostration, discomfort, and moral exhaustion, into this darkness into which you have plunged me, let a glimmer of your triumphant brightness shine. Or rather, since the darkness of Gethsemane and Calvary is fruitful, use all these afflictions for the good of all. Help me to hide my inner suffering and spiritual poverty beneath a wealth of smiles and the splendors of charity. When the cross grows heavier, put your gentle hand under the weight you have placed on me.

O God, I adore you, and I am still, and always, in your debt, for against my sufferings you have put the Holy Eucharist and heaven.

The Journal: Part 2 (1911–1914)

"It is no longer I who live, but it is Christ who lives in me. And the life I now live in the flesh I live by faith in the Son of God, who loved me and gave himself for me" (Gal 2:20).

October 19, 1911

Three days ago, on my birthday, I began a new year. I want to make an act of adoration and thanksgiving, to confess my faith and in some way to confess to myself, by expressing what God has been for me and what I have failed to do in God's service, first through my ignorance, then through my great weakness. When I look at the past, I see that my childhood and even the beginnings of adulthood were lived unaware of God and far from him. I recall early graces received while I was still young, although they did not penetrate very deeply; flashes of light, shining occasionally on a path of indifference and superficiality; this call—a transient light glimpsed in my youth and swiftly extinguished, perhaps by God's mysterious will; the abandonment of every tie, even the external ones with God and the decisive forgetfulness of God; then the slow, silent action of Providence in me and the wonderful process of inner conversion, initiated, guided, completed by God alone, outside all human influence, sometimes through the very means that should have caused me to lose my faith, a process whose intelligent and loving beauty I could discern only when it was finished. Then, when that divine task was done, my spiritual director crossed my path through circumstances that were gently and truly providential.[25] Then my reconciliation with God followed; the journey to Rome, and, at the tomb of Saint Peter, my consecration to Jesus Christ, whom I carried in my heart through communion; then years of testing, and the greatest sorrow of my life up to this time,[26] and my ill-health; and the decisive consecration of myself on October 2, 1908, in the church at Jougne, where I prayed so deeply. Finally, this last year full of suffering: spiritual sufferings and deprivations, heartrending pain, problems with my health, progress sometimes slow and feeble through the hard path of renunciation. Then peace returned; the feeling of having grown in God's service in spite of all my struggles and weaknesses; my total abandonment to Jesus Christ in confidence and love, offering myself in the future for "all that he might want of me," asking in return for the graces that I desire so deeply and whose complete accomplishment I hope for from him, for those dear to me, for everyone, and for the church.

That is a quick review of my life. But what I cannot say, my God, what will be known only in eternity, is the greatness of your love, the wonderful graces you have given me, which I did nothing to deserve. Neither can I describe the extent of my misery and weakness, known to you alone. Blessed are you for everything— even for my faults, since they have served to make me unassuming and to transform me—for your gifts and your unspeakable mercy. Blessed be you for the affection you have put in life, for the trials that were perhaps an even greater grace. Receive the renewed gift I offer you, my soul, my life, wanting to love and serve you alone, joyfully, everywhere, always, with all my being, wanting to do nothing but your will in health or illness, poverty or riches, happiness or suffering, life or death: I ask only that you use me as a simple instrument for the good of others and for your glory. May my grief and spiritual joy, my whole life and even my death proclaim the greatness of your divine love, the holiness of the church, the tenderness and love of the heart of Jesus, the existence and the beauty of the spiritual life, the reality of our Christian hope. I believe, I adore, I put myself under the special protection of the Blessed Virgin, and I have loving confidence that, offered by her, my unpretentious offering, with God's grace, will serve the church and the spiritual well-being of others and of those I love in this life.

October 21, 1911

What will this winter bring: sickness or health, joy or suffering? I do not know, but I know that I shall welcome everything because everything comes from God for my good and the good of those for whom I have surrendered myself into God's hands. In my weakness and weariness, by God's grace, I always want to be joyful, to smile for everyone, and to hide my pain as much as possible; to forget myself, to give myself, and to try to be attractive—that our good God alone may be praised.

I busy myself with clothes and furs…and talk about them so as to give no hint of asceticism. How afraid the world is of suffering and penance, and how carefully I must hide both of these as much as possible! My friendliness and love will, with God's help, draw hearts to him who is so good; my sufferings will accomplish his conquest of them; my prayers will give them to him. Or rather, it is God who will do this blessed work of conversion and sanctification through my prayers, my trials, and my simple efforts at charity.

My Savior, I am all alone spiritually, as you know. You know, too, how I suffer from the hostility or indifference of certain persons. I think that is why you have done so much for me and given me so much in your goodness. And now with your gentle gaze you are dispersing the clouds that in these last months have so often overshadowed me. You are kindling my heart again after leaving it in painful dryness; you are chasing away the darkness and the confusion. Thank you, my beloved Savior, my God! I know that sorrow will return, for effort and struggle are your will for us. Your love has conquered, and I know that you will not abandon me and that deep peace will remain with me. To love during the storm is very consoling, and my love grows stronger after each sorrow, each setback. Complete abandonment to you, offering my heart and my life in your service.

November 5, 1911

I try to keep my resolution of outward "worldliness." When I long for recollection and prayer, when I want to act for God and my neighbor, when I hope for a life totally detached from the world, consisting of contemplation and fruitful activity, devoted to my family, to the poor, and to others, I must give myself to people, activities, and even pleasures that are often superficial in order to fulfill God's will and my obligations. What self-denial—with God as my only witness! God wants me to receive joy and comfort only from him. Perhaps God will wait until he has taken me to heaven and pressed me against his heart, giving faith to those I love; perhaps he will then give me the unspeakable joy of seeing in his light what my sufferings, deprivations, and spiritual isolation will have obtained for others. This morning, coming from church after communion and thinking of Félix and my great longing for his conversion, I said more explicitly to Jesus what he sees unceasingly in my silent depths—I offered myself to him entirely, for my beloved.

November 14, 1911

I renew my resolution of silence, seeing more clearly than ever the need for reserve with everyone, especially concerning God. I must hide my spiritual life and the graces I have received from everyone and speak as little as possible of my difficulties and poor health. The edification of others around me, which (apart from less pure motives) sometimes tempts me to say more, should be only a result and not an end in itself, as Father Faber says so well.[27] The only end I want to have is God's will, and my surrender should be complete, unassuming, and full of love. Other people's complete lack of understanding or ignorance of the spiritual life is a good reason for practicing the silence that is recommended so much by spiritual writers. Interiorly, then, I want more complete recollection and to be in closer union with our Lord. Exteriorly, I want to spend myself more lavishly, become more pleasant and smile. And when my task of unpretentious charity and daily effort is finished, God will know how to use it for others and for his glory. For me, the work, unknown to others; for him, the realization of the good I long for....The worker brings the work, the employer uses it the way he wants; it is enough to know that this work is never unfruitful. To work, then—and joyfully. And if I must continue to suffer because of my faith and my spiritual isolation, I will offer this peacefully for my usual intention and in a spirit of reparation.

January 3, 1912

A new year, which through God's grace will be the beginning of a real change in me.

For this year I ask for the grace of an inner life that is stronger and entirely spiritual and an outer life entirely dedicated to my neighbor. May the serenity of my heart increase and shine upon all; while being more strict within, may I become more hospitable to each one, and gentle toward life, other persons, and difficulties. Use me, O my adored Master, according to your will, for others and for your glory.

...To be silent about God's grace, and to hide my spiritual life. For others, to speak and to act, to be warm, even when it takes great effort.

With God's help and by the gift of myself, I have been seemingly "worldly" and outwardly happy; I have denied myself much for some time, especially recently. And while I talk and smile and force myself to be gracious, in my depths there is an unspeakable longing for solitude and recollection, and I utter a silent cry to our kind God, You see how I desire prayer and tranquility, and how much I want to live only for you and for a few who are dear to me. You know how heavily the world weighs upon me, how I hold the spirit of it in horror; but since it is your will that I should live not for the world but in the world, since my obligations and my intense desire for this ministry keep me there in spite of my longing to be free, then permit these many sacrifices, these constant efforts, these renunciations, and these profound sufferings to accomplish your work in others and to obtain grace for them. It is for this that I offer you so much boring conversation, so many tedious activities, so much costly cheerfulness. Accept it all, take it all, use it all for others and for those I love. Then at the first opportunity, I withdraw quickly into my inner "cell," and there I pray and adore and lie at the feet of my Savior. My three communions each week and the few minutes of meditation each morning prepare me for my daily activity; every day when I offer in advance all the activity and suffering that fill each day, everything that later happens is gathered up by our good God, and nothing is lost, not even this great boredom with worldly activities hidden beneath the veil of charity. Tender confidence in Mary; abandonment to God; prayer, mortification, charity.

February 23, 1912

I have jotted down in my notebook my Lenten resolutions,[28] but I want to confirm them here. I must truly renew my life, and it is God whom I ask in all simplicity to transform me. I want to live interiorly more spiritually, exteriorly more gently and lovingly so as to make God better loved, who is the beginning and end of my spiritual life. More than ever I want to hide in the heart of Jesus my good works, my prayers, my self-denial, to preach only through example, to speak not at all of myself and little of God, since in this sad world one only gives scandal or annoys others by showing one's love for God. But whenever someone approaches me, or whenever it seems to be God's will that I should approach another, I will do so simply, very prudently, and disappear as soon as the task is done, mixing no thought of self with God's action. And should I be misunderstood, criticized, and judged unfavorably, I will try to rejoice in remembering our divine exemplar, and I will seek to be of no consequence in the esteem of others. I who am in fact so poor and little in the eyes of God.

March 6, 1912

A short conversation with my dear Félix a little while ago deeply stirred my hopes and desires concerning him. Oh, yes, my God, I must have him, you must have him, this upright and truthful person. He must know you and love you, become the humble instrument of your glory, and do the work of an apostle. Take him entirely to yourself, my troubles, my sufferings, and my renunciations the path by which you shall come to him. Is there anything that belongs to me alone that I would not be ready to offer you to obtain his conversion, this grace so longed for? Gentle Savior, between your heart and mine there must be this pact of love, which will give you Félix and give me for eternity him whom I cherish, whom I want with me in heaven.

March 27, 1912

"While the angels fulfill their function of watchfulness at our sides, they never cease to contemplate God." This thought of Father Faber struck me during my meditation and made me make a new resolution: to imitate, on earth, our friends the angels. Before all activities, even in the midst of them, to remain united to God, to dwell in his presence, and to offer him everything: words, charitable deeds, work.

April 20, 1912

God, permit that after my death and burial with you, I may rise again to a new and completely spiritual life.

I want this Easter-time to become both more "interior" and more "exterior," however paradoxical that may seem. I want to live in a more complete, intimate union with God. I want prayer to be the foundation of my spiritual life, my surest means of ministry, my best form of charity; my suffering, with my usual voluntary mortifications, will also be the means I will use for doing some good for others and drawing near to the heart of God.

But exteriorly I will become through God's grace, more gentle, more loving, engaged always and exclusively with others, their pleasure, their good, and above all, their spiritual well-being. This in all simplicity, forgetting myself, and making of my entire spiritual life a life hidden in Jesus Christ.

And then I want more and more through prayer and my simple effort to establish in myself and manifest to others the joy, the holy, tender, unspeakable joy of Jesus. My immense weakness allows me to approach him only with great effort. He often makes me walk in darkness, on a dry path where the flowers of joy can scarcely grow. Yet my will to be his is stronger than ever, and he will accept, as a sacrifice of love, the gift of these struggles, these multiple sufferings.

My spiritual isolation, the constant and painful injuries caused by those who are hostile or indifferent, especially when they are near and dear to me, the sadness of feeling not up to the great work to be accomplished, the sufferings of my heart, the difficulties of my life, the misery of physical weakness—this is the rocky soil, my God, in which you will cause joy to grow. And out of all of this you will make, for many, salvation and graces of every kind; for me, expiation and holiness; for you, glory.

All my work of reparation will be accomplished according to my vocation, between us, through these sufferings, through prayer, and through whatever unassuming, lively charity you will put into my heart and enable me to share with others.

May 18, 1912

Difficult days because of [my nephew] Maurice's illness.[29] Renewal of my offering. This morning, communion, with all the sensible consolation that the divine Presence has rarely given me for many months.

September 25, 1912

Returned to Paris, where much sadness awaited me. Loving and fervent communion this morning. I asked Jesus for the virtues he most prefers, his own virtues, without which there is no true spiritual life:

Purity of heart, renewed in the sacrament of penance often, and every day through contrition and a spirit of repentance;

Gentleness, unalterable, strong, and peaceful, in spite of all exterior and interior disturbances;

Patience, in spite of everything, toward all, toward myself, very lovingly;

Obedience to God, to spiritual and temporal authorities in all but matters of conscience, to God's will revealed in all the events of life;

Humility, the foundation of all interior life, the virtue loved by the Heart of Jesus; both interior and exterior humility;

Self-denial, through daily circumstances, through health, through others, through penances carefully chosen and silently performed;

Spiritual poverty, through inner deprivation consistent with family life, renunciation made effective through carefully concealed personal poverty and detachment. To neglect none of my responsibilities, on the contrary, to be more careful about externals—clothes, care of the house, food, even elegance—to make myself more attractive, the better to hide my personal asceticism.

Wholehearted renewal of my offering. I want to dedicate this year to God's winning over those I love, through prayer and suffering especially: my husband, my mother, my dear nephews and niece, my sister, all our relatives. These are the ones for whom I wish to make this offering to Jesus, no matter what the cost; that is the goal of my life. And along with these beloved ones, I wish to give others, by the same means, to our God. I will, therefore, increase my prayers and sacrifices and will begin truly to practice penance for sinners, for the dying (for whom I feel a special tenderness), for unbelievers, and also for those in purgatory, all of whom I deeply love.

October 7, 1912

To love, to be unpretentious, to simplify my life—to go joyfully to God, seeking nothing for myself, in complete abandonment.

Never to lose sight of the intentions for which God wants me to pray, to suffer, and to act. In the midst of exterior activities and my obligations, to keep my inner attention fixed on God, to offer everything for those I love, for those Jesus desires, for the church.

To be always ready to obey the inner call of this gentle Jesus to action or to suffering, or to eternity, too, when he wills, and to reply always with joy and generosity, "Here I am, Lord, ready to do your will." The day will come, will it not, O God, when it will be your will that I come to you, when the darkness and the sorrows shall vanish, and the burden of the body will no longer weigh on me, when my soul will fly at last, freely to your beauty, to plunge itself into your holiness, to drink in your love. When I have been delivered, I will love inexpressibly in you all those I will have rejoined, and those I will have left here below, when the true life will finally begin, to last forever. Blessed dawn of eternity, I greet you, not knowing whether from near or far! I must not hope for you because my only wish is to do God's will "in life or in death." I know that I must first climb up to Calvary and hang upon the cross before knowing union with God; I know that I possess, and hope to possess still more here below, this union through the grace of God, in a great spirit of abandonment. I wait and, like the worker who does not know when he or she will receive the final reward, I want in the meantime to fulfill my responsibilities radiantly and peacefully solely for the love of him who has done everything for me.

October 17, 1912

Yesterday [was] my birthday; behind me stretches a huge expanse almost devoid of any good work, filled only with an abundance of divine grace. O God, may the future, short or long, with your help be rich in effort, sacrifice, and prayer. I ask nothing for myself, not even spiritual joys. I ask...only for the fulfillment of our secret agreement, the realization of all that I hope for, and all that I will then owe you. And now, beloved One, take the first payment, if that is your will, and leave the fulfillment of your promises until later. Should I only behold the realization of my desires from heaven or from an abyss of suffering, may you be praised in advance for having heard me. I renew all, offer all, ask all. For these intentions, for others, for the church, I give myself to thee, my Savior and my God.

In what relates to God: recollection and prayer.
In what relates to my neighbor: charity and loving dedication.

In what relates to myself: penance and asceticism.

A spirit of reparation. Reparation through prayer, suffering, self-denial, and good works.

October 20, 1912

Spoke too much about myself; too self-absorbed. And I caused others to share in my preoccupations. Renewed resolution of silence, self-denial, spiritual and, to the extent possible, even actual poverty.

Total abandonment and offering of myself to God. Greater cheerfulness and graciousness with my neighbor. Nothing difficult or strict with others. Greater strictness and asceticism with myself alone.

January 15, 1913

A new year began, which seems as if it must bring the fulfillment of my pact with God, or at any rate my part of it. O God, do whatever you wish with me so that you will fulfill your blessed promises for those for whom I make this offering, for many others, and the church. I abandon myself to you and desire that your will be done: suffering, poverty, illness, life or death, action or fruitful inactivity—all surrendered to you. Is not this inactivity the image, the reflection of your blessed passion, more powerful with you than all our good works? You know the three graces I ask for: the conversion of my husband, of my mother, and the happiness of my [niece] Marie.[30] If you give me these you can indeed ask much from me; I am prepared to give everything. Give me also many graces for many others, those everywhere whom I love with you and for you. And...and make your church holy and full of life. Recollection, prayer, union with God and with the heart of Jesus; confidence in and love for Mary, my Mother; to plant myself deep in heaven, to live in the Eucharist, to be gently inclined toward my neighbor and toward those on whom the overflow of light and love that the gentle Savior placed in me may fall.

January 29, 1913

Suffering and renunciation through the burdensomeness, discomforts, and exhaustion of the body, through the darkness or at least the dimness of mind, and through the interior suffering of spiritual isolation and aridity. Pure and solid faith. To ask, as I have been advised, for the grace of "simplicity in suffering."

Material concerns, sometimes too heavy for my already burdened body, time wasted, relationships that hold no attraction for me, the effort to be pleasant and to smile when all of me longs for recollection and for only close friends—all this constitutes my hidden cross, the best cross, which does not elicit sympathy or admiration as illness or misfortune does.

Well, I will carry it "joyfully" until God changes my obligations. Yes, joyfully in spite of dryness, weariness, the costliness of these efforts, gently united to the heart of Jesus, aided by Mary, my Mother, sticking to my usual rule of devotions, meditation, and so on, always strict with myself, yet more gracious to everyone, attentive to remain open, trusting, and abandoned, without narrowness, self-centeredness, or subtlety.

To accept equally the impossibility of an active life through good deeds, relationships, and regular work, and the impossibility of a wholly contemplative life that my family obligations, the preferences of those around me, and my circumstances prevent. To do all I can for others, to take refuge often in my "inner cell" to pray, to adore, and to unite myself to my beloved God. To make of everything—prayer, suffering, self-denial, and action—an interior offering for others and for God's glory, as well as for those I love.

O my God, "give me an adoring soul, an atoning soul, an apostle's soul," and do with me what you want according to my pact with you.

February 6, 1913

In my meditation I clearly saw the worldliness remaining in me. In asking God this Lent for a spirit of retreat, I resolved to pray, suffer, and act in union with God's will, for God's glory alone. May his will be done in me, for me, in my whole life, and by me in regard to my neighbor and many others.

To live spiritually hidden; to fast as much as possible, to abstain faithfully, to seek mortification and endure it silently; to speak no more of my suffering, my pain, myself, and to accept the real contradiction of looking so well when I am actually overwhelmed and exhausted. To be gracious, completely serene, and to practice the forms of charity and almsgiving that are most difficult for me. Contact with the world is surely one of these.

God, you have worked with me recently through inner deprivation, suffering, and painful hardships. You must be preparing me for an end known only to you. Whatever it is I accept it....Make me holy if you plan to give your heaven to me; make me holy if you intend to leave me here to labor and bear the cross. All I ask is that you use me for your glory; let me love you more and more, uniting myself completely to you forever.

February 17, 1913

The cross lies heavily on me. May all be as God wills, provided that I am heard. To love, suffer, and pray, always with the joy that comes from Jesus. *Fiat! Deo gratias!* I want to be eucharistic, a hidden apostle of the divine heart. To practice complete, confident, and loving abandonment. To go to God through the cross, through the heart of Jesus, under the tender protection of Mary, my Mother. May I welcome whatever the future holds, since it comes from the heavenly Father and the one Friend. As the future arrives, it will bring its own graces. Until then and even afterward, I must remember that "today's trouble is enough for today" (Matt 6:34), and that I can work and suffer for others and for the glory of God only today.

February 19, 1913

This morning, after communion, in a fleeting vision I thought of the three tabernacles where Jesus dwells. First, the depths of heaven, the heart of the inaccessible Trinity, in the ineffable union of his humanity and divinity; this is the tabernacle of his glory, where we can contemplate him only after death. Then the Eucharist, in which he veils himself in order to come to us and live with us, always ready to welcome us and hear us; this is the tabernacle of his love.

Finally, inner depths, where he comes in communion, wonderfully uniting himself to us, making himself our guest, our friend, our spiritual food, living on in us spiritually after the actual presence has ceased; this is the tabernacle of his heart, the place of his delights, his repose, and his joy. Oh, how I long to be for him at the same time a heaven, a tabernacle, and this appearance under which he comes to me! From beneath this veil where my Savior hides, I will let him shine forth, drawing those he wants to save.

February 20, 1913

Increasingly, I see that God does not want me to be active unless things change. He seems to expect from me a ministry of prayer and suffering. What a blessed vocation, and how much I will try to respond better than in the past, loving the cross of Jesus, "taking up the cross daily" (Luke 9:23), always placing my burden of pain, deprivations, and weaknesses in God's heart. Strict with myself, I want to be only kind and gentle with my neighbor. To live in interior union with our God, and to make of all the monotony, triviality, and simple duties of my life so many prayers for others. To have a eucharistic heart, never losing sight of my vocation of prayer, suffering, and reparation.

Holy Thursday, March 20, 1913

How well you know, O God, how to shape us and how suffering purifies us! Perhaps you have accepted my interior offering. In spite of inexpressible vexations, trials, and deprivations of soul and body, I can say a joyful *fiat*, if by so much suffering I obtain the fulfillment of my desires and all the graces I have hoped for, and if my sufferings serve others. I offer all to you—dryness, deprivation, spiritual isolation, the lack of pastoral care at the moment, overwhelming physical distress. To others I can only talk about some of this. Only you know how costly some efforts are, how certain weaknesses humiliate me. I want to welcome even these trials; and I want to be cheerful and smiling the next time toward suffering, in everything and for everyone. During these four painful weeks a visit from our Lord illuminated my life and my heart.[31] I am at present an exile from the tabernacle, and I hunger for Jesus in the Eucharist. Will I be able to go on Sunday to tell him my joy in the resurrection and renew my offering? I shall spend these holy days in spiritual isolation, in deprivation, in destitution....Yes, but my beloved Savior is close to my heart, I am united to the cross, and I wish only for the fulfillment in me, for me, through me, of God's will. Is it not a great honor to be chosen by our Lord to suffer, on the blessed anniversary of his passion and death on the cross? Yes, through all the shocks, pain, and sacrifices of life, I want to give complete and joyous assent to his beloved will from the depth of my being.

March 25, 1913

Today is the tenth anniversary of the day when I began my new life. I thank you, my God, with all my heart for so many graces. What love and sacrifice could pay my debt of gratitude? The heart of Jesus alone can accomplish this; it is to it that I entrust my burden of thanksgiving. Yesterday I was able to go to Mass for the lovely, great feast of Easter; my fatigue and physical weakness deprived me of any conscious joy in communion, but Jesus' action in me will only have been the greater, as I can feel today. And that is enough. What does even spiritual joy matter to one who feels alive! In my meditation I made the following resolutions for this joyful Easter-time; may God help me to fulfill them despite the great fatigue and discomfort of my aching body.

Toward God: More tender and confident love.

In myself: Greater inner peace and joy, in spite of everything.

Toward my neighbor: More cheerful than recently, a friendlier and more smiling exterior; more self-forgetfulness so I may think of others; to think and speak of myself as little as possible, and yet to be careful not to attract attention by an exaggerated silence or indifference to my own sufferings.

Lord, help my weakness!

April 22, 1913

Ten years ago today I experienced some of the most important and consoling moments of my life. That morning at St. Peter's in Rome, my communion in profound closeness to Jesus, my decisive consecration to God, all the joy, all the love, and all the consolation of that hour when I knelt at the tomb of the apostle: how can I thank you for all of this, O Lord? How can I express my gratitude? I tried to put some of this into words this morning in communion, but it is through my love, my deeds, and my sacrifices that I will try to repay my debt. Only through the heart of Jesus will I be able to pay it off, through the gift of God's gentleness and holiness. To work, then, to act and suffer according to God's will!

Ascension, May 1, 1913

Sharp, intense pain, going straight to the core of my heart, is what I have had to offer to Jesus glorified, together with the struggle against myself and outside disturbances. During this month dedicated to Mary, which is also dedicated to Jesus in the Blessed Sacrament, to the Sacred Heart, and to the Holy Spirit, I want to move courageously toward holiness. To be silent, to forget myself; to think of others and dedicate myself to them; to care for and accomplish nothing but God's will; to be the apostle of the Sacred Heart, an adoring and atoning person; my eyes and my heart fixed on the tabernacle and on heaven, to seek only Jesus there, and to bring to him all of those he places on my path. Above all, a ministry of prayer and suffering. Unpretentious, prudent action; constant gentleness, friendliness, and kindness.

June 14, 1913

My God, may you be blessed for all the graces you have given me: earthly graces through the engagement of my niece and family joys;[32] spiritual graces through much consolation, spiritual joy, and inward illumination, and the compassionate kindness to me you have inspired in my spiritual director, who has done me so much good. What a debt of gratitude I owe you, my God! Give me the fulfillment of the four graces I have asked for this year; grant health and real holiness to those I love; save and convert many, especially those you have entrusted to me; pour out your greatest blessings on your church. Then, Lord, accept my offering, keep our agreement, do with me as you want. I only ask for your love and your grace, the deep and lasting peace necessary for the flourishing of my interior life....I want to abandon myself to you with confidence, to bring you a generous spirit, always peaceful, and to think less of my faults than of your love. You are my Father, my Friend; be also, O Jesus, the "Companion of my solitude." You know how spiritual isolation weighs on me; with you I shall never again be alone. If I am not on earth to see my beloved ones united to me in my inner life, may I from heaven unite myself with them, who shall then become yours and be made holy by you.

June 26, 1913

Recently I have been able to live a more active life and keep some of the resolutions I made. In the future I want to be gracious and warm to everyone; to show more interest in the things of daily life that absorb the energies of so many people; to look after my home and my clothes; to complete all my duties. No one must suspect the trouble and sacrifices that this loving effort means for me. I will guard that full, tender union with God, which is my life, deep in my heart. Be, Lord, the dear companion of my inner solitude, my divine interior guest, and in communion and in prayer give me your grace. Make me the apostle of your Heart through prayer, suffering, and action.

July 16, 1913

Lord, may you be blessed for my present suffering because I dare to hope that it is your gentle answer.[33] I offer all of it—sufferings of body, heart, and soul, all my deprivations, my interior desolation, my great spiritual isolation. Use these unassuming offerings for the intentions...you know, for others, and for the church. Accept a tithe of it in atonement for my sins and for the work of reparation that you entrust to those you most love. It is not pride, is it, to call myself your friend, one you have called, your chosen friend? I see the traces of your love everywhere, the divine call everywhere, my vocation everywhere. You made use of trials, suffering, and illness to make me completely yours and to make me holy, first drawing me to you solely by your action within me. You have done everything. Now complete your work; make me holy according to your will; use me for others, for my beloved ones, for all your interests; use me for your greater glory, and let all be done in silence and in an intimate encounter between us alone. From the depths of my being and my misery I say, "Lord, what will you have me do? Speak, your servant listens; I am the handmaid of the Lord; I come, Father, ready to do your will" (Luke 1:35).

Patience, gentleness, humility, silence, kindness. To hide all that I can of my physical suffering, and all my moral suffering, my spiritual deprivations. To cover everything with serenity and smiles: all my discomfort, sadness, and renunciations. To try to reconcile the tastes, desires, and needs of each and to take no account of myself, not to think of what I might wish; to sacrifice even my greatest hopes, when, misunderstood, they might irritate or displease another. I shall have all eternity in which to contemplate him whom I adore, to unite myself to him, and to pray. Here, I must think of my neighbor, of others; I must sacrifice myself, and practice contemplation in action. There is plenty of material for renunciation and profound and constant self-denial in this unending abandonment of all that is my deepest longing.

January 9, 1914

Six months of suffering: painful suffering of the body, suffering of the soul, deprivations of all sorts, much pain and humiliation. Oh, so long as it is the divine response to me—is it not so, Lord? And so long as nothing of my pain is lost! Stronger than my poor action, stronger than my imperfect prayer, may it reach your Heart and become the most effective form of supplication. Do not delay; listen my God, to these desires you know so well. Give great, Christian happiness to these beloved young people and make all of them holy. Quickly finish the interior conversion and profound sanctification that I so desire. Unite with mine the souls of all I love, the one I love best of all, and end this sad spiritual isolation that weighs on me so much. And then make me holy, too, through this suffering; bring me close to your heart and teach me to love and serve you better.

I resolve (asking for your grace) in the future to give in no more to the lapses I have had in hours of intense pain, to be always gentle, unassuming, full of love.

Help me, dear Savior![34]

Daily Thoughts (1899–1906)

"After this, when Jesus knew that all was now finished, he said (in order to fulfill the scripture), 'I am thirsty'" (John 19:28).

"Then Jesus, crying with a loud voice, said, 'Father into your hands I commend my spirit'" (Luke 23:46).

Through the cross to the Light *(Per crucem ad Lucem)*.

To pray, to suffer, to act.

The future will be what we make it; let us reflect on this thought so that it may motivate us to act. Especially, let us realize that all collective reform must first be individual reform. Let us work at transforming ourselves and our lives. Let us influence those around us, not by useless preaching, but by the irresistible power of our spirituality and the example of our lives.

Let us give ourselves generously and try to strengthen our faith and expand our understanding, confident that all will come to us to be rekindled and to enlighten their hearts and minds.

The world is unable to recognize spiritual reality; it does not know how to penetrate the outer covering that veils our inmost self. Any unconquerable strength, purity, and truth in us is seen in our depths only by him who lives in us and judges us with more justice and love than men and women. What a reason to be faithful and courageous in daily life! Nothing goes unnoticed by our eternal Guest; the least of our actions has a profound effect on others.

Let us love. Let our lives be a perpetual song of love for God, first of all, and for all human beings who suffer, love, and mourn. Let deep joy live in us. Let us be like the lark, enemy of the night, who always announces the dawn and awakens in each creature the love of light and life. Let us awaken others to the spiritual life.

Why do we put off doing the good until tomorrow? Why do we wait to be wealthy before giving? Is not the gift of ourselves better than money, and is there any time when we could not offer a tear or a smile to someone who is suffering? Cannot a word from us strengthen someone in distress? Cannot an act of pure love coming from our depths brighten a sad life? How many times, forgetful of the divine Word, O God, have we carelessly neglected one of our brothers or sisters and refused to respond to human suffering!

O Light, Beauty, total Love, O my God, when will we love you, you alone, letting go of all that distracts us from this pure union with you, seeing only one thing: the soul that you have given us and you, O my God, who live in it and should be the sole guide and judge of our actions and lives?

Let us try to protect ourselves from the useless stimulation that so often disturbs our lives. May those who are ever more serene and filled with God be sanctuaries open to every troubled conscience and every weak will.

Fanaticism frightens me, and I cannot understand how it can exist with sincere conviction. Can anyone who loves Christianity passionately and wishes to see it flourish think for one moment that one can use any method to achieve this goal other than persuasion? Can one instill conviction through force or deception? Besides, is there not in the use of such means something completely repulsive to the upright, loyal spirit that should mark every sincere Christian? And yet how many small acts of fanaticism we commit unconsciously. Apart from personal pride, we have the pride of faith, the most evil of all. We complacently scorn those who hold different beliefs and think ourselves scarcely obliged to extend our charity to them. We consider that Jews, Protestants, or atheists are hardly our brothers and sisters in the true sense, beloved brothers and sisters for whom we should sacrifice ourselves and embrace with a delicate love. In relation to them we seem to think anything is allowed, even calumny sometimes, and we seem less concerned with convincing them than with offending them. The gentle words of Jesus, and of Saint Paul, too, declare that in the future there will be neither Jews nor Gentiles; all that will be forgotten (Gal 3:28). Let those who have inscribed the great law of love on their hearts at least learn to practice it toward all their brothers and sisters, whoever they may be. Weak and small as I am, I will never cease to protest against fanaticism and to proclaim to all Jesus' law of love.

This burning need for justice, this loving flame within us, this deep love for suffering and groaning humanity, all this is and can only be an unconscious turning toward this infinite Love and infinite Justice, toward the ultimate Goodness that is God.

We must give ourselves; that is, we must bring forth from this interior sanctuary where we keep the best of ourselves, some thoughts, chosen from among the best and most noble, that, once we have shared them, will become acts of love and words of life. We must firmly desire to try to give our best, to do all the good we can. The unknown reservoir of strength, energy, and nobility lying within our depths must become the property of our brothers and sisters through courageous effort and a generous surrender of our inmost selves.

Let us despise nothing: not any person, for in the worst of them there is the divine spark, which can always flame forth; nor ideas, for in all of them there is a grain of truth, which one must know how to discover; nor other peoples' actions, for we often are unaware of their motives and always unaware of their far-reaching and providential consequences.

Sometimes the very desire for action leads to neglecting action. In looking for some wonderful opportunity to give oneself, to devote oneself, one forgets the unassuming brother or sister at one's side who is waiting for a word of comfort, a saving gesture. Instead of contemplating the road ahead, let us follow the narrow path. Let us look neither too far ahead nor too high but right in front of ourselves, right next to us. The good to be done is perhaps there.

Sincere convictions and the ardent longing that others should share them can coexist with complete respect for every conscience and every conviction.

All that life reveals each day, all that we acquire by constant, energetic, and persevering work on ourselves, all that constitutes our inner being; all of this should one day become words or actions that reveal our depths. This is what it truly means to give oneself, which is the purpose of all human life. It is a difficult task, a great effort, to express our innermost thoughts, but we must do it, breaking open our souls as we might break open a sacred vase so that others may breathe the divine perfume.

Is it not terrifying to see what the human heart can harbor so easily and reveal as fanaticism and hatred? What thoughts and courageous resolutions this sad situation should inspire! A clear mission presents itself to every good person imbued with the ideas that Christianity has given to the world—to promote unity among people, to sow a little love around one, and to take the trouble to give one's time and all one's heart to bring to birth the light and life of the spirit.

There is a way of living and thinking that I would name negative, another that I would name active. The first consists in seeing always what is defective in people and institutions, not so much to remedy them as to dominate them, in always looking back, and in looking for whatever separates and disunites. The second consists in joyfully looking life and its responsibilities in the face, in looking for the good in everyone in order to develop and cultivate it, in never despairing of the future, the fruit of our will, and in understanding human faults and miseries, expressing that strong compassion which results in action and no longer allows us to live a useless life.

Whoever searches for the truth will find God.

As we go along, let us spread ideas, words, and desires, without looking back to see who gathers them up. There are so many beggars for ideals!

We long for truth; we love it and endlessly search for it, because it is the goal of our being. And one day we will possess it completely. We want to live the spiritual life intensely and deeply, the interior life, the beginning of eternal life, and we wander blindly along this path of good, which we find most lovely, and upon which we sow our efforts, our struggles, and our desires.

A voice resounds near us, the all-powerful Word of invitation that lifts us up and transforms us: "I am the way, and the truth, and the life" (John 14:6). Let us walk in the awareness of this voice. He who can speak such words will never deceive us.

Let us develop in ourselves "divine" compassion for all men and women; only then can it be truly "human."

All that we do to transform and improve ourselves serves the divine cause. When our inner selves expand, only God can fill them.

Let us develop our wills even more; let us try harder to train all our faculties to accept responsibility freely and to fulfill it joyfully; and let us become more gentle toward others, more patient and interiorly serene.

The gratuitous search for beauty, the passionate concern for justice, the love of truth are so many paths that lead to God. Sometimes we make many detours; we even get lost a little. And yet we always reach the goal toward which we walk without recognizing it.

There is nothing so great or ideally beautiful as the action of God in the human soul. If we knew how to discern it in ourselves, our lives would be transformed. If we could see it in others we would love even more him who is always in our midst, who acts in us, and who works marvels—these spiritual renewals that we shall understand only in eternity.

Charity! Saving word, since it includes all light and strength, since it transforms life and the soul, since it means love; and only love will last forever. We must fulfill our responsibilities daily, without worrying about what fruit God will draw out of them. For

us, work, sacrifice, the offering of ourselves. For God, the immediate or remote effect that the least of our thoughts and actions
will have on others. Nothing is lost, and it is this close unity, this
solidarity in work and prayer, that constitutes the wonderful,
blessed communion of saints.

In spite of sufferings of body and soul, life brings unspeakable joys, fleeting glimpses of the ultimate joy to come. But these
loving glimpses cannot be life itself. Life is effort, firm and persevering action, and duty accepted and accomplished, the heroic
conquest of the body by the soul, the serenity nothing can disturb,
and eyes fixed on God. It is charity taking possession of us little by
little, banishing everything that is not love.

Not to accept everything, but to understand everything; not
to approve of everything, but to forgive everything; not to adopt
everything, but to search for the grain of truth that is contained in
everything.

To reject no idea and no good intention, however awkward or
feeble.

To love others as Jesus Christ loved them, including suffering and death.

The first responsibility now for every one of good will is constantly preaching, by word and by example: the divine law of charity. Every Christian should be a voice crying in the desert, "Let us
love!" Perhaps some heavenly breeze will carry these words farther
than we imagine.

In arid times, when duty seems difficult and daily responsibilities have no attraction, when all spiritual consolation is denied us
and the beautiful light that illumines life is veiled, in these times
humble prayer alone can steady us and give us hour by hour and
day by day the determination to act "against our will."

To reveal some of the good we have done so that others may know Who inspires us to all good, and to conceal carefully the rest, which shall be for God alone.

Never to speak of one's health, material concerns, or moral suffering, for that uses up the energy to bear them. But always to welcome with kindness the confidences given to us by others and to seek to relieve their sorrows, thanks to our own experience.

How few people know the meaning and value of the word to *live!* To live is to love, to think, to suffer; to give oneself; to make out of everything—joys, desires, loves, and griefs—a lovely poem that others might hear and that perhaps will awaken them from sleep, from the moral apathy in which so many unfortunate people live.

A few moments of recollection and meditation every morning in the presence of God transform and perfume the whole day, like flowers scattered when night comes, whose fragrance at dawn permeates everything they have touched.

Little duties, small efforts, the better for being seen by no one, except by him in whose eyes nothing is insignificant.

What vivid suffering not to be able to help others understand the beauty of what we love and believe! No one can reach another's depths in which loves and simple and true ideas are born. Only he who sees and knows can penetrate those depths, he who brings with him light and life. Our role is only to make some gesture of appeal and humble supplication: "Come, Lord, to this person, so he may live."

How can we not try to give when we have received so much? How can we not love when infinite Love has renewed and transformed our life?

The action of God in our depths: something intangible, profound, strong, to be understood fully only when the divine work is finished.

141

ELISABETH LESEUR

Through all the turmoil, all the fatigue, and all the distractions of life, we must try to preserve a certain inner peace, which is not always joy, but which alone gives a beautiful unity to life and all its courage to the soul, without which in times of distress we would not know how pray or to think or to act.

The further I go, the more convinced I am of the complete uselessness of religious discussions with unbelievers. The intellectual and historical point of view, which is all they can have, is inadequate to the phenomena of the interior life. All that is profound, subtle, and alive in the human soul is unknown to them. They are even unaware of their own interior depths. Let us look for ways to arouse in them a sense of eternal things; let us search with them for the divine spark; let us open wide for them the path of the good, which leads to God, without encumbering them with barriers and obstacles. That will be enough. Then let us ardently pray, and Providence will do the rest.

To give of oneself only what will benefit others; to keep the rest jealously hidden in our depths as the miser guards his treasure, but with the intention of sacrificing it, of giving it away, when the time comes.

What sadness to comfort, misery to relieve, prejudice to destroy, and hate to transform! How many workers are needed for this task! At least do everything personally that one can.

Christ, our adored and freely chosen Master, at the hour of inner renewal and freedom of consent, fashions and transforms us in such a way, by continuous and intangible action, that the words of Saint Paul become true and we experience this triumphant reality: "It is no longer I who live, but Christ who lives in me" (Gal 2:20). That is, the Christ of interior souls, the Christ of the little ones and of the poor, the one and only, eternally living Christ, whom we can never forget once we have been in his company and communicated with him.

The absence of any deep, extended, Christian conversation is a great lack. Let us know how to offer it to God, with so many other hidden longings, secret desires, and sad reflections that each day brings.

Home—that marvelous word—expresses comfort, tenderness, intimacy, and belonging. I want to make my home a center of light, of beautiful and generous ideas, and of deep feeling, to make it loved by Félix and by many young people, upon whom it might exercise an enlivening influence. For that may God make my beloved husband a Christian!

Which of us can fully say the words of Christ "I have compassion for the crowd" (Mark 8:2)? And who, above all, can give life to these words, making them penetrate our being and every one of our actions? *To have compassion!* What meaning these words hold!

Never forget the distinction between the ideas that we have to defend and get others to love, and ourselves, who represent them so badly; between the ideas professed by others, and those others themselves, who are our neighbors and who should be loved in spite of everything. Treat with deep respect all that belongs to the realm of conscience. Never knowingly harm a sincere conviction. And yet adhere firmly, without any capitulation, to what we consider truth or duty.

It is a difficult thing to know how to reconcile apparently conflicting responsibilities, to tolerate ignorance and prejudice without, however, seeming to accept them, to discern between that which concerns ourselves alone and, as such, should be resolutely sacrificed, and that which is part of the realm of the absolute and belief and, as such, should be defended through struggle and suffering.

To organize one's life with a rule, and to depart from one's rule, once it is established, only for serious reasons of family or charity. To do as well as possible whatever one is doing, not abandoning it for something else without a real need.

At certain times, when the body and soul are both suffering or the divine presence seems distant or hidden, we must take refuge in intellectual work or some peaceful action that gradually restores our inner balance. As far as possible, no one should know about these painful times or suffer because of our suffering. We have no right to add to another's burden. As Christians we should, on the contrary, seek to lighten these burdens, which will make our own seem less heavy.

To take Christ, always living and present in our midst, as the model of our life and our friend at all times, the sad times as well as the blessed ones. To ask him to make himself loved by others through us, and to be, following a metaphor I love, "the rough vessel that contains a brilliant light and through which this light brightens and warms everything around it."[35]

Unwavering serenity, true simplicity, profound charity: the three foundations of every strong and intense interior life.

What a bitter trial is the utter incomprehension of certain people about the things of God! Ignorance, prejudice, and irrational hostility are a heavy weight to lift. No matter: "The true light that enlightens everyone was coming into the world" (John 1:9). Let us strive to dispel the shadows that stand in his way.

To take refuge in action at those times when one's mood is weary or sad, and to lead oneself gently back to interior recollection when action becomes too engrossing and threatens to overwhelm our inner life.

Christ must live in us, so that we may give him to others.

In times of anxiety and suffering, God sometimes gives, in that deep place in the soul where human torments can no longer reach, movements of joy and an intense awareness of spiritual realities, so that one can return to life with its struggles and sorrows.

Divine illumination makes the road more luminous and enables us to see our destination.

We must know how to recognize the important responsibilities contained in the monotonies of everyday life and how to transform them through a lively spirit and love.

Christ has planted his cross in humanity, and nothing can uproot it, if we do not uproot it ourselves from our hearts. We can attack the outer form of Christianity, impede its exterior manifestations for a time at least, in our efforts to diminish it. But who can reach Christ himself, living and triumphant within us?

What a wild dream to think one can destroy the church! It is possible only to those who have not understood the wonderful distinction between its soul and its body. The body may sometimes appear weak and injured, but it lives as long as the soul animates it, and the soul is immortal.

We should make each day a short form of our whole life by filling it with prayer, work, and charity.

Let us never look for the result of our efforts for others. It is good for us not to know it, for if we did, pride in doing good, the most subtle pride of all, might follow. Let us entrust to God the prayers, sacrifices, and efforts that we make, without looking back at what we have already done. Let us continue to work and to act for our brothers and sisters and for the coming of God's reign in them.

Not to be understood brings acute suffering. To know that God understands is a more vivid joy than any suffering.

A simple human connection can sometimes be the best sermon; a spark can ignite a great fire.

More and more I understand how much respect is needed in order to touch the innermost depths of others and their beliefs. In all of these there is a "soul of truth," a spark of life, which must be recognized and revived. That is evangelical work par excellence. To

145

accomplish it one must be possessed by and filled with the truth, and through one's own interior knowledge, know how to reach hidden depths of others. And then one must love. Charity, always.

"The harvest is plentiful, but the laborers are few" (Matt 9:37; Luke 10:2). The masses are waiting, multitudes of poor people are living in evil and ignorance, and yet we can continue our daily life in indifference. Oh, the gentle compassion of Christ, the tears he wept for the miserable, abandoned crowds! Shall we, his disciples, never know how to love with all our hearts and act with all our determination for these little ones, whom Jesus blesses and whom he wants entirely for himself? There is great work to be done. What does it matter? If only we do all we can and leave behind actions, words, and prayers that will multiply wondrously until the end of time and do good spiritually to distant or unknown people!

Suffering works mysteriously, first in ourselves through a kind of inner renewal, and also in others, perhaps far away, without our ever knowing here on earth what we were accomplishing by it. Suffering is an act. Christ on the cross has perhaps done more for humanity than Christ speaking and acting in Galilee or Jerusalem. Suffering creates life; it transforms all it touches, all it reaches.

"Today's trouble is enough for today" (Matt 6:34). We must prepare "today" in recollection and prayer and live it in struggle and suffering.

To shut one's heart to any complaints and regrets that could escape it; to open it wide to pour out all it can of human compassion, strength, and kindness.

Socialism promises to guarantee and transform the future; Christianity transforms the present....It gives to humanity its "daily bread" and does so always.

We must never reject anyone who seeks to approach us spiritually; perhaps that person, consciously or unconsciously, is in quest of the "unknown God" (Acts 17:23) and has sensed in us something that reveals his presence; perhaps he or she thirsts for truth and feels that we live by this truth.

Those who seem to be spiritually dead are not always those least accessible to the divine word; when wood is dead, it needs only a spark to set it afire.

Many people live on the surface of their lives without ever penetrating their profound and sorrowful depths. If we knew how to center ourselves, how to look clearly into ourselves, and how to understand the meaning and fruitfulness of suffering, then the slightest gesture, the most imperceptible movement of the most unassuming of human beings, would reveal to us these abysses of sorrow or tenderness that remain open interiorly until the day when another pours light into them and causes life to burst forth.

Silence is sometimes an energetic act, and smiling is, too.

To defend oneself against the multiplicity of external things and the agitation they bring, make firm resolutions and carry out faithfully the fruit of our meditation.

Look around oneself for proud sufferers in need, find them, and give them the alms of our heart, of our time, and of our tender respect.

Pride in suffering! To distrust even that.

To let our inner depth fully bloom. To reject everything that impoverishes or confines it. No meanness. Life in its fullest and richest expression.

If all of us tried in good faith to see our brothers and sisters as they really are and brought a little indulgence into our relationship with them, then hatred and fighting, private or public, would quickly cease. But when we look at others we are generally nearsighted or farsighted, and so we either scrutinize their errors too closely, or we exaggerate their faults from a distance. Only charity gives a correct view of people and of things.

A thought from outside, suggested by the spoken or written word, is received by the intelligence more or less passively. For a long time that thought remains purely intellectual. Then one day, under the influence of grace, it comes to life and becomes not only present to the mind but alive for the soul. Does this not explain and justify human participation in God's work? Grace alone brings about a conversion; without it we can do nothing. But can we not prepare the materials for grace? Can we not put into people's minds new ideas that, when touched by grace, may one day spring to life? It is very humble work, demanding much patience and tact, and it must be done without expecting any result but that which God wills and is known only to him.

In order to become fruitful, work must be regular and represent real effort and a deep exploration of things. We must guard against the habit of staying on the surface, which is dangerous to the mind and useless.

It seems to me that recollection is especially lacking in this generation. To meditate presupposes intellectual strength, a profound insight into spiritual things, of which this generation is, for the most part, incapable. And yet it is only by this means that one can have an interior life, of which outer life is merely an expression; only by this means can action become fruitful. What can we give to others if we have gathered nothing for ourselves? Let us first create a reservoir of thought, of energy, of prayer. Our abundance will overflow to others, and this stream of life will never exhaust itself, because its source is in God. Let us renew our strength in deep contact with the Eternal each day. May the heart of Christ, in a communion that is daily more intimate with us, tell us some of his divine secrets. May the light of the Spirit guide us. Having God within us, we will surely do the work of God, or rather, he will do it himself through us and better than us.

Let us not be dilettantes of divine love, and let us not cultivate even this sort of egotism. We must know how to share with our brothers and sisters the gifts that God has given us and to give a tithe of the graces we have received. In this effort we may lose a bit of the joys of recollection, of interior union with God; this is a sacrifice every Christian must make. What we give will in this way have only more value. Is this not, to a small extent, what it is "to lose one's soul" (Matt 10:39; Mark 8:35; Luke 9:24) for the benefit of others?

It is relatively easy not to be absorbed in our own suffering, but the suffering of those we love is apt to become a constant and unhappy preoccupation, against which we must struggle: first through prayer, entrusting those we love to God in complete, filial abandonment, then through work, and also through an occupation chosen outside the center of our thoughts and affections. Finally by doing some good for others, we can forget a little of our dear ones' burdens, which we find a thousand times more painful than the ones we carry alone.

Let us keep silence as much as possible about our sorrows and anxiety; if someone sees that we suffer, may God alone, at least, know the extent and the deepest causes of our suffering.

There are times when we can more fully understand Saint Paul's sublime meaning when he tells us to rejoice always (1 Thess 5:16). There is a joy that the worst sorrows cannot destroy, a light that shines in the darkest night, a strength that sustains us in all our weakness. Alone, we would collapse and fall, like Christ carrying his cross; however, we continue on, for our falls are only passing, and soon we are standing again. For we "can do all things through him who strengthens us" (Phil 4:13). Although weak creatures, we have an infinite strength within us, and in our depths shines the light that never goes out. How can we not rejoice, in spite of everything, with a deep spiritual joy, when we have God now and for eternity?

The influence we can exercise is something subtle, penetrating; its strength cannot be measured. What powerful preaching there is in simple connection with another! A single spiritual person can change the whole moral atmosphere by its solitary light.

Let us not think that we can personally hasten the coming of God's reign in others. As soon as the divine hour comes, our efforts are useless, or rather they are only an active prayer, an appeal to him who transforms and saves. Nevertheless, let us appeal to him with the simple conviction that he alone will do what must be done and will bring spiritual life to those for whom we act and pray.

What joy to discover suddenly in others resources that we did not suspect, an instinctive need for the higher life, an unconscious seeking for the unknown God! We then respectfully draw near to share with them some of our inner treasure and must offer for them some of our daily suffering and effort. But with what delicacy must we approach them, so as not to impede divine action! A single word that lacks the spirit of the eternal Word might destroy this interior work that God alone accomplishes. We must let God speak, and we must show by our example and our lives alone the fulfillment of his deep, subtle, and fruitful action in us.

Never must our injured sensitivities make us indifferent and hardhearted. The wounds that bleed are still alive; let us rejoice if an unconscious hand, by touching our wound, proves that the tissues are full of life and will one day experience complete healing through continual interior action.

Christ's church needs apostles. But how much we need before we can claim that name, what subordination of our sensible being to the strong and sovereign soul: what humble consciousness of failings and faults, what calm and intelligence, what burning faith, and, above all, what unalterable and lively charity! We must become "another Christ" among men and women, bringing, like our divine model, a message of peace, a teaching, and freedom through truth.

Why look so hard for someone who understands us and a voice that knows how to speak to us of God and spirituality, when the heart of Christ is open to us and no one in the world knows how to love us and understand us as he does?

Catholic spiritual direction, which is so poorly known or so severely criticized, is a wonderful strength that serves the inner life. Practiced as it should be, it gives to Christians an incomparable energy and may even reveal the soul to itself.

We never speak to God without hearing a response, if the language of our souls is made of humility, suffering, and longing for the good.

Those whom we encounter on our earthly path often only see in passing the outer wrappings of our being and go their way, confident of knowing us well enough. Let us be careful not to do the same with the companions of our life. Even in a brief encounter we can touch others' depths, or even more, achieve profound insight into that which is hidden beneath appearances: a whole person, a whole life, of which others are completely unaware.

I believe in the creative, powerful, and constant action of the Holy Spirit in us and in the church.

Practical materialism is as dangerous as philosophical materialism. Every day it makes further inroads among the masses, and without a set agenda, simply through the free play of evil influences, it is now establishing itself in our democracy. Therefore, in the face of egotism, it is up to Christians to proclaim the fundamental notion of sacrifice; in the face of raw pride or even intellectual pride, the notion of humility; in the face of sensuality and indulgence, the law of duty, not made by humans but coming from above.

Why should a word, which most of the time would remain on the surface, sometimes sink to a great depth and inflict a cruel wound? Perhaps in such moments we are already bruised by other sufferings and ready to overflow, and thus we find ourselves nearer the surface, closer to painful blows and brutal misunderstanding.

To know how to be silent is often wisdom and an act of virtue.

It is sometimes necessary to disclose more of ourselves than we wish to those who will never completely understand us and to hide our inner depth from those to whom we would like to open it wide.

Charity, a supernatural virtue, is rarely considered as such, even by Christians. It is life, love, action; let us be careful not to practice it in a sluggish, passive, and lifeless way.

To transform one's suffering into joy for others, to cover it with a veil that only allows to show through what could become consolation or affection. May God alone know what he alone desires for us and the burden he has given us.

From all sides human affairs crowd upon and absorb us, and if our will, aided by divine grace, does not counteract them, we soon deserve our Savior's reproach to Peter: "You do not savor the things of God" (Matt 16:23; Mark 8:33).[36]

To savor the things of God is to have God in our life, to be penetrated through and through with Christianity, to see everything in the light of eternity, which the Holy Spirit never refuses us; it is to transform ourselves and to establish ourselves in peace and charity; it is to love, along with the works of the human intelligence, the ultimate Intelligence from which they spring; it is to look for what goes on beneath the surface of people, to reach those depths where we can gently try to bring them to God; it is, finally, to live, through our devotion, in loving, strong intimacy with him whom we call our Father, who is the life of our soul.

There is little suffering that can compare with this: to love, and to be repaid with hatred or at least hostility; to dream of doing good for someone, of giving a little of oneself, and to find that this person does not appreciate you, judges you unfairly, and misunderstands everything about you. What should one do then? Not be unjust in return; remember that the Master suffered misunderstanding and contempt; and, without reproaches or self-centeredness, continue to speak, act, and love, not to gain the affection denied us, but in the higher and spiritual thought of charity.

To think is excellent; to pray is better; to love is everything.

We should not scrutinize ourselves too closely but try to live simply, bravely, and joyously beneath the gaze of God and for him.

We must always, in spite of everything, be indulgent. In all the wrongs that others do to us, there is always some fault of our own. May the offense received from our neighbor always be an occasion of a sincere examination of conscience, and may the wrong of another disappear in the light of what we discover in ourselves of our own weaknesses and faults.

To know how to forgive is the special mark of the Christian. Forgiveness should not merely be passive; it should be a lively act of love.

Human knowledge becomes more delicate and more interesting to the extent that the Light that comes from the Infinite penetrates it. Second causes, when linked to the First and only Cause, become harmonious. The world and history are transformed when one discerns the Energy that guides them in unknown ways to an unknown end. Humanity appears very significant, to those who know how to see the soul—this soul to whom Infinity lies open, this soul who thinks, loves, and can fearlessly regard everything that happens, sure of its immortality.

The chasm between souls can only be filled by God.

The world approves and allows nearly everything. To the squandering of time or fortune or one's heart, and even to the most blatant acts of foolishness and guilt, it closes its eyes, smiles, or applauds. On the other hand, do not try to consecrate some of yourself or your time or money to God's cause. Such a way of living your life is not pleasing to this superficial world, which considers itself to be deprived of all you give to eternal things and to your brothers and sisters; it will not tolerate such theft. The love of

God is the only eccentricity the world does not and will never accept.

The intensity of certain sorrows makes them almost sacred and compels them to be hidden from view. In our innermost depths where they take refuge, with God as their only witness, they can be discovered only by spiritually sensitive people who know how to penetrate the living depths of a person and who, as kind visitors, leave behind them religious empathy. These persons are rare, and "he who sees in secret" (Matt 6:18) is usually our only confidant.

The Eucharist truly transforms us from within, almost without our knowing it, as ordinary bread and wine, earthly nourishment, strengthens our entire body and blood without our being aware of it. By his contact and his grace, Christ gives us moral health and creates new life in us. It is not in vain that we lean for a moment upon his heart and entrust our burden of suffering, weakness, and anxiety to him.

To refrain from action is sometimes the greatest sacrifice and the most fruitful of all actions.

God does for us, better than we can, the things we dreamed of doing ourselves. The influence we want to exert he uses for the good of others, while we offer him only our silence, our weakness, and our apparent inertia.

The world does not understand grief; it is ignorant of compassion and unaware of consolation. How shall the worldly grasp the endlessness of suffering when they do not experience an infinity in love and in joy?

We must humbly and lovingly accept the superficial consolation and encouragement that come only from the lips, words that do not spring from the heart and that stop before they reach our heart. But we must open wide to receive the empathy and words that bring something of God and speak to us living and eternal words.

April 13, 1905[37]

✝

Per crucem ad Lucem.

In the final moments of Christ's passion, when, with pierced hands and feet, he poured out all of his precious blood on human soil to make it fruitful, lived his last hours, and experienced human suffering to a greater extent than we can understand, the Gospels tell us that the earth was covered with darkness (Mark 15:33).

> Lord, in our lives, there are also hours completely covered in darkness, sad hours in which the veil cast over our hearts hides even those things that could give us comfort, hours in which we suffer in such a way that nothing on earth can console us.
>
> Happy are those who during such times of outer darkness can still at least contemplate you, Jesus Christ, the only Life! Happy are those whose weak arms can still clasp your feet on the cross, who can lean their weary heads against your pierced hands and their bruised hearts on the heart that has suffered so much and is filled with such compassion and love!

I believe that God allows human suffering with a great intention of love and mercy.

I believe that Jesus Christ has transformed suffering, made it holy, and almost divine.

I believe that suffering is the great instrument of redemption and sanctification.

I believe that suffering is fruitful, as much as and sometimes more than our words and actions, and that the hours of Christ's passion did more for us and were more powerful with the Father than his years of preaching and earthly activity.

I believe that there is flowing through us—those on earth, those in purgatory, and those who have reached true life—a great, unending stream made up of the sufferings, merits, and love of everyone, and that our least sorrow, our slightest efforts, can through grace reach others, whether near or far, and bring them light, peace, and holiness.

I believe that in eternity we shall find again our beloved ones who have known and loved the cross, and that their sufferings and our own will be lost in the infinity of divine Love and the joy of final reunion.

I believe that God is love, and that suffering, in his hand, is the means his love uses to transform and save us.

I believe in the communion of saints, the resurrection of the body, and life everlasting.

Jesus on the cross said these beautiful and sad words: "I am thirsty" (John 19:28). Since then, throughout the ages, all of humanity has echoed these words. They have cried or whispered them, and every human being in turn speaks them either in despair or faith.

My day has come, O my God! It began a long time ago, through the authority of your word and the influence of your love, and through the slow suffering that you have used for your work of renewal.

Misfortune came, breaking my heart forever, taking from me one of my greatest loves, one that nothing can replace, an affection formed of maternity, friendship, and sisterly feeling.

Now, O God, with all my heart, I say the sorrowful words: "I am thirsty."

I am thirsty for the peace you alone give, which transforms life; for the stability and living refreshment that only exists in you.

I am thirsty for light, thirsty to know, to see, to possess, as we shall see and possess in eternity.

I am thirsty for the profound sensitivity and the tenderness that can read hearts, and for a close and strong union with you.

I am thirsty to devote myself, to give myself, to be understood and loved, to understand and participate in everything.

I sigh for that which endures, and I sometimes want to shake off the burden of misunderstandings, hostility, and narrowness that weighs on me and hurts me.

I am thirsty for immortality, that complete flourishing of the soul beyond this transitory world.

I am thirsty for life, the only Life, abundant and eternal, with all our loves restored in the heart of infinite Love.

My God, I am thirsty for you!

I utter this cry right now; I will speak it again many times, O Jesus, before I come to you. I will say it with you: "I am thirsty."

As soon as you had spoken, you had accomplished your mission in this world. You prayed, labored, suffered, and "those you have given me I guarded, and not one of them was lost" (John 17:12).

Let it be so for me, and in solitude, in those times when I come to you as a loving friend, I again express my sorrowful appeal; let me nevertheless, with your help, accomplish my mission and be a courageous Christian and apostle. May my secret love of eternal things never allow me to forget those who suffer on earth. May I always increasingly love my human brothers and sisters and those who are close to me. Only then will I have the right to say with you "those you have given me I guarded, and not one of them was lost." I have not asked you to take me from the world but to allow me to do your will and the work that you have given me. Now, having purified me, you can draw me to you in your light and your love, where those I have loved so much already live, and where others will rejoin me one day. More than ever I am thirsty to find them again, my beloved dead; I am thirsty to live with them, to know, to possess, to love; I am thirsty for you, my God!

Spiritual reality has become so strange to certain people that they imagine that anyone who is called a mystic is useless in practical matters, and their astonishment is great when they see that same mystic capable of bold initiative or persevering will. Ah, poor people! Those who rise very high see earthly things all the more clearly, and as "the soul is mistress of the body it animates," the body obeys its stern commandment. Continue on, skimming close to the ground, birds with heavy wings, but let the swift-winged birds fly high into the sky, whence they will return to collect spoils on earth. One can breathe better, on this poor earth, when one has gathered a provision of pure air in the heights.

When prejudice and opposition attack and hurt us, we too easily forget that Jesus Christ also suffered this. He who penetrated everything and could see into all subtleties and nuances of feeling must have suffered greatly sometimes from the misunderstanding and narrow-mindedness of those whom he yet loved with incomparable tenderness. And yet we do not know how to endure the least blow, even when those who inflict it are not, as with Jesus Christ, our friends and loved ones. Let us learn from him to be always kind and patient with people and with ideas.

To give oneself and yet reserve oneself. All Christian duty lies in this.

God, in giving us life, gives each of us a mission to accomplish and a role to fulfill in his eternal plan. The most important thing, then, is to recognize this particular mission, to discern the divine will in our life, and then to work to make of our entire life and death a means of salvation for ourselves and our brothers and sisters.

We are the good God's humble workers, the laborers of the Father, and when the night falls, we must be able to say confidently that the harvest is ready and that the living Sun may now cause the seeds we have sown to grow.

"Thus you will know them by their fruits" (Matt 7:16, 20). God knows us in all our depths; he is aware of our least desire, the least impulse of our hearts, and the least movement of our will. But others see only what we show on the outside. That is why our actions and words and even our bearing must be the harmonious and truthful expression of our interior depths. Others will judge our depths, or, what is more important, God will judge them on the basis of the fruits he produces in us and the works he inspires us to do.

Martha and Mary! The continual conflict between external, material existence and the imperishable needs of inner life; the demands from without, urging us to reveal the hidden forces of our innermost being, to abandon inner recollection for the activity that is more pure, more fruitful, or so it seems. But the Master answered the question and ended the conflict. Mary wins; and if our bodies must often be given to the unassuming tasks of Martha, it is only on condition that our soul, like Mary, devotes itself to the contemplation and adoration of him who speaks the divine word, and that we know how to listen in silence to that word in our depths. The value of activity lies only in the meditation that prepared it and in offering it to God.

Christianity is based on the idea of sacrifice. Christians should imitate Jesus' model in their own times and make their sacrifice, amid human silence or indifference, to be joined to that of the Master. They should know Gethsemane or Calvary to the small degree that their strength supports. They should offer themselves for the salvation of all, and stretch out their hands, which are often weary, to the cross in supplication for all. Their lips should proclaim their sublime union with the Crucified, and they should give what is most pure in itself for sinners and the disinherited.

Souls who have lived for a long time withdrawn into their depths, and who have not been able to pour out their abundance, sometimes need to give to others a little of their interior treasure. This is the secret of some writings, and it is perhaps the mysterious reason for this lack of Christian understanding that sometimes causes suffering. Exterior deprivations make the interior life more intense and the gift of self richer.

We must give the least possible place to our self-centered self, avoiding that which brings us praise and esteem without serving God or our neighbor. And yet we must not neglect the least opportunity for doing good. It is a difficult thing to reconcile these two duties, and yet indispensable. The divine light will guide us if we ask for it when it is needed. According to whether the need or duty at hand is one that requires our self-forgetfulness or our charity, we must be prepared to sacrifice either our pride or our humility.

When blood no longer flows from an open wound, it appears to be healed to the indifferent eye. Nothing could be more wrong; the wound that no longer bleeds is one that may never heal.

It is surprising to see how much spiritual progress we make in times of aridity, when no conscious joy of any kind unites our souls with God. It is then indeed God himself whom we love, and not his consolations; and whatever we do then, requiring constant effort and appeals for grace, is indeed duty in all its starkness. Then, when the dusty road is over and the way becomes easier, we are astonished to see how far we have come; sometimes we arrive at a gentle resting place, in peace, near the heart of God.

Observe great reserve concerning everything about my interior life. Whatever I disclose, without the absolute duty of charity, will be of no use to others. We must not foolishly distribute even the smallest amount of our fortune and waste what the Master has given us.

When physical or moral suffering threatens our very soul, we must say to it: "You shall go no farther." We must allow the waves from outside to beat against us, without using too many of our resources to resist them. On the contrary, we must avoid any disturbance and strengthen our defenses against it. The agitation, bitterness, and all that attacks us from outside or from our sensible nature quickly pass if we create in ourselves a little silence and take a deep breath in the presence of God.

If God wants me to see old age, I fully accept his will, asking only that I may love him and work fruitfully for the coming of his reign in others and for his church throughout my life. Otherwise, why would anyone wish the road to be shorter when one knows where it goes? I can wait for the hour appointed for me, for I am confident of finding again, through divine grace, those who have gone before me into eternity.

I know that I cannot now possess the fullness of life, such as we shall know in eternity. I am imprisoned by a thousand human ties that do not allow me truly to know, possess, or love. And yet the divine light that illumines the darkness is enough to enable me to wait and hope for everything.

To put more energy into the struggle with myself; not to allow external influences to go beyond a certain point, and to strengthen myself against the wounds that are endlessly inflicted on me.

One deception alone is admirable: that which allows us to ignore the evil done to us, our suffering, and the deep place in ourselves that belongs to God alone; the deception that, without hiding what we are, does not reveal everything and does not exhaust our reserves of charity, of energy, and of kindness.

To act while physically exhausted and to suffer without any felt consolation is perhaps to earn what our prayer would not have been worthy to obtain. Only sacrifice is certain to go straight to the heart of Jesus.

Silence is a Christian duty. When it is a question of ourselves, our trials, our graces, we should remain silent, unless charity requires us to speak. And even when it is a question of divine things, it is good to be reserved, "to treasure all these things in our heart" (Luke 2:51), until the time when this heart opens itself to someone who is unhappy or in doubt.

What good is there in entrusting one's sufferings, miseries, and regrets to those to whom one cannot say at the end, "Pray for me"?

Before acting, establish interior peace; banish all that could disturb or agitate you through recollection, strengthen your will through prayer and meditation; and then get to work humbly, energetically, joyfully.

Some laughter is like tears; some tears are like a song of thanksgiving.

Many people know so little of their own interior reality that it is indeed difficult for them to understand another's.

August 1906

I now stop writing down my thoughts. The evolution in my spiritual life these notes marked is completed. Or at least, because nothing is finished on earth, I have entered into this great, divine peace, an undeserved grace for which I bless him who willed and accomplished it. I believe, I hope, I adore. It is in a spirit of profound humility and gratitude that, looking at my life and the grace I have received, I give myself to God, I consecrate to him my soul and the new life that is opening before me.

My Spiritual Testament

For Félix

Jesus said to her, "I am the resurrection and the life; those who believe in me, though they die, will live, and everyone who lives and believes in me will never die. Do you believe this?" She said to him, "Yes, Lord, I believe that you are the Messiah, the Son of God, the one coming into the world" (John 11:25–27).

This, my beloved husband, is my spiritual testament. I wish you to be my principal and dearest heir. Especially to you and to all who love me I leave the mission of praying, and of having prayers said for me; and of having Eucharist offered for my intention for thirty consecutive days after my death, and many times a year during your life. May your good works and almsgiving speak to God of her who served him so imperfectly but who loves him with all the strength of her being and the full affection of her heart.

Try during your life, as much as is possible for any human being, to pay off my immense debt of gratitude to the adored Father, whom you shall know and love through my prayers in heaven.

When you also shall have become his son, the disciple of Jesus Christ and a living member of his church, consecrate your life, transformed by grace, to prayer and charity. Be a Christian and an apostle. All that my prayers and sufferings have asked for our poor brothers and sisters here below try to give them in your turn. Love others; pray, suffer, and work for them. They deserve all our sorrows, all our efforts, and all our sacrifices

I leave those whom I love to you so that you may surround them with your care and affection. Accompany through their lives our nephews and niece, who are also my friends and whom I love so much. Be their spiritual guide, their soul-friend, the example of their lives. Help them, morally and materially, at the time of their marriage or vocation. Consider them to be our beloved children and never abandon them. To their parents always be the brother and the loving, devoted friend that you are now, but in a more spiritual way. Even increase your affection, for I leave you mine to pour out upon them.

If I should die before my mother, I do not need to ask you to care for her; but you will have a great task if to your own tenderness you are to add all of mine for my beloved mother.

With your mother, too, who is also so fully mine, I ask you to replace me.

I leave in your hands "Juliette's work," that is, the installation of a chapel in some poor quarter. If the name has not already been used, it should be dedicated to the Holy Spirit, otherwise to Saint Teresa or the Sacred Heart.

I also leave you my various charitable works and the payment during your life of my regular donations or others to replace them.

I remind our nephews and niece never to forget how much is owed to God and to the poor out of what we shall leave them.

At my burial I want a simple service, without any kind of ostentation, with only religious music, and no display either at the house or outside the church. I would like the mourners to meet at the church, and that my relatives and friends, instead of sending unnecessary flowers, should have Masses said and give some alms for my intention.

And now, my beloved Félix, I tell you once more of my great love. And I charge you to tell our relatives and friends how much

I loved them all and how much I shall pray for them until the hour of reunion. Close to God, where so many of our beloved dead already await us, we shall one day be eternally united. I hope for this through my sufferings offered for you and through God's mercy.

Your wife forever
Elisabeth

October 15, 1905[38]

WRITINGS ON
CHRISTIAN VOCATION

Translator's Introduction

Elisabeth Leseur began formulating her reflections on the vocation of lay Christians when she embraced the "new life" that began for her in 1897 with her recommitment to Christian faith and practice. She experienced a call to love in a special way those who were different from her in thought and in matters of belief. She recognized both the limits of women's social roles and their power for good. And she vigorously thought about the social and political concerns that affected Christians in the world and developed her own approach. She embraced both a philosophy of the hidden force for good Christian men and women can be in the world and their responsibility to do what they can to reduce evil and suffering whenever possible, yet she recognized that only God can reach the inner spirit of human beings. These reflections are scattered throughout her writings. Letters written to the Duvents in 1901 and in 1904 suggest how much she was thinking about these themes and living them in her own life through the first five years of the twentieth century. In her letter of September 10, 1901, to the painter Charles Duvent she wrote:

> Yes, there is much evil, much meanness in the world, and the great error of socialists and other reformers is to imagine that through violence, through the theories they develop, humanity will discover how to regenerate itself and enter into an era of endless happiness. These fine illusions last a long time; then comes the time of disillusionment and of discouragement when one becomes pessimistic and gives up. This is all because the point of departure is false. Besides, since others as well

as you have said, even the sincere exploit the situation. Even among the sincere there is often such arrogance, such a desire to play a role, to be the leader, a subtle form of pride among the refined.

My dear friend, I am starting from a different point of view. I am persuaded that evil and suffering will never completely desert our poor earth, but I am also convinced that it is everyone's task to work to reduce evil and suffering as much as possible, in our own sphere, humbly, simply, without concern for our precious personality, through dedication, love, the gift of ourselves to that which is our duty. I believe that to accomplish this mission, the first thing to do is to try to become our best selves, even perhaps without knowing it. And God will do the rest. Our effort, our sacrifices, our actions, even the most hidden, will not be lost. This is my absolute conviction; everything has a long-lasting and profound repercussion. This thought leaves little room for discouragement, but it does not permit laziness. We are poor day-laborers of life; we sow and God gives the harvest. You understand...I am unable to despair of humanity.[1]

When her niece and godchild, Marie Duron, made her first communion one month after her aunt Juliette's death (April 13, 1905), Elisabeth composed an essay for Marie in which she shares this vision of the Christian woman's vocation, which at that historical moment began to offer greater breadth of action in the world as well as in the domestic sphere.

Elisabeth had earlier written to Aline Duvent on October 30, 1904:

I believe, my dear friend, that if faith leads us to the good, the good will multiply and that you will be a Christian woman. I mean, a consciously Christian woman, and not only as you are now through morals and generous instincts. You would have a reason to live, an understanding of suffering, a spiritual idea of duty that would make you a special person by transforming your precious and natural qualities. Above all, I do not believe in indiscreet proselytism; I know only too well that one cannot give another faith.

In her essay to Marie she develops these themes further in the very personal voice of a loving aunt who has great hopes for her niece. This is one of the many occasions that enable her to share a little of what God has given her.

In the second essay in this section Elisabeth writes a parallel essay to her nephew André, Marie's younger brother by a year. Since Elisabeth had several other nephews, she envisioned giving a copy of this reflection to each of them as they approached the rite of Christian passage marked by first communion and confirmation at that time in Catholic life in France. She understood only too well how difficult it was for any young man to emerge through adolescence and young adulthood with his faith intact. In these essays she tries to open a way for her nephews to do so with integrity. Both of her essays assume that the Christian vocation includes a strong intellectual component. Ideas, thought, culture, and politics are not to be avoided but engaged in, reflected upon, and entered into with sufficient knowledge and understanding of faith realities that one can do so without fear or loss of faith. She recognizes that the modern world must be met on its own terms and at the same time from a thoroughly Christian perspective.

❦

The Christian Life of Women

An Essay on the Christian Life of Women

(Composed by Elisabeth Leseur for her niece, Marie, for her first communion)[2]

A good tree cannot bring forth bad fruit, nor can a bad tree bring forth good fruit. Every tree that does not bear good fruit is cut down and shall be thrown into the fire (Matt 7:18–19).

Dedication

To my beloved only niece, my godchild, through a precious and sacred bequest, and my adopted daughter, I offer this expression of my deep and Christian affection.

My beloved child, for a long time I have planned to dedicate to you the months preceding your first communion. I want in a special way, and the thought of it alone has been a joy for me, to give you on that day, the happiest and most important in your spiritual life, a little of what God has given me. I want to show you what every Christian bears within herself, a treasure that increases by our personal experiences, our sufferings, and our daily more intimate contact with him who is the Truth and the Life.

I did not dream this up by myself. It was shared by another who was holier and more lovely than I. Your dear godmother [Juliette] eagerly looked forward to this day and hoped for a complete union of all our souls during your first sacramental encounter with Jesus.

Who among us, if we are really Christians, can say that her hopes were mistaken, and that Providence did not fulfill her intense desire? If only we knew how to withdraw for an hour into our depths, where God dwells, and how to contemplate the eternal realities, as much as our weakness allows, we should grasp how much love and how much fulfillment of our desires is really hidden in our great sorrow. It only seems to feel more painful because it happened so close to your eagerly awaited first communion. No, dear, none of us will really be missing from our family gathering. What would have happened if your godmother had been far from you, lying on her sickbed, will not occur. In the fullness of her faith and love she longed for you to be united with her in God. This union will now be greater than it could have been were she still alive. In this life many things separate people, but those who live in the one true Light are indeed near to us. They know and understand us more deeply than they could ever do here below, where the best and truest part of ourselves always remains hidden in the depths of our being; some things cannot be expressed in human language.

From now on, we will continue to experience your godmother's influence throughout our lives. She will guide our consciences, strengthen our wills, obtain the peace and strength to accomplish our work in the world and to fulfill the particular mission given to each of us. Your godmother will do more for you than if she were still on this earth. She protects you and will continue to do so, and her love for you is greater now that she lives in God's infinite love.

As for me, my dear, I do not deserve the happiness that she enjoys. My life and heart have been devoted to her for months, and so I have not been able to be involved with you. But now, I want to talk to you and pass on to you some of my most important thoughts and deepest convictions, which by God's grace and inspiration are the fruit of the effort, meditation, prayer, and work of many years. All the good in me I owe to God alone, whose parental and continuous action is so visible in my life that, in spite of great trials and this most recent and greatest sorrow of all, I can still fervently thank him and try to transform myself and my life for his service in the future

If it is all right with you, I will talk to you about your first communion, and especially about your Christian life that will follow from it. I will talk about what you can and ought to do to become spiritually strong, to make your life fruitful in good works, and to share with others, according to the great law of Christian solidarity, the gifts that you have received.

In speaking about Jesus, Saint Peter says that "he went about doing good" (Acts 10:38). Happy are those who at the hour of death and new life feel they have done a little toward spreading light and love among their brothers and sisters, and, to use a maxim your godmother liked, that they have raised the level of the human race by lifting themselves to a higher point.[3]

You are reaching the age when, with each successive year, you are able to do good. You are coming to that decisive time when you will make of your life one of two things: either, as many people do, something purposeless and vague, without any strong moral discipline, useless and consequently harmful (for neutrality is impossible where it is a question of doing the good); or something beautiful, harmonious, and purposeful, sowing good seed on the earth and preparing a rich harvest for eternity. Every person is an incalculable force, bearing within her a little of the future. Until the end of time our words and actions will bear fruit, either good or bad; nothing that we have once given of ourselves is lost, but our words and works, passed on from one to another, will continue to do good or harm to later generations. This is why life is something sacred, and we ought not to pass through it thoughtlessly but to understand its value and use it so that when we have finished our lives we will have increased the amount of good in the world.

Your first communion is your first step on this path of doing the good, and I am not going to say much to you about it, because others will tell you better than I could; you will soon see for yourself what the mysterious encounter is between you and Jesus Christ. Nothing can be compared to this union, and later you will experience even more fully all the strength and joy imparted by this divine contact. You will understand that all human happiness, all sorrow, and all repentance are transformed in the heart of him who alone gives pardon, consolation, and peace. True communion is, strictly speaking, a communication of life by God himself. You will come to know this personally, and nothing that I could say about it would be as valuable as your own experience. I will simply tell you that if I have been able to bear the sufferings of the last few months, ending as they have in this agonizing loss, without sinking under the burden, it is because I have been strengthened from this same source—the holy Eucharist and union with Jesus Christ.

After your first communion, and after having received the sacrament of confirmation, which will bring you illumination and the gifts of the Holy Spirit, you will really begin life, and I want, as far as my weakness allows, to tell you what I wish for your life.

Humanly speaking, I hope and pray constantly that your life may be happy and that you may enjoy all its joys. I hope that you will someday be a wife and mother, that you will have a husband worthy of you, as good a man as your own father or your uncle Félix, and that you will pass on to your grandchildren the good example and teaching that you have received. I hope you will have good health and trust that the sufferings of your loving godmother and her prayers will obtain all this. Finally, I hope you will live to old age, and that, in the words of the marriage service, you will see your children's children to the fourth generation.

But it is not this purely human aspect of your life that I want to discuss. I want to speak about the spiritual life and the effect that this inner life will have on your actions and on those around you.

In the first place, a Christian woman is a human being like everyone else. Every individual is a thinking, reasoning being, illumined by that natural light which is the first degree of the divine intelligence, as you will learn later from Saint Augustine. This is the light that Saint John says enlightens everyone who comes into the world. Those who know no other will be judged by God according to this light. We, too, possess it, and it leads us to the place where the light of faith begins, to that point where, as Pascal says, "reason's last step is the recognition that there are an infinite number of things which are beyond it."[4] This light of faith comes directly from God and shapes our supernatural existence. It gives our actions, which appear to resemble those of other people, an end that the actions of others do not have, and it gives an incomparable value to ourselves and to souls. Our bodily and rational lives differ in no way from those of the other members of the human race, but there is something "beyond," not, as all too many people imagine, antagonistic to this life. There is a higher life, which permeates our entire selves, transforming them, giving them motives for action, supernatural like itself, and fashioning our outer lives into the likeness of our innermost being, so as to create an harmonious unity.

This supernatural light never overshadows the human mind and its learning. Rather, shedding its rays upon them, it illumines them more intensely, and it is superior and exterior to them, as it were. Shining on humble as well as powerful minds, it reaches the soul within and gives it a motive for living and acting, the meaning of suffering, an explanation of death, as well as revealing to it the beauty and usefulness of our activity in this world and its supernatural fruitfulness.

ELISABETH LESEUR

There is no peculiarly Christian kind of learning—learning is the same for all, whether they are believers or not—but there are Christian scholars who, while using methods common to all in the scientific domain, advance beyond the domain of sense-knowledge, and, by quite another method, well suited to its object, reach those mysterious realities that constitute the whole of our humanity. In their wholeness, men and women seek to discover these realities behind the veil hiding them from their view until the day when they will at last behold in eternity the one light of Truth.

A Christian is, therefore, in one sense complete, since her field of thought and action may be as wide as that of the greatest scholar (that depends upon her intellectual faculties) and at the same time the sphere of the infinite and eternal lies open to her, revealing not merely the world of sense, the knowledge of the changes and events that take place, but also the infinitely greater and unchanging world of God and the human soul.

This is the life of faith, understood not as passive acquiescence on the part of the mind, but as an active acceptance, a lively assimilation of truths that surpass the mind and which constant experience, suggested and directed by grace, impresses upon us. You will possess this life, and it is now going to begin in you.

What others have received and passed on to you, as it was passed on to them, will become real and living for you. You will be a link in the long chain that Christian tradition is slowly forming and that will last to the end of time. You will, in a greater or less degree, enrich the collective consciousness of Christianity by your effort, energy, and sacrifices.

From now on you ought to prepare yourself for this great task that is required of each of us, or at least of those who are inspired by faith. You are a Christian, and from a purely Christian point of view your responsibility will present itself to you under various aspects when you consider the particular circumstances that affect Christianity in our times. All Christians have the same aim and ideal, in every age, to whatever race they belong and whatever may happen to them, but circumstances require them to adapt their mode of action and the form of their ministries. As a matter of fact, our Christian duty appears under a threefold aspect—intellectual, familial, and social. I do not add its spiritual

172

dimension because the other three are only different forms of the religious responsibilities imposed on us all.

In the society in which you will live, you will have an intellectual duty to perform that is more important than ever. You ought to be a woman of real worth, well educated, with your mind open to every argument from outside. You ought to know how to discern among incoherent and varying ideas and systems that which is true or fruitful in each. The fathers of the church said that each of these systems contained "the soul of truth," that must never be allowed to die. Never be put off by words and always go beyond appearances. In this patient search for the truth and a habit of fairness that we ought to have toward others and their ideas, we need integrity of mind, clear judgment, and solid learning. You will gradually acquire these things, and you will do so more easily when your convictions become more consciously developed.

Consequently, you need a serious education; there should be nothing superficial or mediocre, not only in your literary and scientific studies, but also in the intellectual knowledge that you ought to have of all things Christian. I am sometimes shocked to see how completely ignorant most women are of the religion they profess. Its very spirit is totally foreign to them, its living and imperishable dogmas are to them a dead weight that they drag around, and their appalling narrowness in matters of doctrine shows how completely they fail to recognize the heart of Christ beating for them under the veil of rituals and symbols. They have even lost all appreciation of our wonderful Catholic liturgy, which accompanies us from the cradle to the grave and is made from the most beautiful impulses of people in every age, inspired by the Holy Spirit. They are that heartrending thing, a body devoid of a soul, which people call a woman who "practices" her religion, but who has nothing of that nobility of spirit, that interior beauty and liveliness of soul that every Christian woman ought to display.

In saying this to you, do not imagine that I have any desire to condemn "religious" practices. Nothing is farther from my mind. But devotional practices ought never to be anything other than the manifestation of what lies in one's depths. We must first thoroughly grasp the truth that such practices help to enliven within us. So, too, we must grasp the harmony of the church as a whole, the vitality and power of Christian teachings, and the moral and social value of Catholic doctrine. I hope, my beloved, that from an intellectual point of view you will be a thoughtful Christian and that you will understand the reasons that undergird your faith and the grounds that you have for hope and worship. Then, when you will have matured sufficiently to grasp the great thoughts that Catholicism presents, you will bring a real spiritual and theological awareness to your religious practices, and you will reject all that might lead others, who have no faith, to suppose Christians to be eccentric and narrow-minded. Saint Vincent de Paul makes this exquisite remark: "Evangelical practices ought to be no more burdensome to a Christian than wings are to a bird: both of them are means of leaving the earth and rising to heaven."

You must also make every effort to increase your depth of human learning; I should like you to be very well educated or even learned. The word *learned* does not bother me, in spite of Molière, for whom learned women are nothing but silly pedants.[5] In our times a learned woman can do much good.

A woman is responsible for her intellectual development and ought to increase the breadth and depth of her knowledge and enlarge her intellectual horizon, so as to be capable one day of simultaneously fulfilling her role as a mother and her duty toward the society in which she lives. For it stands in need of illumination, faint though it may be, from all of us. When we work not for trivial satisfactions but to strengthen our minds so that others may benefit from our work, we can be sure that it will be fruitful, and that God will bless it. One day, sooner or later, it will bear more fruit than we can imagine. Once more let me remind you that none of our disinterested or generous efforts is ever lost.

Your second responsibility is for your family; it is certainly not new, but so important that I want to speak about it again. With the church, I believe that the whole structure of our moral, national, and social life is based on the family, and I am convinced that everything done for the family enhances the greatness and strength of peoples and societies; on the other hand, they are irretrievably destroyed as soon as the family, the cornerstone of the structure, is attacked.

174

Thus, you will do all you can to strengthen in every way respect for family life. Later on, when you have your own family, you will make your home a warm and lively center of influence, and you will be a guiding spirit for those who live in the light that you spread. You will be a friend and companion to your husband, and a guide and model of moral strength to your children. You will possess that precious treasure that your dear godmother and I have so often discussed, and that she preserved amid all her sufferings—a serenity and peace of mind that nothing can destroy, neither trials nor losses, since God is their source, and God gives them sometimes in proportion to our sufferings. This is one of those mysterious compensations, unknown on a purely human level but known only in God who alone reveals the secret.

Then, and even now, in the midst of your extended family, you will develop the habit through daily effort and the help of God's grace to "possess your soul in peace," to be gentle and lovingly composed in your attitude toward events, people, and life itself. Sometimes managing to smile requires true heroism; may your smile, whether thoughtful or joyful, always do good. You will meet many people throughout your life, but by preference go to the weakest, the most embittered, and the most marginalized, and regardless of your trials and sorrows, you should know "to rejoice with those who rejoice," and to share in the happiness of others.

Just as important, every Christian woman has a responsibility to society. Because of your education, you will be able to accomplish more and must work with all your strength to improve the material and moral condition of others, especially of the dispossessed masses that, though often deceived and taken advantage of, are, nevertheless, still good hearted and are the great reserves of the nation and of the church. You see, we must never forget the tender words spoken one day by Jesus on seeing the crowd gathered around him, "I have compassion on the crowd" (Mark 8:2). Like him, let us be compassionate, and love these people who are deprived of so many material goods, and above all of the supreme good, which alone could reward their sacrifices and hard daily work, namely, the knowledge and love of God and of spiritual things. Let us go to them as brothers and sisters, not as superiors or benefactors, and show them that real equality is found only in the teachings of Christianity, which recognizes the same human dignity in all people, assigns to them the same end, and promises them the same happiness. Let us demonstrate that the church alone carries out the ideal of fraternity and imposes it as a law upon her children, and that she alone, according to the sayings of Jesus assures us true freedom: "You shall know the Truth, and the Truth will make you free" (John 8:31).[6]

Quite soon, to the extent that your parents think advisable, you will be able to share to a greater degree in the social action that is emerging everywhere, choosing those [activities] that are at the same time the most spiritual and the most practical. You should bring to this collaboration a generous spirit of adaptability, devotion, and energy; a sense of the need of discipline; and little self-centeredness or selfishness. Never be one of those who want to be the commander and not an ordinary soldier, who want only to participate in the good projects they create and only recognize as good anything that is done in their particular way according to their own procedures. Here, as elsewhere, you should have a broad mind and generous heart; put up with the contradictions and difficulties that are the price of success; work day by day without looking for results, but be confident that God will make something of your efforts. Remember, however, that in order to become involved fruitfully with the questions so important today, during this period of transition through which we are passing, in order to work to bring about a new Christian social order, you must prepare yourself by making a serious study of these difficult problems, bringing to any attempt at their solution very great prudence together with Christian courage. Catholics are not afraid of democracy; they know that the church baptized, transformed, and civilized barbarians, and that the masses of our people still retain a rudimentary seed of Christianity, capable of growing and developing into a tree with spreading branches. Catholics love these sister souls and long to make them Christian. Even if they make themselves liable to be thought to be socialists or revolutionaries by their embittered opponents, they would continue their work of social progress, saying to themselves that after all they are content to be socialists in the company of Saint Thomas Aquinas, or revolutionaries with the fathers of the church, and that only the people who do nothing at all can hope to avoid being called unpleasant names. At this cost, what Catholic worthy of the name would want to avoid such epithets?

You and I are at this moment casting a very rapid glance over Christian life as a whole. Our survey would be altogether incomplete were I not to mention two serious and holy things, which it would be painful to contemplate if a gleam of divine light did not illumine them. I am talking about suffering and death. One is the path leading to a higher life; the other is the gate opening to the only true life.

Never, I assure you, in the case of a really Christian person will the anticipation of suffering and the thought of death cast too deep a shadow over life. The strongest people, who with courageous hearts face struggles, losses, and trials, who can meet death with a smile and make it for themselves and others a supreme offering, are those who once and for all have grasped the fact that suffering is closely intermingled with life, is part of God's law and works our redemption and sanctification, and that death destroys nothing but sorrow. They rest in the serene belief that God alone is beauty, truth, and love, and that death is the road leading to him and in him to fullness of happiness and life. They know, too, that in him we shall meet, never to lose again our beloved ones whom he has called before us.

Like everyone else, a Christian suffers, but she does not suffer like others "who have no hope." Our hopes are great and beautiful, my darling, and, over and above the happiness that our trials prepare for us, we have the Catholic doctrine of the communion of saints that helps us to bear them.

About this doctrine I will only tell you what I told you about the holy Eucharist, that you will not understand it until you have, so to say, experienced it in life. The communion of saints brings about a sweet communion and mysterious interchange of prayers and merits among all God's people—those who have already received their reward, those who are still being purified, and those who are struggling here below. Our sacrifices, actions, and efforts, when they have a supernatural intention, possess a purifying and sanctifying power we can use for the good of our brothers and sisters living and dead. It is indescribably beautiful and consoling to feel that, when we weep, our tears may be bringing peace or conversion to some beloved or unknown soul, and that we are not suffering or acting for ourselves alone, for this, as your godmother used to say, "would not be enough." She suffered a great deal and offered up many of her sufferings for you. Only in eternity, when all secrets are made known, shall we learn all that she thus obtained for you. Then you will discover what she won for you through her suffering, faith, and Christian life—perhaps also through those human joys that she did not live to taste.

We shall all die, but, because you are a Christian, you will not fear death, and you will remember that the best way to prepare for it is to live and act in a Christian manner. Tell yourself that death is the child's return to its Father, the creature's return to its God, and that only through death shall we ever possess the happiness and enjoy the realities of the world to come, for the affection and joy of this life are only a shadow of what shall follow.

Circumstances force me to stop writing sooner than I would like, and at the present time you will understand very little of it. When it has once been read aloud to you, you will put it aside and quickly forget it. With your soul transformed by our Savior's first visit, you return to your work and play, and your daily occupations, and my little notebook will lie forgotten in some corner.

But as the years pass and you mature, and also later in life at times of joy or sorrow, or when you need some special inspiration, you will, I hope, read my little book again. Although it has no exterior merit, you will find in it the trace and reflection, as it were, of a heart that loves you. You will feel yourself encircled by my affection, and, if God allows, a little of what fills my soul will pass into yours. Then, if you feel consoled and strengthened, if, after reading this book, you have greater love for your brothers and sisters and can make a more intense act of faith and love, whether I am still in this world or in everlasting bliss (provided that I attain to it), I shall be able to sing a canticle of thanksgiving and say with boundless gratitude: O Lord, you have tried me by suffering. You have withheld or withdrawn from me many earthly joys, but you have repaid me a hundredfold, inasmuch as you have revealed to me, in addition to your love, the comfort of human affections, and have allowed me to do a little good for the child whom I loved so much, and whom our Juliette had, in a way, entrusted to my care before returning to you.

The Christian Man

A Little Essay on the Christian Life

(Written for André Duron for his first communion)[7]

Blessed are they who observe justice, who do righteous-
ness at all times (Ps 106:3).

Dedication
To my dear godson, the child of my heart, I offer a little of
my heart, which will always be open to him.

My Dear Child,

Last May we went through a time together that we can never
forget. You, a young child, still immature, received for the first
time a visit from God, and we were happy to join you in this
unique and great act of communion so full of blessings.

I am sure that you were not alone at the altar. Mary was
there, blessing your young heart; your guardian angel was there,
praying for you, and with them was [Juliette], happy in the joy that
can never be taken from her. While you were making your thanksgiving, one of those prayers that God never fails to hear was made
for you close beside you, by her who has loved you so much and
who loves you now more than ever.

If we consider the great mystery of the spiritual life, the powerful communion of saints, perhaps, when you were beginning
your true and profound spiritual life, your beloved aunt Juliette's
reminding God of some of her sufferings that are over now but
that, nevertheless, remain fruitful, asked him in return to give you
the grace to be always true to Christ, and, better still, to be an
apostle. You will understand later that holy people like your dear
young aunt, through their trials, sow the seed of holiness in others. When you become a man, a mature Christian man, you will
realize that the good you accomplish is like a flower growing in the
fertile soil that others have watered by their tears and cultivated
through the their painful labor.

Although my offering is not worth as much as Juliette's, God willing, some of the sorrows of my life, softened by so much love, may also result in interior graces, peace and salvation for you, and that my unceasing prayer may bring you divine light and the fullness of supernatural life.

When I have gone before you to our blessed and final meeting place, I want to leave you a remembrance of the blessed day of your first communion as well as of your godmother, who loves you more than you know. That is why I am adding to the copy book containing the notes of your retreat a few pages, which I suggest you keep and read over occasionally at times of joy or sorrow, and especially at times of doubt or temptation.[8]

My dear child, the words *Orare et laborare* ought to be the motto for our whole life. They were spoken by the holy father and repeated by the parish priest of St. Louis d'Antin on the first day of your retreat.[9]

If you can understand and practice these two things and make your existence one of work and prayer, there is nothing to fear. Your life will be useful and your death blessed and your influence for good will last for years to come.

To pray is to believe in and worship God and to acknowledge that our existence has a supernatural goal, and that we have not only a bodily but also a spiritual life; we put God first, others before ourselves, and ourselves before worldly things, before all that is transitory and that is not as valuable as our immortal souls.

To pray is to live in constant, calm, strong, and lasting union with God, to look at everything from God's point of view, and to be so peacefully anchored in eternity that annoyances, unavoidable struggles and continual activity have no ability to disturb us or to drag us down.

Do not think that, when I speak to you in this way about living in eternity in advance, that I forget that though you are a future citizen of heaven, you are at the present time a young citizen of earth. I am not encouraging you to neglect your human responsibilities. When life is established on a solid foundation of faith and when grace sustains us daily, we can live on earth and do our part in building up society. We are still able to enjoy the happiness and love that come our way to a degree scarcely known to those who do not put a little of eternity into their love and pleasure. Nothing human is foreign to us, and we possess the priceless privilege of being simultaneously members of the human race and sons of earth, and also members of the heavenly race and sons of God.

The first part of what your motto should be necessarily complements the second. Prayer calls for action, just as action requires prayer to inspire and direct it. *Orare*, yes, indeed, let us pray a great deal. *Laborare!* Let us always work with courage for ourselves, for our brothers and sisters, and for God. I want to say in a few words how prayer and work ought to exist together in your life and never be separated, and how spirituality and work ought to be combined together during the three major stages of your career.

Right now and for the immediate future, according to circumstances, you will continue to live from the Christian point of view influenced by your first communion. Make the most of this time; you will be strengthening not only your intellect but your heart for the struggle, and the preparation that you make now will enable you perhaps to pass through the difficult periods that await you without weakening. I say this regretfully but with great certitude. Store up reserves of spirituality, of humble, confident faith, of intense charity and kindness. Someday you will see that I have not misled you, and that you must have an abundance of good grain stored up in the granary of your heart if you are not to die of hunger during the lean season.

Thus, we pass on without dwelling on this period of your life. You will recall it later with pleasure and will remember with emotion the days when the great Christian, that you will then be, was only an innocent, young, and pious child.

How long will this period of your life last? I do not know. A year, two years, or perhaps a little longer, but certainly not much more. Then, too quickly for your dear mother and all of us, you will begin the time of moral transformation and of individuation, a time of temptation and struggle.

What is the use of denying it or of trying to hide it from you? You will experience temptation under many forms, as varied as the forms of evil itself, and, if you desire to overcome it, you will undergo a harsh struggle from which you will emerge strengthened and prepared for the task God wants for you to do, which is,

181

in the precise sense of the word, your vocation. This is a thought that I wish to impress upon your mind: there is for every young man, every young Christian, a time that is absolutely decisive with regard to his physical and moral being, his future here and in eternity. One who wants only to save his soul and who has no higher ambition can always entrust himself to God's mercy. And even those who have wasted the gifts of nature and grace may hope to become laborers at the eleventh hour, provided they do not die before this hour strikes.

But you, son and grandson of Christian women, for whom your beloved aunt Juliette suffered and for whom she desired something more than only personal salvation, you may possess holy ambition. You ought not to be a laggard in the Christian army but one of those courageous leaders who encourage others to plant their standard, the cross, more or less everywhere in the world and in the souls of others.

Therefore, when the crisis of which I am speaking comes, you must remember that it is a serious time and that your own future and that of many others influenced by you depend upon your hard work and the decisions you make then.

This crisis may take two different forms; it may be exterior, due to human temptations, or interior, affecting your mind and faith. I think I can tell you that, apart from a very rare and special grace, temptation will attack you under both these forms.

First of all, you will have to struggle against the world, evil suggestions, bad companions, and a terrible thing that few resist—sarcasm. To be able to stand firm in spite of a disdainful smile is a sign of great moral strength. For you, dear child, I dread a companion who makes fun of you more than one who attacks you. The latter will disgust you, but the former will disturb your peace of mind, and this agitation is often the first sign of defection.

Later, God willing, I shall deal with this delicate topic at greater length, for the sake of my dear nephews.[10] For the present I only want to tell you that every thought and deed that you would not like your mother to know may be regarded by you as evil. This is the great criterion. At the same time, I wish to advise you never to be afraid to tell to your mother everything that might disturb or surprise you. She will understand everything, share and explain everything; she will always be ready to do this, and this loving confidence will certainly protect you against many faults and failures.

Let us turn now to the other form that your moral crisis may assume, namely, the intellectual.

The time will come when you will encounter, more or less unexpectedly, the shock of hearing our doctrines contradicted. Even if the shock is not violent, you will, nevertheless, be aware of the intellectual atmosphere of our times, and perhaps unconsciously you will breathe in the air that surrounds young men of the present day, and in time you will be surprised to find that it has intoxicated you, and that you feel uncomfortable in the atmosphere of faith. You will notice that an outwardly spiritual life does not correspond with your interior reality, and undoubtedly, in your surprise and discouragement, you will be tempted to leave behind what will seem to you burdensome and a hindrance to the free development of your intellect.

Few people, especially few young men, escape this crisis of faith. Perhaps we should not regret it, were it not that so many become depressed and irremediably disturbed spiritually. Those who by God's assistance and by the means about which I now speak pass safely through this dangerous time, possess from then on a courageous spirit and really understand what faith is. They have what Saint Teresa used to call "experimental knowledge" of spiritual things; they understand the sphere of faith and how it differs from that of science, which it may be said to extend beyond, since it possesses methods and experiences proper to itself. These young men arrive at that stability in faith, certainty in intuition, and vigorous charity that God alone gives when we have earned them by our previous work and humble good will. These men are strong apostles; a single one can influence all around him, the members of his own family, of society, and also the hearts of others. I am sure you will be one of these strong men, not a coward or a weakling, as are unhappily only too many of those who call themselves Christians.

But before you can reach this goal, you must face the struggle, (and we must discuss the methods to be used) if you are to pass through this crisis unharmed. This accomplishment will make your faith conscious and mature.

Above all, never forget that you have a mother to whom you can always unburden your heart; do not hesitate to tell her about the ideas that come to mind, the doubts that arise, the difficulties that you encounter, and all that affects your moral and spiritual life. Do not forget that I, too, can help you on the basis of my experience, the fruits of long, interior effort, and the grace God has done in me with no merit of mine. He refused me a son like you, but I think he intended me to be your spiritual mother and perhaps of others as well. He prepared me for this task by giving me experience of spiritual things and bringing me into contact with people of all sorts who either deny the faith or are hostile or indifferent to it. By his grace the world within and the world without have made my faith indestructible. I say this humbly but confidently, since God is never the first to withdraw from us, and I can no longer live without him, after having known the reality of his presence and the happiness that he brings.

I ask you, therefore, to come to me any time that intellect and faith appear to conflict. You have no idea how easy it sometimes is to disperse the clouds that confuse the mind. It is quite possible for a beautiful harmony to exist among all the powers of our being, when we have carried our human knowledge (such, at least, as each of us can acquire) as far as we can, and then we pass beyond this barrier, that is after all not far off, and enter the sphere of the supernatural and infinite. Nothing on earth is as beautiful as this union of human reason and faith, of earthly and divine knowledge, of an intense spiritual life and a very active outer life, entirely dedicated to the good. A man who has achieved this exquisite unity of his entire being is truly strong. He exercises an influence over others that cannot be measured. He does this merely by coming into contact with others and by his example. Without any premeditation perhaps, in the milieu in which God has placed him, and under the circumstances desired by Providence, he is an apostle in all the dignity, beauty, and strength of the word.

So that you may in a few years time pass through this critical period of physical, spiritual, and intellectual development without harm, you must make use of the two means at your disposal; there are no others either from the human or the supernatural point of view, but the first is all-powerful, and the second, which draws its efficacy from the first, will also be most useful to you. These two means are *prayer* and *work*.

When you face temptation, doubt, or cowardice, you must not argue or hesitate, or give in to the enemy, but throw yourself into God's arms. We who are baptized, confirmed in the faith, and children of light must call on the Spirit who is love and life and who never refuses to illumine those who turn to him in fervent prayer. I have already told you that the life of reason and the spiritual life do not have the same methods and are not nourished by the same food. The soul lives by prayer, just as the intellect absorbs intellectual nourishment and the body material substances; the soul dies when it lacks divine warmth, just as the body dies for lack of food and the mind for lack of an education. Someone has said so aptly that prayer is the soul's breathing in God. Never lose this breath by abandoning interior prayer, which is called grace in us and which gives us life.

Work, serious work, prepared for and sustained by prayer, will help you to pass happily through those early years that are, as I have said, absolutely decisive. Begin to prepare for your future career by means of rigorous study. It does not matter so much that you achieve brilliant success, for this is often due to innate ability and does not always involve sustained effort and energy. Work conscientiously, doing what you can do, as it has been said. Be convinced that this is your absolute duty. Christianity needs men of solid worth to represent it. In the world few people are able to form a personal opinion about doctrine. They look to its representatives for guidance, and the best way to make others appreciate and love Catholicism is, perhaps, to show simply by one's example what a Catholic is.

You will demonstrate once more that a man may be learned and highly cultured while remaining a humble, fervent Christian. The strength of your convictions joined to a delicate respect for the consciences of others will, perhaps, contribute toward breaking down the absurd prejudice cultivated against us, and you will show successfully that all human knowledge collectively cannot obscure the pure light of God but, on the contrary, can only become more resplendent from its radiance.

By work, dear child, I mean the activities your age and studies allow you to do. Persons of good will always have some spare moments that may become means of saving others. I know no more touching sight than that of young people, students, pupils at the public schools, and artisans who give their free time and their Sundays to visit poor families, to look after young apprentices, or to organize popular lectures and meetings that will bring them into personal contact with their less fortunate brothers and sisters. These young men work for social peace and true charity. They work slowly and patiently at "necessary reconstructions" about which Joseph de Maistre used to speak.[11] These are not merely political pipe dreams, because history teaches us that forms once abolished hardly ever reappear, and that God does not require any set forms in order to direct humanity toward its destiny; rather, they are real reconstructions, built up on the cornerstone, which is Christ, and fostered by the maternal care of the church, which is always the same and yet always new. It is to this church that our Savior promised he would be with to the end of time.

You will be surrounded by affection, which will protect you from evil; you will be sustained by prayer and by the divine grace that results from it and from the sacraments, too. You will be prevented from frequenting bad places of amusement and harmful acquaintances by serious activities and the good works to which you will devote some of your free time. Consequently, I hope that you will happily navigate this period of youth and reach the age when your active life begins, not without having encountered evil (for you must learn to recognize it), but without its ever making you alter your route, and without your giving it anything but a glance of pity, reserving your heart for your future life work.

When you complete this phase of your life and are ready to become an adult, it will be extremely important for you to recognize and follow your vocation. The word *vocation* means "calling:" it is God's secret call to your conscience to follow the path that he has marked out. According to the design of Providence, each of us is intended to do some special work and receives a task determined beforehand. Human society would be wonderful and harmonious if everyone accomplished all the work given to him by the "head of the household," and if we, laborers of the first hour, tried to discover

God's will at every stage of our life. This cannot be, because from the beginning evil entered into the world, but we can at least take our stand among those who desire to carry out God's plans in and around them, among those faithful servants who carry a heavy sheaf to their Father's house and patiently prepare the soil for future sowing and spiritual harvests.

Therefore, when the time comes, try to discern God's will for you. In order to do so, you must pray, fortify yourself with the wise and loving advice of your parents and of others whose character validates consulting them, and especially of the priest, the friend and guide of your soul. Withdraw into your depths alone with God; face the thought of death, which clarifies so much, and try to recognize your tastes and desires and to discern what career and what kind of life will be the most fruitful for you and for others. Try to see clearly where you will be able to do most good while freely developing your abilities. Give as much time as necessary to this patient search; this discovery is worth the effort and refection that help you reach it. It is better to spend a long time looking for the right road than to risk getting lost or choosing a hard and difficult path. Ask God to illumine you; he will not refuse you but will show you the way.

Then courageously begin your work, always trying to discern your true task and the most amount of good that you can do, telling yourself that, whatever your vocation may be, there are always people suffering in mind or body to be cared for, tempers to be calmed, and hearts to be healed. Look for others on this spiritual path and do your best to influence them by your example. During this active phase of your life, let your motto always be *Orare et laborare.*

Be faithful to your morning and evening prayer, and to that honest examination of conscience that strengthens and guides the moral life. However absorbing your occupations may be, every day reserve a few minutes for recollection and solid meditation, which will strengthen you for the struggle. Above all, receive holy communion often with simplicity, confidence, and love. Approach our Savior without anxiety as the friend he is, able to understand and share everything, with whom you can talk about your joys and sorrows, your temptations, and even the doubts that he can remove,

187

your human plans and spiritual desires. Do not imagine, as some do, that, before going to holy communion you must be "well disposed" or worthy of the divine visit. Such an idea is the result of a misconception about the goal and action of the holy Eucharist. When we are physically weak, we eat the bread that restores our life; let us do the same spiritually. If we were saints, the same abyss would exist between God and ourselves; but since he fills it up with his love, let us go to him as friends whom he does not frighten and whom his goodness attracts.

Above all, never stop receiving holy communion because you feel no consolation. Sometimes we deeply sense our Savior's real presence and are tempted to believe that this loving awareness ought to happen every time. This is a mistake, for, if it were so, communion would already be heaven, whereas it is only meant to be the way. The profound effects of the sacrament and the life that it gives exist even when all sensible consolation is absent. Just as food affects the body, so does God affect us without our perceiving it, and our interior life grows stronger the oftener he comes to replenish our inward reserves of grace that he alone gives to nourish us spiritually.

Live your life as a man, in youth and in maturity, filling it with strenuous work and make it holy through prayer. *Orare et laborare:* once more I ask you to make this your motto throughout life, especially during those years of mental and physical energy when you can do so much to further God's interest. Although it may be possible later to make up for wasted years, they can never be replaced. Privileged people like yourself will have to render a strict account of them.

It fills me with emotion to think about the good you can do with the gifts you have received. You are beginning life under the following circumstances: God has given you good health and intelligence; you were born into a distinguished and united family; you have an excellent father and a Christian mother; you have received great gifts spiritually, baptism, confirmation, and the Eucharist, and also many signs of your heavenly Father's love for you. Until now, you have been able to offer him nothing in return except a little love and good will. But from now on, you should think seriously about what you will be able to do for him, and by means of what courageous efforts, good works, and strong spirituality you will become a true soldier of Christ, in the sense in which the words *Miles Christi* are inscribed on Montalembert's tomb.[12]

When you have spent your childhood, youth, and adulthood accomplishing the task Providence has assigned you; when, according to your vocation, you have done God's will; when, both at home and in your professional and civic life, you have generously and scrupulously fulfilled your responsibilities; and when you have courageously practiced that self-denial without which you can do nothing great in this world; then you will be able to enter fearlessly into the final stage of life, the darkness of old age, on which faith can shine its light and beyond which eternity dawns.

You will need to transform this final stage of your life, like the preceding ones, through prayer. Your human activity will be over, or rather will take another form, and you will give a fine example to others, letting them benefit from your advice and from that kindly influence that an older Christian can exercise very effectively. You will pray for everyone, especially for those for whom you are responsible, and having developed a habit of recollection, you will prepare for your final journey. You will make your death holy in advance and make this last spiritual task a work of grace for yourself and others.

Right now, I cannot discuss these important topics at greater length. We have had a rapid look at the Christian life together. May this little essay be a road sign at the crossroads, pointing out to travelers the path that will not lead them astray.

In relationship to the various paths from which you might choose so your journey is faster and more direct, I pray God to reveal them to you and to give you our Lord Jesus Christ as your guide, your master, and your friend on this perhaps difficult journey, for without him we cannot overcome the obstacles we face.

May he be near you in your struggles, temptations, and labors; may he be with you in your joys and sorrows, and may he rest within you frequently through holy communion. May he stand beside you when you have to fight and suffer for his sake and resist evil in and around you, when you strive to be strong in the midst of the morally debased, chaste in an unhealthy atmosphere, and good in spite of hatred and contempt. May he accompany you in every phase of your life: during youth, to keep it pure and holy; during adulthood, to make it fruitful in good works; and during old age, to shed upon it the light that comes from him.

Whatever your age may be, when you recollect yourself to examine your conscience and study the road that you have traveled, may you be able to testify before God that you have been a man of prayer and of action, that you have "fought the good fight," and struggled, worked, and served for the sake of God and humankind and have shown yourself a good soldier of Christ— *Miles Christi:* this is the prayer of one who loves you, your spiritual mother through baptism and affection, who blesses you as she finishes writing these pages, in which God will supply for your good all that she would have liked to have said.

Elisabeth Leseur

LETTERS TO UNBELIEVERS

Translator's Introduction

This small sampling of letters, nominally addressed to "unbelievers," demonstrates quite powerfully Elisabeth's highly developed ability to carry on a sustained dialogue with this group of friends. In reading these selections it is important to remember that the letters are supplemental to face-to-face conversation. Aimée Fiévet captures vividly Elisabeth as a conversation partner.

It was rare that anyone attacked the faith in her presence. When she did not approve of a judgment, an idea expressed and she had reason to keep silent...she neither protested by an expression on her face, nor by critique. From her silence emanated something inexpressible giving the impression that she had withdrawn into her soul, like putting something away in a safe place.

She was a good listener, looking for the truth or wisdom of her interlocutor. Some discussions were very profound and prolonged....At other times in intimate conversations, her face took on an extraordinary appearance, as if she wanted to understand completely what was being said...and expressed it, especially if it was a matter of education, morality, or duty, etc. If they did not come to agreement, she would end...easily, with a smile full of resolve and hope and say, "we will think about this each from our own side."...Elisabeth was very clear sighted and intuitive, often understanding something one had not quite said. If she thought she might be helpful or useful, she would make the perfect

191

response with discretion, without giving the impression
of an intrusive intimacy.[1]

Such was the quality of her dialogue and search for common
ground among a very disparate group. The letters written to
Aimée Fiévet, the most intellectual of the three women friends
addressed in this correspondence, express Elisabeth's concern for
Aimée's health, her need to rest from overwork, and their very different interpretations of reality. Her other two correspondents
were close social friends. Jeanne Alcan, a non-practicing Jew, suffered from depression. Elisabeth offers her practical advice and
encouragement, tactfully drawing on her experience of periods of
despondency and depression caused by loss and illness. In Jeanne
she recognized undeveloped spiritual potential, which she tried to
nourish. Yvonne Le Dantec was like an adopted younger sister to
Elisabeth. Like Elisabeth, she married a man who was no longer a
believer. In Yvonne's case, her husband was a professed atheist and
an intellectual who had written a book on atheism. In this set of
letters Elisabeth maintains ordinary social conversation with
Yvonne, sharing the overlapping details of their family news and
social lives. She offers her as much support as possible, encouraging Yvonne's faith despite her husband's position. She embraces
Félix Le Dantec as the younger brother-in-law (almost) he is and
approaches him with a great deal of charm and warmth. She all but
seduces him into reconsidering his point of view just because he is
so fond of Elisabeth. The majority of these letters are to Yvonne.
However, Elisabeth slips in remarks meant for Félix, and her most
important letter to him, in which she engages him intellectually
about his illogical atheism, is included.

Selected Letters to Unbelievers

Part I: Letters to Madame Emile Alcan (Jeanne)

Letter II

September 3, 1901

My Dear Friend,

Yesterday after you left, I gave more thought to the doubts and scruples about which you spoke with me. It seemed to me that I did not say to you a quarter of what I was thinking and feeling, and that I had expressed to you neither my affection nor some ideas that might help you relieve your actual situation. Influenced by these feelings of regret, I send you this note. I am always divided between two contrary feelings: the fear of being a tedious philosopher or of appearing to preach about things that I have not done myself, and then the remorse of not having done all that I should have. Happily, I am confident that in the context of our indulgent friendship, which understands my affection and which will forgive me so readily, I will do that which I had neglected to do.

I still had many thoughts about you this morning, because you would know how to believe the point that I want to help you see in order to get rid of this trial. I believe that if you are able to manage to be in Ville-D'Avray, or to be in Paris fifteen days, and then leave with your husband, that would perhaps be good. Except, of course, the case where you would feel that your physical strength would not be sufficient to do that. What tempts me about your returning to Paris is that I would have the ability to see you often. That would, I assure you, be very pleasing, and I would profit from that the most.

I have sent you this morning loving thoughts, wishing with all my heart that you will have the strength to summon the necessary will, which is, I believe, needed for your complete healing. Above all, do not abandon the initial effort. Do regularly each day that which you are supposed to do: your accounts, a little personal work, intellectual and physical, and make Adrien work a little.[2] I am convinced that these small, repeated actions will restore the vigor of your will, which is a little anemic, and that you will feel

193

the good effects. Do this, even if it is tedious or tires you a little, and try each day to do it a little better than the day before.

Why would you not look for a way to do that which Christianity recommends so much and that I find so helpful: every day a brief meditation on a thought or an inspiring subject? Of course (you know my respect for your conscience and your convictions), you would know that it would not be a question for you of religious subjects. But there are some thoughts that are common to all of humanity, and some reflections on duty, on usefulness and the meaning of life, on love of one's fellow human beings, that everyone can do, it seems to me, whether believers or unbelievers. This method helps very much to recognize clearly one's responsibilities, to increase the inner life, and to put one's existence in harmony. Lifting ourselves a little higher so that we forget ourselves and our suffering helps us to open our life a little to this poetry that is in us and that transforms so many things. The outer world is very often the reflection of our inner being.

All things considered, you have made me able to offer some simple advice, but in some states of health it is difficult to practice it. This is true. Also, in telling you all of this, I am only compelled to do so because of my affection for you. You will earn great merit and you will win for yourself a great victory in trying on your own to wage this daily battle, which will strengthen your will.

I would need to be with you, full of confidence, and sure of your heart and of your understanding, to speak with you like this. In order to do something in return, you can demonstrate your affection for me by sharing with me the truth.

I send you, my dear friend, a big kiss with all my affection; it is not a small thing to say.

Your
E. Leseur
Regards to your husband.

Letter IV

September 12, 1901

Dear Friend,

...How are you, my friend? I hate to ask how you are feeling: if the fresh air and peaceful countryside has a beneficial effect or if

194

you still suffer from your malaise. It often takes a long time to rid oneself of these unpleasant things, and I am very pained that you have this kind of health problem, you whom I truly love, and whom I know to be so courageous, upright, and robust. Also, I am convinced little by little that your nature will overcome the suffering and the lethargy and that you will recover all your optimism and your liveliness. I think it is necessary for you to live for a while from day to day and to look for a way to distract yourself without fatigue. If reading does not tire you, our expansive libraries are at your disposal. Because of some sad days we have had, it seems to me that I can understand your actual fatigue better. I have had to struggle a great deal against physical and moral depression. Right now, that is over. I have regained my self-possession, through repeated efforts, which have led me little by little to deep interior peace. Now, it seems to me that I leave this difficulty the better for it, understanding all suffering even more, and loving more deeply my family and my dear friends, of whom you are one....I have experienced some very great consolations, and if I say this to you with such frankness, it is only because I have such complete esteem for you. I am sure that you understand the thought and the joy that animate me so that I can risk opening myself with such warmth to you. It is not necessary to think alike about everything in order to love much.

On that note, I have to go. Perhaps on Thursday, until then, in any case. If Maman does not need me to drive her to the Salon on Saturday, I would be able to go to see you. Not having been able to do this, it has been impossible not to write you. When I write, Félix would say to you that one knows that when I begin, I ignore everything until I am finished.

And meanwhile I must regretfully stop writing, embracing you with great affection. Greetings to your spouse. Affectionate kisses to your children. Be assured, dear friend, of all my lively affection.

E. Leseur

I just remembered that I will be free next Wednesday, the nineteenth. If you prefer that I go to Ville-D'Avray that day, tell me. Until Wednesday.

Letter VI

Jougne[3]
July 16, 1902

My dear Jeanne,

I do not know whether or not this letter will reach you and if you have finally found a roof to put over your heads. But I write you all the same so that you will know that the Jougnards are thinking about you and regret that you have been drawn in the opposite direction. Our country is incredibly wonderful. And even more, the charm of these places, where we are happy, peaceful, and enjoy good feelings all around us, has already captured us. The house is large enough for the fifteen of us who are here; the view is beautiful; the surrounding area that we have already explored a little with our guests is very beautiful, and all my dear ones are thrilled with their stay. For me, after the commotion of Paris, I am pleased with the tranquility and the regularity of life, this possibility of working peacefully and "truly." Also, the serene beauty of the mountains renews me physically and morally. I seem to feel better, and I report to you a transformed Bébeth. I dare not speak in a less enthusiastic way because these great views changing so slowly offer a poor idea of revolution, but instead, considering this beauty, I experience a slow and sure evolution that I would like to see operating in humanity, beginning with this small bit of humanity—that is, my poor little person, and which I find develops very slowly. At the risk of your husband's making fun of me, I have to admit that I think and reflect even more here than in Paris. Where can I find a better confidante in such a reliable and dear friend than you? And then, you know that if I do not always tell you everything I think, I always think about what I say and that I feel it vividly; this is because you know that a believing friend has thought about you more than once in her *péchinisation* sessions. (You remember that Félix named me "Madame Péchin.")[4]

We have my mother-in-law here, together with all my immediate family. The children are lovely, and I have such a good time with them. Félix is ravishing. He wore a casual outfit that everyone admired. We are going to have a housewarming soon with the Pelletans and the Ordinaires. The latter are still in Paris and will arrive tomorrow.

Would you be so kind, my dear Jeanne, to tell me what has been done about the subject of Duvent? If your husband has paid him directly, that is perfect. If not, would you quickly let me know so that I can send him the agreed-upon amount? How are the children? It would have been good to have a party with ours; that will have to wait for the winter, when I hope to be able to bring them together a little. Give them a hug for me and convey to their father friendly greetings from all here that you will share with him. But what you are to keep for yourself, dear friend, is a very affectionate kiss from your old and faithful friend.

E. Leseur

Letter VII

August 12, 1902 (Jougne)

My dear Jeanne,

We have just ended one of those weeks that life holds in reserve, but which is very painful and sad. Félix had been called immediately to Vienna on business for the *Compagnie Anonyme de Gestion D'Assurances sur la Vie,* and we had to leave. That was very difficult for me, truly heart-wrenching to leave the countryside and the good life we were leading. I left quite sad, and we returned Saturday at eleven. My sister and her husband were waiting for us at the station, with such expressions on their faces that we knew right away that something terrible had happened. The evening before, my mother's cousin, whom we all loved and treated as a grandparent, who had accompanied us here, being single, died from a sudden heart attack going up to his room. You can guess the sudden chill and our distress and the painful feeling that I suffered returning to our home in that fashion. Everyone in the region has been perfect; one could never imagine a better community, showing such tactfulness, such unheard-of discretion and an extraordinary generosity. They moved the body of our dear relative to a reception room in the town hall, and they decorated it with perfect taste. Throughout each night some local people came to wake the body, and each evening everyone came to pray in the room. I have rarely seen anything more touching. Yesterday was the burial, and we accompanied the body of this loving and good man to the train station. He had arrived here so happy, and we spent some wonderful hours with him. During the sad services, a telegram arrived with the news of my brother's mother-in-law, who had been injured in a car accident in Lozère where she was traveling at the time. My sister-in-law left to care for her. Finally, that night, my mother-in-law had been suffering, which succeeded in discouraging us. Luckily, her difficulties have not been serious and she is fine now. But I assure you, dear friend, that we need some quiet days to put all these emotions in perspective. We have just had three good weeks, and on the thirty-first we had a joyful family celebration here. I have had much pleasure from the children, from the contentment of being with my own family, and from the kindness we received in this region. I assure you that, like you, I have been very reflective during these sad days. In seeing these people so sane, so dignified, and so united, I said to myself that those who sow hatred are very culpable. I know well that they are tainted by "superstition" and to the eyes of some everything is fine like that. But even for those, like me, who do not share these superstitions, one can still wonder if the beautiful and strong local and family customs, the respect of all who deserve respect, the narrow solidarity that binds them together and that manifests itself through some works and a very interesting organization—if all these things that are obviously the fruit of superstition do not have a value that one hesitates to destroy. I would like to bring Georges here and notice with him these spirited people, very proud and free, who have nothing of the "religious" in the bad sense of that word.[5] There are two women religious here who render unappreciated services and who are probably going to leave like the others when the "new order" begins.[6]

Congratulate Adrien for me on his success, which gave great pleasure to the heart of his pseudo-aunt. I saw his name in the paper and wanted to write to him. But my life has been very difficult the last ten days.

I think well of your poor aunt and I am sorry with all my heart;[7] the emptiness for her must be so great. Your mother, I hope, is going to put all these sad feelings into perspective. Me, too, my dear Jeanne. I will be happy to get to know your friend, because from the moment that you loved her she can only be deserving of your affection. I have worked hard to believe that she has a love for you that is even greater and more sincere than mine.

All those you know here, that is to say, those who love you, send you their best wishes. Both of us repeat our love for both of you. A kiss for the children. My dear friend, I embrace you with all my heart and all my love

E. Leseur

Letter VIII

September 13, 1902

My dear Jeanne,

No, you will not be peaceful on your mountain because I must come to lean on you a little. All of that is because I am missing you very much and it is a long time since I have seen you. I think often of you and of the joy that you must be experiencing in this beautiful country where life is certainly more gentle than here. I have had a very hard time getting used to Paris again; the transition has been too abrupt between this full house and my silent quarters in Jougne, where life is so full and at the same time so tranquil. My life in Paris feels more empty and tiring each time we return. Félix has been involved with his business, and I have had in the meantime many hours of a terrible depression in which the little voices of children who give me such joy would have been most necessary to lift it. You do not know that lack, the happy and loving mother of four. Now this awful period is over thanks to an energetic moral effort and a brief genuine retreat that I made. I am going to try to forget the uselessness of my life by looking for ways to be more useful. Do not make any reference to all this when you write me; it is one thing among others that I have to endure, with the exception sometimes of my true and dear friends to whom I can open a little corner of my heart.

Maman has come to spend three days in Paris for the burial of our poor cousin and to put his affairs in order. I have been happy to see her for a while. We always expect to go to Jougne toward the first, and we will be delighted if you can make the trip from Lausanne to see our castle. I can let you know then when our departure date is settled. Don't forget to give me your address in Lausanne.

Your brother-in-law, Viot, had lunch with us Thursday, and we are expecting him again on Tuesday. I often see Alice now. She, more than ever, needs to be surrounded by and loved by friends.[8] Do not make any reference to anyone (especially in writing) to what I mentioned above. We have been to Vaucresson, where sanity reigns.

Félix and I have returned to childhood; we just read the last volume of Danrit,[9] which we find very amusing. I am going back to work and have been busy; that is why I cannot write you more often.

Enjoy your stay there, dear friend; I would love to return to the beauty of nature with you, to the very special and profound emotions that I experience so often during the summer. And all that is inexpressible. Only, I am certain that you would be experiencing something similar and that would give me pleasure. Would you kindly remember us to Madame Hechtole?[10] I hope that the fresh air will do her some good. Share our good feelings with your husband and give him a joyful hug for me. I send you, my dear Jeanne, my fond thoughts and all my love.

Bébeth

Letter XLIII

June 3, 1910

Dear Jeanne,

Thank you for letting me know how you are. I am very pleased. I really hope that this is the beginning of a better time for you, a time of rapid healing. Surely, this time, your depression will not last long, and you will soon be peaceful again, in full possession of yourself and totally ready to resume your life and your daily occupations joyfully. Surely, this is the time to be vigilant and to prepare for the future—as you would put it, "to reform your life." I am convinced that you are able to avoid returning to the same situation again or at least to be better prepared to nip it in the bud. But for that moral discipline is necessary. You will need to lead a life where tranquility of spirit and physical activities are combined in such a way as to create, without lessening your determination, a way of doing everything from your innermost self, with habitual awareness and serenity. That is the whole secret of life. It is precisely that which I have forced myself to work at for a number of years, taking much effort and many sacrifices, passing through many failures, but sustained by a supernatural power that I have prayed to God without ceasing for you, because left to our own resources, we are very little and weak.

As soon as you are completely relieved of your actual miseries, begin this process without delay, and outline for yourself sort of a rule of life, committing yourself never to set it aside. You will clearly recognize your main responsibilities toward your husband, your children, and others. Also, decide on some time that you will reserve for a little more recollection; that I believe is indispensable for good, interior equilibrium. Why not make each morning what in religious language is called a preview of the day? That is, take a rapid look at all the tasks that will fill your day and make resolutions about how you want to do them. And in the evening, you might also make a short examination of conscience to make sure that you have given to others that which they can rightfully expect from you as well as making sure that you have saved a few minutes for some good, fruitful reflection. I am very sure that, if you do this, you will no longer be afraid of the bad hours, and that if they try to return, they will find someone who can withstand them.

But all this is just for the interim (and I will repeat this for you). While you wait for that, begin as much as possible to train yourself wisely in this path. Every day, do a few chosen things very regularly, accomplish these gestures first, even if you are bored or if they take effort. Gradually they will become more interesting. Take care of Maurice; try to chat with Marianne; read a little every day; do some accounts or write some letters; have some hand work that you can do when you are tired. Incidentally, if you crochet some small pieces, I promise to make something from them for the poor. When you feel anguish or anxiety, let these feelings be, without paying too much attention to them. They will eventually end by themselves. This is the approach that spiritual directors suggest for the overly conscientious, and they find it often helps.

Especially, try to remain peaceful. But when you are with others, without straining yourself too much, show yourself externally to think as much as possible about how you can give others pleasure or do them some good. I promise you much good comes from this double exercise.

My very dear friend, let me embrace you with my affection, with my ardent desire to help you, who are so beautiful, so good, and so understanding of me that I love you with all my heart. I absolutely want you to be released from this suffering that so prevents you from flourishing. We will see each other soon, but right now, I do not want to tire you any more and I ask your pardon for having thus tried your patience. Tomorrow morning, before lunch, if I am not too tired, I will come up about eleven o'clock and give you a hug. If that is not convenient, let me know.

Greetings to our good friend, Emile, to whom I hope you offer a smiling face. A little kiss to the children and to you.

Your old friend,
Elisabeth

My patient is recovering from her pulmonary condition; her phlebitis has pretty much cleared up.[11]

Letter XLVI

Second half of 1910

Dear Jeanne,[12]

Christians believe that a mysterious, spiritual solidarity exists among themselves and all other children of the same God. We call this solidarity the communion of saints; the efforts, merits, and sufferings of each individual benefit the rest. A similar law exists in the natural order, and if we think about it a little, we shall be convinced that our words and actions have a deeper and more far-reaching effect than we often imagine. Therefore, it is an absolute duty for everyone who understands what "absolute" and "duty" mean, to say and do nothing that is evil or even indifferent, since there is no neutrality in matters of morality. From that arises the obligation to make a sustained effort on a daily basis to work at interior perfection, because, whether we intend it or not, the effect we have on others will be the reflection and expression of what we are within. Let us create an interior treasure of noble thoughts, energy, and strong, intense affection, and then we may be sure that sooner or later, perhaps without our being aware of it, the overflow will affect the hearts of others.

I am not hiding the fact that this is a difficult task for one who relies on reason alone, which is itself to some extent only a tool, and many circumstances may falsify it or impede its action. I have, however, total confidence in God's ways of working with each person, even with those who never address God personally, and yet offer genuine homage by their love of the good, the just, and the beautiful. I believe that God inspires and directs all true reason and all who walk by its light. Therefore, setting aside all that is "of another kind," as Pascal used to say, and that belongs to another sphere, I want to limit myself to the sphere that belongs to all, Christians and unbelievers alike. For Christians are also "rational beings," and reason brings them just as far as anyone else, namely, up to the point of which Pascal speaks, "reason's last step is the recognition that there is an infinite number of things which are beyond it."[13]

Therefore, every life is a serious matter and ought not to be led carelessly. Whether we consider it to be the prelude or a rough outline of the fuller, better life that we cannot enjoy here below, or whether we look at it as a fruit (a very bitter fruit sometimes) and not as a seed, nevertheless, we arrive at this conclusion that *every life involves responsibility, and we are accountable not only for the evil that we do, but also for the good that we do not do.* We are convinced also that our smallest actions and our most unnoticed sacrifices have a lasting effect in time and space, and that we continue forever the good or evil that we have once begun.

As a result, nothing is indifferent in our moral life; the neglect of the smallest duty has consequences we never suspect. This is why we must live in such a way that no obligation, great or small, may be left undone. That is why we must not lose sight of this desired goal in the clouds, but work in the present in order to attain it. The important thing is not so much to succeed immediately, but to begin and to continue the effort. For that reason, each day, we ought to make a brief review of our life as a whole and bring into it each of the responsibilities that creates our life; these are obligations toward our family and toward society, and, in your case, I would say, moral rather than religious obligations.

First of all, we must clearly recognize our real responsibilities. There are two dangers to avoid: we must not too easily imagine that certain so-called obligations really are binding on us, or we might become anxious and distracted by many useless things; nor, on the other hand, ought we neglect our real obligations, from which nothing can excuse us. We ought to organize our tasks carefully, never letting the less important ones replace those of greater significance. Moral obligations are the most important; if I give them precedence over the rest, it is because they include the rest, and because the way in which we fulfill our obligations depends upon the way we approach this one. You must not think that the moral life does not need nourishment; one's spirit, just as much as one's body, can be ill, strong, or anemic. If you do not want it to waste away, you must provide it with daily food, and instead of prayer, that incomparable source of life, you must practice two things, namely, meditation and examination of conscience. All reflective people recognize that these interior activities are a necessity, and they were practiced by Marcus Aurelius and Maine de Biran, just as much as by Saint Francis de Sales and the most unassuming Christian. Meditation is the gathering of oneself into the very depths of one's being, to that point where, as theologians tell us, in the silencing of outward things, God is found. There you will find the source of all good (and this is God), strength, and beauty (and that is God). There you will strengthen yourself in the thought of what is eternal in preparation for the struggle; and there you will understand, as your ideal becomes daily more clearly defined, both your own weakness and all that you can do here below in the cause of good. A very definite theme must be taken for meditation, which otherwise is likely to become vague and dreamy, and in that case the remedy would be worse than the evil. Meditation should end with a resolution that can be immediately put into practice. Finally, it should be done every day, all the more when we are not disposed to it. It is when we are sick that we most need a doctor. Examination of conscience is also indispensable every evening; it ought to be clearly focused, equally avoiding vagueness and scrupulosity. It takes little time to examine oneself about the use of time and the accomplishment of various obligations when you have prioritized them well and organized your time.

After this most basic duty that tends to renew and strengthen your spirit every day, we come to exterior responsibilities that are, as I have already said, the outward manifestation of our inner spirit. You have responsibilities for your children and have to look after their lives, their work, and so on. All this should be done without exaggerating anything or allowing yourself to be absorbed by one thing at the expense of another, or by one child to the detriment of the others.

The responsibilities of a mother, who has household help in taking care of material needs, is to provide for and organize everything, watching over all, without trying to do everything herself. These household concerns, as well as the organization and arrangement of her home, the accounts, and so on, do not need to absorb her completely when things are done regularly day by day, and everything is in the right place. What a mother ought to do, and what she alone can do, is to foster her children's moral development, to discover their unique personalities, and to awaken in them their highest aspirations. By simply coming into contact with them, she can gradually give them a sense of strength and serenity that is not easily disturbed, and thus she becomes a second conscience for them. When a mother has the good fortune of being able to pass on to her children the effects of her own interior experiences, she has the duty to do so.

Toward those whom we lovingly call neighbors, you, who enjoy a privileged life, have obligations and responsibilities. The responsibility of wealth, intelligence, and moral worth. You are a cultured woman, whose heart and mind can grasp and share many things; you enjoy the privilege, in this age of hostility, of hating only hatred, and so you can do much good, if you know where to look. The heart has an intuitive sense, more or less intense, that enables us to perceive needs or sufferings that others would not notice. My own experience of life has convinced me that never a day goes by without our meeting someone in distress of body or soul, some form of sorrow or poverty, and there must surely be many more that we miss. Look around you, my friend, and you will soon see that your good heart does not need glasses.

I should like to talk to you for hours but prefer to see you in person, although I often feel more shy in speaking than in writing. Let me give you this little essay, written in haste, for in it I have given you a small piece of my heart. It still contains an abundance of affection, sufferings, and personal experiences, for which I thank God daily, and which my heart offers you whenever you want to draw upon it. What comes from God must be given back to him in the form of love for all our companions on our earthly journey, and this is a very enjoyable duty in the case of a companion such as you.

E. L.

Resolutions

> *On awakening:*
> Concentrate my mind on devoting myself to what is good
>   and to the day's duties.
> *Make a quarter of an hour's meditation* upon some very definite
>   moral topic, and make a practical resolution.

> *In the evening:*
> Focus of examination:
> Examination of conscience:
> My responsibilities toward my family.
> My household responsibilities.
> My responsibilities toward my neighbor.

> *For a short time, lift up my soul.*

Part II: Selected Letters to Aimée Fiévet[14]

Letter XLVIII

January 29, 1905

Dear Mademoiselle,

Madame Pontrenioli gave me your address, which I quickly made use of to send this letter. I hope it was not indiscreet of me. You are somewhat isolated and, of course, depressed; I, too, have been burdened these last months with sadness and concerns.

Perhaps, in connecting our trials a little, we will be able to strengthen one another in them. I will be the one to benefit the most from what I will receive from you. We do not have the same ideas about everything, I know, and my beliefs are not fully yours. I say "fully yours" because love of the good, constant concern for truth, and love of our fellow humans—all that we have in common, which allows us to accompany one another on our journeys. And if the star that guides us does not shine for both of us with the same beams, at least it offers the light by which we are able to walk toward the truth that unifies and calms our hearts. I speak to you so candidly, dear Mademoiselle, because there are two things that are equally deep in me: the convictions that guide my life and the interior life that has made me vibrant and strong. I have a total and absolute respect for each person's conscience and convictions. For me, that which transpires between God and human beings is something sacred, and nothing must intrude from an undiscerning hand. Besides, I feel that I am too imperfect and fallible to judge, and I am too much in need of competent care myself to be strict toward another. Now that I have made my confession, I will be more comfortable chatting with you frankly and warmly about all the beautiful and great things that make life better and help us to get through sad times, transforming that suffering into joy and love for all.

Your letter did me much good; you show me an indulgence that I know is excessive, but that only demonstrates your generosity. What has been so loving is the sense of your genuine compassion; finding this feeling is so rare in close connections between minds. Thank you, dear Mademoiselle, since, thanks to you, I felt a little better and stronger.

The beautiful sun of the Midi will dispel all your sorrows and heal your worn-out throat. This is the desire of all who love you, especially me. By the time you return, I hope you will have recovered enough of your voice to speak many good and comforting words; but you are among those who do not need to speak in order to do good.

We have had dinner the last two days with the Alcans, the Viots, and the lovely Pontrenioli family. My days caring for my sister prevent me from seeing them; later, if my dear little invalid improves, I will be a little freer. The days pass quickly, even those which do not bring joy. I am often too sad to do much of anything.

My husband has a case of the flu right now but does not have to stay in bed. He asks me to send you his respectful remembrances. Dear Mademoiselle, I send you the expression of my deepest and most profound sympathy with every affectionate thought.[15]

E. Leseur

Letter XLIX

April 28, 1905[16]

Dear Mademoiselle,

Your heart spoke profoundly to my suffering and it inspired these loving words, so lofty and beneficial. After so many months of sorrow, my sweet memories flood me now. My heart has been terribly broken, the worst of my whole life. I lost not only a beloved sister, but a friend, in the full sense of the word, and a daughter, because I loved her as a mother. The long hours spent with her, in such loving intimacy, the outpouring of our souls to one another, the same desires, the same loves, growing more and more each day, all that united us so completely that life now seems impossible without the strength, I hope, she will obtain for me.

Dear Mademoiselle, such a long ordeal of the soul has given me such great and supernatural certitudes that it seems as if they have now imposed themselves on me. The life of my dear sister has been fashioned from sufferings, sacrifices, and love. She knew every noble aspiration without being able to satisfy it. She ardently desired to do good without being able to put it into practice, at least as she would have wanted, because I believe in the fruitfulness of suffering. She achieved nothing here below, and this dear one, so vibrant (I have a consoling conviction of this) finally found her ultimate flowering, and the true life, that we only begin in this world and that we get glimpses of in our better moments, those when we unite ourselves with that which is infinite and eternal.

Since she died, in my times of recollection and prayer I feel the soul of my beloved sister very close to mine, and she will help me wait for our reunion, to make my sorrow serve the well-being of others and to become perhaps what she already was.

She died like the saint she had already become, through loving and praying, accepting suffering and death, and saying in a tone of voice I will never be able to forget, after having received communion, to my sister who was speaking to her about God: "I love him and I have abandoned myself to him." She died with her dear eyes fixed on mine, and I had the terrible sorrow of closing them and of kissing her one last time after everything was over.

Forgive me for opening my heart to you in the depth of my sorrow. That is only possible for me with those with whom I feel a deep bond, and you have well shown me yours. Meanwhile, I wanted to say to you that I think of you, in the trial that you are experiencing. Even when it is entirely normal, death always causes suffering among friends. I have had neither enough time nor the courage to send you a loving thought, but I hope that you have felt it a little yourself.

How are you finding your stay in Hyères? I want to know that all is well with you and in the note you sent, so openhearted, you did not tell me enough about your health. When you are able, let me know if you are feeling better. And if you come to Paris, let me know ahead of time. It would be so good to see you, and I would come to see you if it would not be too tiring for you.

My husband sends his respectful greetings. From the depths of my heart, I say again, thank you, and I send this with a little of the complete love and affection that I feel so deeply for you.

Yours,

E. Leseur

Letter LI

March 26, 1907

My dear Aimée,

As people say, "I feel sorry for you." Have you received the letter that I addressed for your arrival at Cepoy?[17] It was not all that important, but what I most wanted to know is how you are feeling and what you are doing as well as to convey some small expression of my love and affection for you. I have often thought about you

209

since you left and not seeing you has been a true mortification the end of this Lent. I have fasted for you and this fast (from our visits) is harder than the other; like the heart that lives and expands for the one it loves. There is some sadness in the absence of those from whom I have been separated the longest, but at least I know that there will soon be joy on their return. I also know, is it not true, in the other case, that the wait is longer. Life would be very cruel if one would not have done a little good and loved another deeply in order to replenish oneself and if one is not walking toward the light that shines on the end of the road. But when one has all that, my dear friend, I say this with great conviction, despite all suffering, life is beautiful, very loving, and one can wait for the reunion. I love life, even what is hard, since, according to a saying, "death is only the continuation of life." This makes me remember another saying that I like of your teacher, Monsieur Pécaut: "To believe in eternal life, it must already have begun in us."[18]

It seems that I have gone further than I should have and that I need to return to my more usual style. But these ramblings do express some things I really feel, and I believe that you love me deeply and will forgive me.

We have a bright sun, which makes me happy for you and for me as well; this brighter light is good for us from every point of view, and I fully appreciate it. With praiseworthy perseverance I continue my treatment, but I am still not very strong; and you, how are you finding your rest and the country air? Don't write a long note in reply; you are supposed to be resting, but do give me some news of yourself on a postcard. And then, anticipate for me the moment of your return when I can come to your house whenever I want.

The health of everyone around me is good; Maman's is less satisfactory. I had hoped the summer would have helped her more. These days are very sad for her; they are for me too, but thanks to God I have great serenity. You have been faithful in thinking about us, and I will return the favor in hours of recollection when those I love rest deep in my heart.

A solid kiss, dear Aimée. Would you kindly pass on my respects to your mother and believe the deep affection of your old friend?

E. Leseur

All the best from my husband.

Letter LV

August 16, 1907
Jougne

An annoying crisis of sufferings and of unexpected vomiting for three weeks has once again prevented me from writing to you, my very dear Aimée. I have been made altogether remiss by this warning but have been able to benefit from the very good weather we have had up to now, and from a thunderstorm that gathered yesterday, momentarily, I hope. Despite very strong wind, I am writing you while resting on the terrace, which will not improve my poor writing.

I joyfully received your long-desired letter, especially since you have received this new assignment.[19] First, I am happy for you despite the fact that this measure is insufficient from some points of view, and then for those for whom your intervention will be helpful. And then, there is another consideration, entirely personal; this scheme takes you from Paris, and I dread seeing you leave this winter. How I will miss my visits to Tournelles Street, and how happy I will be to resume them. This winter I intend to eliminate all social visiting, and you needn't doubt that it is not a sacrifice. But my health will most likely impose other ones for which it would have been a sweet recompense to spend some time with you. We will return to Paris the first of September, and we are already anticipating a too-rapid end to our time in the country. I would have liked to stay here longer and to create some new activities and duties. Will I be able to accomplish these plans in the years ahead?

Perhaps I am going to shock you by telling you that I understand perfectly your impressions during the baptism of your grandniece; something witnessed from outside seems to produce a very strong effect. I only object to your observations relative to the modern mentality. One can easily admit the Christian conception of sin, and thus time changes nothing because evil always exists here below. For instance, I suppose in your case, one denies this conception, with the result that there is no reason for baptism. But if you had, my friend, once studied thoroughly the structure of Christian faith without any preconceived antipathy, you would at least be able to recognize how it all fits together so well, so solid, and how many different parts are connected one to another to the point of touching upon

211

parts of the building that could make it crumble were one to take a part out. Thus, in the whole building there is an admirable solidity. But I understand that one must admit the bases and that faith is the foundation of everything. I have only wanted to defend in the presence of your loyal spirit a great thing that we contemplate from two different perspectives. When you see the exterior windows of a church, you only see some unformed fragments, but from inside, it is colorful and harmonious. Thus we both see something different at the same time. I add that this comparison is not my own; I read it, and I can't remember where. I like it very much and share it thus with you, adding only that we have at least the same point of view about things of the mind and of the heart and that your soul must be better than mine. They will always be united in this life or beyond, in this beyond that your dear religious mentor, Monsieur Pécaut, spoke about in such noble terms.

I am better and all my dear housemates are in good shape. How beautiful are all our mountains this month! Nothing can express the effect of the light, which changes the forests by the hour and illumines in a different way the hills that form the horizon. I would have liked you to see and admire all this with me, chatting about everything in a good heart-to-heart talk....

A solid kiss from your old friend,
Elisabeth

Letter LVI

September 17, 1907

My friend, Aimée,

You really deserved to be scolded for having sinned in thought. How could you have imagined for an instant that your candidness toward me would have annoyed or pained me? Meanwhile, it is this frankness that I love in you, and thus, I am the same in your regard without human respect or without any trouble. I forgive you, but for your penance you must write me soon, unless that would make you too tired.

I was going to forget my second grievance; how, old friend, you came two steps with me and went no further because of a troubling scruple. How could you not see you would only have been refreshing for me and a better influence than all others? One other time, especially, you did not resume again. Anyway, this time I would be annoyed if it were true.

Since my return I have been fine, except for a case of fatigue accompanied by fever, but that passed in only two or three days. What prevented me from writing was that, in order to avoid returning to Paris too directly and experiencing the rapid change of air quality, Félix wanted me to spend some time outside of Paris at his brother's, where we stayed from Saturday to the following Monday. These last few days we were with friends at Louveciennes. I will be in Paris this evening….I will be happy to be back in my own home, because if I left Jougne with deep regret, suburban holidays, as pleasant as they are, cannot replace it, and nothing is as good as being in one's own home, especially when one is not very strong.

My health is better, but I still have some complaints and I especially need to avoid commotion and movement. This last point is very painful for me, because it will disturb my active life. But I will be forced to rearrange my priorities without suppressing activity altogether.

Félix is fine; my sister and her husband have returned to Paris. The children are still in Jougne with my mother until about the twenty-fifth of September. I long for their return.

And you, my dear Aimée, how are you? You do not tell me about your health, and this may be a third grievance, but being loving and generous, I forgive you again.

We will return to our friendly quarrel over baptism, but I cannot wait for our next and much desired conversation without protesting strongly against one idea expressed in your letter: You seem to believe that I have made my convictions to my own size and that I have, these are your expressions, "elevated, purified, and divinized" them. But, dear friend, it is entirely the opposite that is true. You would no longer say that if you knew my inner life a little and how much it was worth before the blessed hour of *fiat lux*, an interior light, and the slow, deep transformation that my innermost being has undergone through the action of God. You have felt, you say, that "there were no longer vaulted ceilings veiling the sky, nor walls constricting the air you breath." In what way is my sky obscured, or where are the walls that limit my horizon? What represents an obstacle, a hindrance for my human nature, is also one for you, since you are not among those who deny the moral law, since you fight against self-centeredness, hatred, and evil under all its forms, as I do. Is it because I recognize and accept doctrine, an entirely spiritual law, which diminishes nothing in the field of my thought and of my human activity? But you, dear friend, accept (as I do) scientific law, you proclaim the moral law without your freedom being curtailed. If you tell me that scientific laws are controlled and verifiable, that you only admit certain knowledge, I would reply that the truths in the spiritual order are verified by the soul, with the aid of other methods, without doubt, but also certain. And they are assimilated like our human organism assimilates nourishing bread. Religious truth is not a passive thing; it is alive and we sense its all powerful reality when it has taken possession of our being, illuminated it, transformed it, strengthened it. To continue, and this is a certain point, the little that I value must be in my faith or I will not be me.

And I, too, love you, my friend, with a very strong and gentle love, that nothing is able to extinguish because it is so planted in the depths of my heart. This is the cause of this same tenderness that I recognize in you, that enables me to share my thoughts and show you my faith, because usually, I keep to myself what renews my soul and inspires my life.

Receive a very loving kiss and Félix' respectful greetings. Share mine with your mother, and believe, Aimée, that not a day goes by that I do not think of you and offer a prayer. This is the best I can give to those whom I cherish.

Elisabeth

Part III: Selected Letters to Madame Félix Le Dantec and to Félix Le Dantec

Letter LXXVI

December 27, 1904

My dear little Yvonne,

To say that I have been profoundly moved by your communication to Maman is an understatement.[20] I love you so completely as a little sister who took the place of our Marie that your happiness is one of my greatest concerns and that such an important decision can only evoke an entirely sisterly feeling. I have asked God, in this serious matter, to accomplish everything for your happiness and your greatest good. I hope that my prayers will be heard, and I know in advance all that you will discover in Mr. Le Dantec—his nobility of heart, generosity, and great intelligence. You can say of him that already he is a brother for us and that we love him, considering that he has come to love and understand you. We congratulate him in having such a charming new wife, and I rejoice, my dear one, in feeling your happiness, after so many difficult things and emotions.

Can you join us for luncheon next Monday, January 2? Convey this friendly invitation to Mr. Le Dantec, and in order not to be taken a villain, let him see in advance that his future adoptive sister-in-law is not "a servant of obscurantism." Moreover (at least, I hope), that I have not been made into a fanatic or a frightful reactionary.

Your dear maman must be happy to have a son without having to see her beloved daughter move away. Give her a hug for me and tell her how much we love her.

Monday, is it not, my little sister? It will be so nice to see all three of you. We send you a kiss in which I put all my love for you.

Your older sister,
Elisabeth

P.S. The address of the dressmaker is Depré, 8 Place de la Madeleine. Madame Hennequin thinks that she has had to raise her prices some, since she lives in such an elegant neighborhood, but nevertheless will still give you a good price.

Letter LXXVIII

March 3, 1905

My dear little Yvonne,

Félix, who is very absorbed at this time by his work, has had to schedule an event at home on Tuesday at one o'clock. It will hardly be possible for us to meet you. Would it be possible to reschedule for Thursday the ninth or Saturday the eleventh, whichever is better for you? You see how much I want to be with you. You can let me know your response Monday evening at our aunt's.

It seems to me, my dear, that yesterday, very moved by your news and by your distress, I expressed my affection for you very poorly.[21] Meanwhile, I have been feeling it very deeply ever since yesterday. We share so completely the sufferings of those we love as much as you. In our helplessness to do something for you and our Juliette, and in the sadness that I feel, seeing the two of you suffering, first one and then the other, I take refuge in prayer so intense and full of love that I hope it spills over on both of you. Do I need to tell you that I include your fiancé, that nothing separates him from you right now? In a moment, I am going out. I intend to make a pilgrimage to Sacré Coeur, for Juliette. I will bring with me at the same time your intentions and those of your ill fiancé. Certainly, God is the same in every church and his Heart is open in every tabernacle, but I want to make this pilgrimage so that my prayer might be more ardent and express my desires better to him.

My dearest, in these sad times through which we are passing, we will be there for each other. We will rekindle our hearts in our mutual love, especially confiding ourselves to the great Power that is, at the time, the great Love and who accomplishes through us, ignorant workers, a result that only he knows. Let us at least be workers of good will and try to make of our lives all that they might be, beautiful works of peace, intelligence, and love.

These works are created from suffering. If, at least, mine can be transformed into joy for my two sisters, Juliette and you, I will be happy.

I clasp you against my sisterly heart; and I send your dear maman a hug. Send us your news. My dear little one, the heart of your older sister will always be open to and you will always be able to share your joy and your suffering, especially your suffering, with me.

Your older sister,
Elisabeth

Letter XCII

June 3, 1907

My dear little sister,

What must you think of your old Bébeth, who not only has not written you since your arrival at Ty Plad but has not even replied to your affectionate letter, which has given her such pleasure? You see, I have not been very well, and my obligations when I can summon my strength sometime prevent me from doing the things that I would ordinarily want to do. Happily, it is not harmful to my precious health to think a lot about those I love, and I am not deprived of that. That is why when you do not receive news from me, you feel, I hope, a little of my deep sisterly love wrap around you, and when you receive it to pray for and to think about, in all serenity, your dear absent ones. Our hearts must often meet like that.

The tone of your letter pleased me; I see that my little Yvonne is completely happy to have found her Félix and to see that her dear maman likes being in Ty Plad. The dark point is the health of your poor godfather. At least you can both talk to him and do all that you can to relieve his suffering. Do you know that poor Mamie just had another erysipelas and is well on the road to healing?[22] Maman has more and more pain when she moves. And I anticipate with fear the time when she will be completely immobilized. God willing that may be as slow as possible. Amélie and her children are fine. My Félix is, too, except for some small annoyances.

Me, hum! Hum! It could be worse; it could be better; it is just so-so. But when the bad times last a long time, when there are many things that are very hard, I take a hold of myself so that from my part these miseries will not have any repercussions on those around me and those I love will not be preoccupied with them. I believe very much that rest and affection from Ty Plad will make me better. And if you want to explore the works of Georges Goyau,[23] only for this year, Goyau will remain at both your house and mine. I expect my health will improve greatly in time.

Meanwhile, I hope that we will be able to take a long vacation this year. I would love a lengthy stay in the country, and it is one of those things thing that we do not know much in advance. Friday morning, I went to see a woman in Passy involved with work and who incidentally is a very remarkable and attractive woman. She lives in her own little peaceful house. There is a garden in which some birds sing, the sun shines on the greenery. I wanted not to return to Paris but to live like that.

What do you say about all these disturbances: the strikes, the extraordinary activity of the vintners?[24] All that suggests so well a spirit of anarchy. Those who see the middle way are not able to do anything for the ones who are hurting. Meanwhile, I am not a pessimist and believe that the future will be better than the present because of the religious awakening that is beginning. Without it we will go quickly into complete anarchy.

Are you familiar with the Picpus convent?[25] We were there recently to see Martha Darcy before her departure. The garden is pleasant and it is a true oasis of peace and of recollection in the quarter of wine merchants, of the railway, and of just plain ugliness. Only such charm and religious serenity can infiltrate the consciousness of the locals at the Place du Trone and remove their taste for taverns. One will, no doubt, rid them not long from now of these "last traces of superstition." (See Môssieu Ranc.)[26]

I wrote to you about Amélie la Bruyère, didn't I? I do not doubt that she is much better, and that at the moment it is a question of courageously accepting life and of believing for herself in the little happiness that we are permitted. I find very true the words of Madame Swetchine: "Happiness is something that we find only on the day when we stop looking for it."[27]

In this grand provisional view of existence, it seems good to contribute as much as possible to the greatest happiness of others. The more good sown without keeping track and without disturbing any portion of the joy that one is able to collect along the way, the more you will welcome it when it returns. I assure you my dear sister (and I would not say this to everyone for fear that others would not understand), I assure you that in spite of more and more uncertain health, of all the uncertainties in the future, of the suffering from separation in which only time can lift the bitterness in some kind of external way, despite passing regrets and often the sadness of the years ahead, I have never been more truly happy than at this moment. I do not speak badly of life, and I would have much more to say about it if any glimmer beyond this would have sweetened the sadness or illumined the joy.

Thus, my little sister, to conclude: really enjoy your happiness, your love for Félix, the love that surrounds you, and never look back without turning your view toward the future, which will console us in helping us to recover from everything, or rather in returning to us those who are living.

You must see us in the beginning of July if at all possible. Give your mother and Félix a hug for us, and say to them that all three of you are never separate in my heart. Greetings to all your in-laws; I feel very sorry for poor Madame Le Dantec and Madame Beguin. I give you, my dear, the most tender kiss.

Your older sister,
Elisabeth

Letter XCIII

July 8, 1907

My dear Félix,

Here are the brief notes about which I spoke.[28] I have put to the test a lively interest—my ignorance does not allow me to follow you in your usual studies—in taking up this time, in the measure that is possible for me, to contact a mind like yours. I am not able to discuss with you some of your scientific ideas, but allow me to place myself on the only terrain that is familiar to me, the terrain of religion, to which you have some objections. I have reduced these to a minimum, because if I had wanted to try to analyze your observations or your critique from this perspective alone, I would have written a book. And knowing you, you would have thought you had to read it. I prefer to limit to one stroke my ambition and your punishment.

Let me first repeat how much I enjoyed not finding you to be a logical atheist because you would not be the charming person whom we love so fraternally. Is it not unusual and striking to think that finding for the first time in my life a true atheist, that I must establish the admirable qualities of this latter that are his due, not only an exceptionally rich nature, but even more these "ancestral errors" that enliven many souls and upon which mine has nourished itself.[29] I, too, my dear Félix, I, like the apple tree,[30] produce and give my humble fruits, but I do not confuse myself with the warmth of the sun, which brings them to maturity, and I only desire one thing, that I become more enlightened so that this fruit

219

becomes more abundant, more substantial as well for some enflamed or exhausted hearts.

I admired, in all sincerity, what your book contained in subtlety and great intelligence, what it demonstrates, and what it permits one to imagine knowing. Meanwhile, I can surely say, since above all, we value frankness, that it created in me a real sense of sadness. Certainly, it will not harm true believers and only push those who are already three-quarters atheistic to atheism. It is not them, except perhaps for a few very simple minds (but they will not read your book), that got me thinking while reading your book, but you. Often, when I make my own examination of conscience, I wonder why I did something and I ask myself why I wrote this? I do not really accept your apple tree theory, which maybe leads us to a tree that produces bad fruit, under the guise of bad books that you, of course, do not consider, but that a neighboring tree easily produces something else. In spite of yourself, the notion of conscience, of duty, of moral responsibility exudes from all your pores, and I believe that you often think about the immediate and distant consequences of your actions. What good has destined you to attack the idea of God, speaking only from a scientific point of view? I thoroughly understand that you, an atheist, do take this idea into any account in your wise research and that you search uniquely for the truth without any religious preoccupation. But I will add, without any antireligious preoccupation, despite your detached tone. You want to study scientifically that which escapes the scientific domain and convince us of our absurdity through arguments that do not convince us, because we will be able to respond that whereas you argue in order to persuade us that we are unreasonable, we "live" from a higher life, entirely interior, so penetrated with faith that our moral being is transformed by it and that at the same time we are able to remain very humble, since we feel that this life has been given to us and that we do not believe this on our own. You will have beautifully explained to a poor child that its mother, whom it adores and from whom it receives its nourishment and care, does not have all the virtues he imagines, and it will say to you: "In that case, she is still my mother, I love her, and it is because of her that I live." This is what I say to you, my dear Félix, knowing very well that I am not capable of discussing these questions effectively with you, but knowing also the little of this faith I have just spoken about you do not possess.[31] Others than you (who are too modest) would be able to say that you are worth more than I because of your generosity and altruism: "Much more," I would say, "because without the faith that animates me, I would not be worth much." But if I humble myself in comparison with you, I can see the action of grace in me, thanks to God, having thus transformed an average nature and having given me for now this peace here below, and for much later, some hope that illumines life.

If I thus open my heart to you in such a totally friendly way, it is above all so that I can feel your confidence and affection again, then so that I judge you worthy of my frankness, and finally that I have put to the test my need to make known to you my most intimate and precious beliefs. This is not, I truly believe, because I have some pretension that you will fully understand this, still less share it. No human being can accomplish this work of persuasion. This belongs to God alone, and it is only to him that I will address myself, or even more, that I do so after obtaining for those whom I love this serenity and this faith that he most wants me to communicate.

And in conclusion, I simply but very lovingly embrace you with all my fraternal affection and ask that you pardon me for this small expression of "mysticism." You will not take my words in a poor or wrong sense;[32] I truly believe, moreover, that you are a bit of a mystic just as you are a bit Christian, just as you are especially one of the best hearts I have known.

Your older sister,
Elisabeth

LETTERS ON SUFFERING

Translator's Introduction

The relationship Elisabeth Leseur developed with Sister Marie Goby from 1910 to 1914 was one of the most important spiritual and human events in her life. Drawn together by a shared love for and care for the poor, each in her own way, and their deep relationship through prayer and Eucharist with God, the women experienced an intensely evolving spiritual friendship. Elisabeth describes in one of her letters how God sometimes directs people himself. She goes on to portray the formal relationship she experienced with her confessor and spiritual director—support during difficult times, moral guidance, assurance of being on the right path. In Père Hébert's introduction to these letters, he comments that Elisabeth came to confession every two weeks when she was healthy and in Paris. Even after she was diagnosed with breast cancer and became increasingly ill, Père Hébert never initiated pastoral visits unless he was sent for, he explains, out of deference to Félix Leseur, whom he did not want to alienate. Hébert recognized himself in Elisabeth's description of a formal and moderately helpful experience of spiritual direction within the context of confession. He notes that Elisabeth rarely wrote to him in between her personal visits, maybe three times over ten years.

The contrast with Sister Goby is remarkable. These women had only two face-to-face visits, a one-day visit in Beaune and a longer visit when Sister Marie was under doctor's care in Dijon. Yet they found in each other a real soul-friend. The letters that follow not only provide a more sustained glimpse into Elisabeth's theology of the communion of saints and its corollary, the value of suffering for accomplishing spiritual good, but they also give privileged access to an intense, epistolary friendship. In some of Elisabeth's letters to Sister Goby, she is reassuring her correspondent of the fully Christian quality of their mutual love and respect. Elisabeth includes Sister Goby among her beloveds. Her husband is just as impressed as Elisabeth was with Sister Goby.

Both women faced different kinds of personal suffering—Sister Goby's mother had a life-threatening illness and Sister Goby herself was threatened with the loss of her eyesight. Elisabeth was diagnosed with breast cancer in 1911. Both women experienced certain kinds of isolation. Sister Goby was away from her community, nursing her mother in a tiny village, while Elisabeth repeatedly mentioned her isolation from other religious-minded people. Both women discovered they were no longer alone on their respective spiritual journeys but were drawn to share more fully with each other than with anyone else in their lives the central reality of their lives—their spiritual journey and their love for God shaped by their respective vocations. They console each other, accompany each other, pray for each other, and offer each other spiritual counsel as each situation presents itself.

History has preserved less about Sister Marie Goby than about Elisabeth Leseur. The community has only minimal information about her in its archives. We do know that she was born in the village of Savigny in 1865, making her one year younger than Elisabeth. She boarded in Beaune at a school run by sisters and entered the Hospitallers of St. Martha of Beaune on March 19, 1888. She received the habit June 24, 1890, but for unspecified reasons did not make vows until June 27, 1895. She was much loved by her patients and the people in her village. She died rather suddenly on April 20, 1922, at fifty-six years of age. The community necrology describes extensive witness to her goodness and care from soldiers and patients she had nursed. The entire village as well as the medical and hospital staff attended her funeral. She was sufficiently admired in her nearby village that Savigny named a street after her.[1]

ELISABETH LESEUR

Selected Letters on Suffering: Part 1

Letter I

December 19, 1910

My very dear Sister,

How can I thank you for your long and welcome letter, received this morning?[2] You did a real act of charity in writing because in spite of the deep emotion I'm feeling because of the death of this dear one, your letter helped me achieve a deep sense of calm: realizing how happy the child is now, the remembrance of all that God has done for her, in great part because of you, dear sister, and of the confidence we have that this pure soul is now praying for us. Yes! May she obtain for me graces I so ardently seek, above all, conversion, the main purpose of my life; and may she ask God to give me the grace to be faithful to my spiritual calling, to this intimate work that God alone has done within me who am so unworthy of it.

Fortified by the prayers of dear little Marie, I hope you will join me in asking for all these things. How beautiful and how touching her death was, so filled with God's fatherly love! And how much good the gentle and holy remembrance of her has done for me and will continue to do. The little holy card has been carefully put away with your letter, both reminders of this touching episode in my life.

But, dear sister, I hope that the spiritual bonds created between us through this encounter will remain and that our souls will never be separated again.

I'm sending you the latest copy of a picture of me, taken at the time of my sister's death five years ago. And tomorrow I'll send you the little book I told you about.[3] This too will be a reminder for you to pray for me and for all those so dear to me.

Thank you again, dear sister, from the bottom of my heart. If you haven't already given it away, keep the little plaque from Notre Dame des Victoires. Again, my deepest thanks and fond good wishes.

E. Leseur

Letter VI

June 7, 1911

Our letters would have crossed in the mail if I hadn't had to interrupt mine yesterday, but our hearts were certainly in unison. Thank you, dear sister, for your long letter. You cannot believe how good you are for me, or how much I value your friendship. My husband and I are currently reading *The Little Flowers of St. Francis of Assisi*, and I was telling him this morning that my meeting little Marie was certainly a "flower" in my own life. It is so reassuring to have such experiences from time to time. Your affection is another example, so sincere and so helpful to me.

I prayed for you during this feast of Pentecost, and together with you, I will ask the Spirit to enlighten us and to enable me to put to good use this new life that I have received through his providence. How long will this life last? The years ahead will reveal God's will in this regard, because in spite of my fairly healthy condition, I have had and continue to have such dire illnesses that my entire physical well-being is greatly compromised. Well, let's not worry about that but rather live in the present moment, doing our work as well as we can while we wait for the good God to let me know what he wants from me: sickness or relative health, joy or suffering, a long life or an early arrival in heaven. Ah, yes, how good it would be to find ourselves in the hereafter we so dearly want to attain and to find there the One for whom we have lived and suffered. Wouldn't this be a wonderful way for our hearts to be united?

In the meantime, let me share with you another piece of good news. My husband can't leave until the end of July, and we're also constrained by my radiation therapy treatment. We're going to go to my brother in Yonne for a few days, and from there to Beaune, and at that time we'll come see you for a short visit. It will be sometime between the August 1 and 15....Will you be free to see us? The thought of this fills me with joy, and if it is possible, I will receive communion in your little chapel, which I remember so fondly. Then we will leave directly after that for our house in Jougne, where we'll spend our vacation.[4]

I must stop, since I still haven't regained full mobility in my arm.[5] Be assured, my dear sister, of my affectionate wishes and my deepest friendship. Pray always for my intentions, and let us remain united in the spirit of our Lord.

E. Leseur

Letter VIII

Jougne, Doubs
August 15, 1911

My very dear Sister,

This beautiful feast of the Assumption inspires me to send you my loving wishes. This morning we were, indeed, united in the Sacred Heart of our Lord. I was thinking of you at seven o'clock as you were about to receive him, recalling those warm moments I spent with him in your company just two days ago.[6] Then, in my own communion, I thought of you and knew you were praying for me too and for those I love.

How can I describe for you my thoughts about last Sunday, and the good that it did me and which now gives me the strength to go on. Getting to know you a little better, having the experience of your deep love, and spending a few hours in the warm, peaceful atmosphere of your dear hospital, this is for me a treasury of graces for which I thank God.

God gave me there one of those smiles rarely given to one somewhat advanced on the spiritual journey, where it is necessary to take a more difficult path. In this way he can enable one who is having difficulty ascending the barren road to feel the gentleness of his tender presence. Then one can begin anew, and if the beloved host remains there in the intimacy of the heart, providing strength and guidance, the fleeting joy may pass but the deep life-giving effect remains.

My dear sister, in the best sense of the word, isn't it true that in God we will love one another and find one another in him?

We have much cooler air here, so welcome after the intense heat, and I'm hoping it will be good for my niece. She was so touched to receive your message—as was her aunt. Do continue to keep up your good prayers for her, as well as those you've promised for my dear husband. How happy I would be if through your efforts and prayers he would be able to give himself to God.

I would be pleased to receive news from you when you can, even though I'm reluctant to take you away from your dear patients for even one hour. Tell me about poor Catherine, and about the mother of the three children, and be sure to let me know if I can do anything for them.[7]

Ask our Lord to make me more and more attuned to whatever he desires of me, and to continue to use me in his service.

My warmest embraces to you, dear sister, and my sincerest prayers.

E. Leseur

Best regards from my husband and a hug from my niece.

Letter IX

Jougne, Doubs
August 31, 1911

My very dear Sister and friend,

How can I thank you for your prayers and for those you had said for us at Ars? It would seem that my deepest intentions are in good hands, and that the holy Curé of Ars will obtain for me all the graces I so ardently desire,[8] especially the one for which I would so willingly give my life.[9]

Your letters are so good for me that you do a good deed by writing to me from time to time. The good God has tested me so much this year, in heart and spirit even more than in body, and in a way that affects me so very deeply. After all the outstanding graces he has given me, all the spiritual consolations, I can only thank him for treating me more as a friend of his heart by sending me the suffering that sanctifies and allows me to offer a very simple act of reparation. Don't ask him to relieve me of a single pain, but rather ask that I may use these sufferings for others, for the church, and for those so dear to me in this life and in the next.

My niece is leaving tomorrow, and we are going to miss her. On Saturday, my husband's nephew will be coming, and around September 10, André, Marie's brother, and perhaps also my brother's son. All these young people whom I love bring us such joy when they arrive, and then sadness when they leave; such partings are among the most painful of life's trials. I experienced that anew when I said goodbye to you at the door of your hospital. My mother and sister are presently in Wissant in Pas-de-Calais, and the news from them is good. My husband is resting and thoroughly enjoying the tranquility and fresh air; our weather is very pleasant and at the moment my health is as satisfactory as possible. Since that can change from one day to the next, I abandon myself to Providence and live only in the present.

I'm thinking that you probably haven't yet returned to the hospital;[10] for this reason I can't refer a friend to you who will be leaving us soon and will be passing through Beaune, perhaps Sunday or early next week. Would it be totally inappropriate to recommend that he see Sister Marion through a note I would give him?[11] Although he has no faith, my friend does have religious inclinations and has suffered deeply during the past three years: he lost both his mother and father; his young wife whom he deeply loved became insane and has been institutionalized; and he has had serious professional difficulties. He would like to see the entire hospital and, if he's at Beaune on Sunday, would also like to attend Vespers, the service that so moved my husband. I'm looking for anything that can help this friend in distress, which is why I'm writing this to you in confidence. If my request is indiscreet, just let me know. If not, I'll give the note to our friend.

I think of you as I read one of Father Faber's books; his sermons are so beautiful. Are you familiar with this book? If not, I'll send you a copy as soon as I get back to Paris. We received the book you sent us, and I'm very interested in it but am so busy I can only read it a little at a time.[12] My husband wants to read it too. Can I keep it until the end of the month?

Yes, you *must* call me your friend,[13] since the truth must always be told. Thoughtful wishes to your mother, whom I love without knowing her because she is your mother and because she too must be a beautiful person, having given her daughter to God. We've agreed that we will not come into the Franche-Comté again without visiting you. Our one visit with you created a warm and I believe good impression on my husband. For myself, it's impossible to tell you how much good it did for me; it was a gift, a ray of sunshine sent by Providence amid the little or great shadows of life, both interior and exterior.

How good God is, my friend. When I look over the years, the graces I've received, the way he has taken me and led me to himself, I can only say a deeply grateful "thank you." I earnestly feel now that I must go further and faster along the path leading to his heart, even if this path is strewn with hardships and at times somewhat obscure. This is a good darkness, nonetheless, since it allows God's penetrating light to reach me.

This year, then, I want to practice greater renunciation, develop a more complete spirit of sacrifice and reparation, be more charitable toward all, and pray more earnestly than in the past. That is a fine proposal, and it now needs to be put into practice. Pray for me that I may receive the necessary graces, above all the grace to desire, to love, and to do only the divine will, and to accomplish this *with joy*, because God loves such generosity of heart.

When you get back to Beaune, you must tell me very honestly what would bring happiness and well-being to your patients, poor Louise and Catherine,[14] so that I can assist you as much as possible in relieving their pain or being helpful to them. It's so little compared to what you are giving them yourself: the fullness of your heart and your entire life.

Renewed thanks for the remembrances from Ars. Once again I am placing my intentions in your heart. On behalf of my husband, my mother, my beloved nephews, my sister, never stop asking God to grant the intentions I've made known to you. And for me, say simply: "My God, I offer you my friend so that you may use her for the good of others, for your glory, so that we may meet again in eternity."

I embrace you warmly, my sister and friend, with the assurance of finding you often in the heart of him whom we both wish to love and serve, in differing degrees and in separate ways but with the same good intention. My husband sends you his good wishes; my niece thanks you and sends her love. Again, a loving remembrance from your friend.

E. Leseur

Letter X

September 2, 1911 [Jougne]

My dear Sister and friend,

...I was saddened to learn of poor Catherine's death and will pray for her with all my heart. I understand so well your sorrow in watching these poor people die, but what a consolation for you to be able to accompany them to the end of life's journey, leading them to the good God, who must have treasures of mercy for these little ones so dear to him. I'll send you Father Faber's book from Paris, because I really want you to have a religious keepsake from me to remind you of me during your meditations and prayers. I must tell you that you didn't make me entirely happy by adding "Madame" to the affectionate term of "friend," and that you would do well to delete it. You will do that, won't you?

I'm glad you were able to have a quiet moment at the sacred tomb in Ars. These are gifts from the good God, and we must enjoy them fully...just as we must also accept, as joyfully as our weakness permits, with God's grace, the trials and tribulations that so often follow consolations.

While you're on vacation,[15] I'd be very pleased if you would tell me more about yourself. I had to miss Mass yesterday because my niece was leaving at the same time and I had to drive her to the train station. However, thanks to the kindness of our young assistant, I did not miss communion and was able to talk to our Lord about all those I love, and about you, my dear friend, who now holds such a large place in my heart.

Yes, we will lead one another along the path marked out for us by divine Providence, you leading the way, doing more good, alas, than I can ever know or do. I say "alas" not because of any envy but rather the regret of having lived apart from God for so long, doing nothing for him. Then, ever since he drew me totally to himself with a goodness that fills me with gratitude and through measures that are both simple and generous, I regret that I haven't measured up to such graces and have been so unresponsive to them. At least now I am deeply committed to living only for God, to doing generously as much as I can in his service, and above all, to abandoning myself entirely to his will. I believe that, for a long time to come, what I am able to do will be fragmented and limited simply to carrying out the demands of my vocation and a few other works of charity. But what is possible and seems to be the will of God for me is to act through prayer and suffering. This vocation seems to be so stamped by the love of our God that I must be grateful and accept it with joy. Of course—since I don't want you to think I'm better than I really am—this acceptance is joyful only in my depths. On the surface there are many aversions, weaknesses, and miseries, which humiliate me. Nevertheless, in spite of all of this, I am moving slowly toward the harbor like a boat tossing every which way on the waves, buffeted or gliding quickly along with the Master of the waves on board; and led by a bright star, I can see (in the distance or near at hand, as God wills) the safe haven where I will be united with him whom we love, and where I will find once again the loved ones I have lost; and where, my very dear Sister, we will proclaim more fully than we can ever do in this world the immense mercies given us by God. How joyful that thought is! But after savoring it for a few moments, we must return to this world and continue to take up our daily responsibilities. But no matter, since on earth as in heaven we can find our Savior and can lean on his heart. You can see that I've allowed myself to get carried away, at the risk of taking up your precious time. But this is good for me, so you haven't been idly standing by. I know you will forgive me.

My niece has left, which saddens me. This evening she will be with her own dear mother as well as my mother. News from there is good. For myself, aside from a few insignificant little troubles, I'm doing well at the moment.

My husband has a deep and respectful regard for you, and I know that will be good for him. He sends his best wishes, and from me, my dear Sister and friend, my warmest embrace.

Your friend,
E. Leseur

Letter XII

September 17, 1911 [Jougne]
My dear Sister and friend,

We're going to be away for three days, and before leaving, I want to thank you for your welcome long letter, which I found truly touched my heart.[16] Along with my loving thanks, let me add too an equally loving remembrance. I was so deeply touched by your words of affection, and even more by the feeling you have of the intimate and total union of our hearts in the very heart of our beloved Master. I too bring you to him whenever he comes into my poor heart, although I am so unworthy of his visit. I feel in these instances that we are together at his feet. Thank you, thank you, for your faithful and fervent prayers for the many intentions so dear to me. Thanks too to your dear mother for her prayers each day for these same intentions. However, tell her not to pray that I will get better but rather that I may do God's will. This is my one desire, and I've asked our Lord to put the health and especially the holiness of those I love over my personal happiness and well-being. In this way, we won't put conflicting intentions before him or ask him both for what I want and what I don't want.

On this subject, dear friend, I wonder if you're not being somewhat ambitious and self-serving. You tell me "the dream of your religious life and the only thing you ask of Jesus" is to love and serve him alone, understanding that this means you will suffer and renounce yourself for him as you work in his service. Just think of the spiritual greed of one who abounds in care for the poor and the sick, while I, on the other hand, am poor and able to do so little in the name of charity. Yet by praying for my recovery, you are forcing God to remove the last resource of my impoverished zeal, namely, suffering accepted and offered up, often poorly, I know, but offered up nonetheless, for others and for God's providence in this life. But I'm not concerned because I know only too well that God will do what God wants, and in my case, I hope it will be only that which can promote God's glory, the well-being of others, and the fulfillment of my deepest intentions, which you already know about.

It's true, isn't it, that physical suffering is the least of all sufferings, and that sufferings of the heart and spirit are so much greater? And all of these are, or should be, the lot of those for whom God has done so much, and who have received so many great graces. So, my friend, in spite of my weakness, leave me my small share in the cross of Jesus, in order to pay my debt of gratitude, offering him a humble sacrifice of love and reparation in an effort to obtain *all* that he alone can give me. If God allows me to live, dear friend, I shall make even greater efforts to do his will in myself and in others. And if such is not his will and he is to shorten my journey, I leave to you, my friend nearest to his heart, the mission of telling my loved ones that I offered my trials and prayers for them, begging God for their souls *at all costs*. I thank you in advance, dear executrix of my will....Perhaps I will live to a hundred, which would be fine, provided that at one hundred I can praise God and work for him as I do at forty-four.

It seems as if this letter is all about me, while my thoughts are all about you. However, I know how much a friend likes to listen to another friend tell her story. I am not telling you my weaknesses: the despondency brought on by my poor health, to which I completely give in at times; my tremendous desire for solitude and silence, which may harbor some selfishness and cowardice along with the higher motives; the frequent disdain for pettiness, mediocrity, and the "encumbrances" of life that make me want to live far away from the world and worldly affairs, in a little place with a few loved ones, in the presence of the Blessed Sacrament. Will that ever be? That depends on the hundred years...or on the *x* number of years, months, or days that I have left.

Yes, take advantage of this pleasant vacation, a time of real rest, fueled by the warm maternal tenderness that surrounds you. Not to do so would seem like a lack of gratitude and appreciation for God's gifts. And then, still smiling, come back to your dear patients, giving them more of yourself and being able to share with them all the light and happiness of our Savior; comforting broken bodies, healing wounded spirits, and embracing, with the gentleness of Jesus who comes to you each day, the hostile or weak, in order to bring all of them to him. Pray, suffer, and act for those unable to do so, for those who suffer without supernatural consolations, for those who cannot pray or who no longer do so. Ask our dear Friend and Master to give me the grace to follow in your footsteps at a distance and not to be a useless servant.

...I've been feeling a little "heavy" and tired the last few days, the usual complaints, which always come back like birds to their nests: reminders of illnesses and surgeries, invitations to sacrifice, and, if I knew better how to take advantage of them, opportunities for rewards and very personal offerings. Please pray that I don't squander these precious graces.

My best wishes for your dear mother, my husband's greetings for her and for you, and the affection of your friend.

E. Leseur

Letter XIV

October 15, 1911

My dear Sister and friend,

My letter of the other day was necessarily brief and undoubtedly somewhat "vague" since I wasn't yet feeling too well.[17] I'm a little better now, although I can't say I'm really recovered, since some rather painful ailments remind me that I can't stray too far from the cross. At the same time, and lasting to some degree even now, I became depressed as a result of these various illnesses, creating an ordeal with which I am familiar, but which I find also somewhat humiliating. By right, this is a good situation. Although God is offering me intimate and subtle sufferings of the heart, with few of the spiritual consolations he had so generously given to me in the past, I tell myself at the same time that he wants to treat me as a friend of his heart, allowing me in a very small way to identify with his sufferings and make reparation close to him, and that this ordeal is in response to the graces I asked him to give to others, as well as to my personal surrender to him for these intentions. Moreover, in spite of the deprivations, sufferings, and sadness, a profound joy exists in my depths, and I express great thanks to God, forcing myself to do so with a smile.

These are very intimate matters that I share with you, my sister and friend; there is not another person with whom I would share them. God has placed you in my path, perhaps because he saw that in spite of his loving caresses, I still remained in spiritual isolation, and he wanted to give me the sweet consolation of a completely spiritual friendship. May God be blessed for that! You have no idea how good you are for me. We don't even need words to express this union, because it is totally spiritual, so don't be concerned if there are long periods of time when you are unable to write to me. Nothing would make me want to take you away from your patients, and no matter how happy I am to receive your letters, they are not necessary to assure me that we are closely united in spirit. We are as one in the heart of Jesus and near the tabernacle, especially at the moment of communion. From time to time during the day, I let myself be carried in spirit to your chapel to offer there my adoration and prayers to our Lord. And I follow you in spirit too as you move among your patients, watching with envy the good you do. But since God's will is what really matters, I tell myself that my depressing illnesses with the privations they entail and the monotony they represent are also a form of action that God will use for others and for his glory. What joy this thought brings, doesn't it?

Dear friend, I've worn your little relic and will do so again before returning it to you in my next letter.[18] However, while I do respect and believe in this religious object and the intercession of this holy person, I believe her protection will assume another and even more useful form for me, for God's will for me seems very clear, namely, a life of suffering to which God called me a long time ago. Hopefully I will respond better now than I have in the past, becoming less unworthy of this significant grace. It is a great thing to be treated in some small way like his servants and friends and to follow him along the way of the cross. With your love, I'm sure you will understand and that you will pray for me and for my dear ones.

I ask you to pray especially for my dear mother, who is in such need of spiritual strength.[19] Also for a friend, who does not know God but who is experiencing great interior turmoil. And, as always, I ask you to remember my husband.

I think this winter will be a quiet one for me. I've started my morning visits to the neighboring chapel again, several times a week; also my comings and goings to visit my mother, who has difficulty getting around and who needs to take care of her bronchitis. At the moment I've started a new series of five radiation treatments, one each week. I'll see my surgeon in November. As you can see, I'm taking good care of myself, and, like you, consider it a serious obligation to do so.

My nephews have resumed their studies, and they are well, thank God. Their mothers are extremely busy and carry out their work with devotion, while I do the same in my own household, outwardly very unassuming and ordinary work, limited and uninspiring, but God will take care of that. Whereas you, dear little sister, are the Good Samaritan of bodies and souls. Isn't it true that each has her place and all are in the heart of Jesus, and that's all that is really necessary?

How is your dear mother? Remember me to her and to your superior as well. Heartfelt thoughts to the Marion sisters. A warm embrace, dear friend and sister, with much love. Don't forget me when you are near the One we both love. A kiss from

Your friend

E. Leseur

My husband sends his best wishes.

Did you receive Father Faber's book? And your book about the Hôtel-Dieu that I sent back to you from Jougne?

Letter XVI

November 7, 1911

Would you believe, dear little sister, that yesterday morning I was so anxious to receive a letter from you I would have been terribly upset if one hadn't arrived? But the good God spared me that minor disappointment and instead inspired you to write one of those heartfelt messages that always bring me encouragement and joy, and that sustain me for a long time…until the next one arrives.

That said, however, I really don't want you to write me as often or as much if that tires your eyes.[20]…It seems as if Jesus, in a very small way, is treating those he loves in the same way he treated his beloved mother, whose every joy was accompanied by an extreme sadness. Your letter was a source of great happiness for me and at the same time caused me deep pain. As I thought of the danger you are facing, I experienced something I had never felt before in dealing with my own suffering. I knelt and earnestly begged our Lord to remove that trial from you—and from me. Oh, dear friend, may the Lord continue to give you light from outside while at the same time he increases his light in you. My prayers will be more urgent, my poor offerings more frequent and more loving, so that the one I love as a soul-friend may not have to drink from the chalice of suffering, but that she may be filled with great graces and savor the most consoling spiritual joys.

Be careful that the comings and goings between Beaune and Dijon don't wear you out. If your treatment isn't successful and they want to send you to Paris for another consultation, you know we will welcome you to our home with open hearts. In the meantime, I'll make a short pilgrimage to the Basilica of Sacré Coeur as soon as I can and will have Mass said for you there as well as one here at our church. Beloved sister, may God answer our prayers and allow you to continue to care for your sick, an act of charity you can fulfill, continuing to serve the poor of Christ, and leaving the vocation of "patient" to your friend.

How beautifully you speak of our beloved heavenly home. There are times I yearn for it; then I tell myself that I must be completely flexible in the hands of divine providence, fully surrendered to the good God, knowing that whatever he sends me is good: joys or sufferings, sickness or health, life or death. We know that that blessed hour will come when we will enter into our Father's house, and that in the Heart of Jesus we will find rest from our labors; where we will know complete joy in being with our loved ones and with the saints of all ages, where we will love, enjoy, and know one another forever. In contemplating this great vision, all the trials of life seem so small, and the shadows of this world are dissipated by the radiant light of heaven!

Aside from the usual problems, my health is good at present. As for my soul, don't think that God has given me any great consolations. I used to experience those at the beginning of my spiritual life, when he wanted to take me completely to himself, and I have pleasant and grateful memories of that time. But it was fitting and right that that should pass and the good God, after giving me the "milk of children," wanted me to drink the wine of the strong, and for many months my soul, like yours, has been "a dry and waterless land." But recently, undoubtedly because of your prayers, I have been strengthened and better able to understand how profoundly good the time of trial and aridity has been for me. Now God is working within me through intense interior sufferings, unknown to those dear to me. May God be praised in everything, and for those who inadvertently are causing them, may these sufferings be transformed into spiritual graces—the fruits of conversion and holiness.

Yes, following your example, dear one, I want to be indifferent to consolations or frequent dry spells, or sorrows too, or exterior joys, so that I can look for only one thing: the will of the One whom alone and always we seek to love. There is one sentence in your letter that pierced my heart like an arrow coming from your own heart, in which you wrote: "The important thing is to follow Jesus and to love him, much more for what he is than what he gives." I'll ponder in my heart this spiritual bouquet you sent me.

I'll be united in spirit with you from November 15 to 21.[21] I dream of making a real retreat someday, although I don't know if Providence will allow it. I have to practice self-denial even in spiritual matters. But my beloved sister, if those who feel sorry for me because of all the physical sufferings I've had to put up with were to know how comparatively insignificant those sufferings are to me, they would probably be very surprised. What I really find hardest is to live in the midst of hostility or religious indifference. For me, it is like inhaling a moral atmosphere in which my soul cannot flourish, or feeling spiritually isolated in spite of the signs of affection, which I truly appreciate, or being unable to obtain any enlightenment and life of the spirit for those I love. These are the deep and unknown sufferings that God is asking of me, hopefully for the benefit of those dear to me, for others, and for the church. Sometimes I tell myself that I will never experience in this life the joy of being one in spirit with those around me, and that this will only occur in the next life when the good God will have accepted my total surrender. As in all things, may his will be done. I firmly believe and eternally hope my prayers will be answered, namely, that before she dies my poor mother will experience the consolations and reassurances of the spiritual life of faith, that my dear husband, so good and so loving, will be converted and made holy, and that my nephews will become Christians with apostolic hearts. You will help me obtain all that, won't you, dear friend?

During the celebration of All Saints and All Souls, I prayed for your dear departed ones, particularly your father. Spiritually, I love the month of November, when the church seems to exercise a maternal concern for her suffering children, and when the communion of saints seems more alive. In addition to my prayers for the church, for souls, for my loved ones, and for those who have asked to be remembered, I especially like to pray for the souls in purgatory, the dying, and also for priests, that their number and holiness may grow.

I'm going to send you a dress for Louise's little daughter, as well as a toy, since the little ones do need some fun.[22] Please give them to her, and let her sick mother know I'm thinking of her, and that we are all sisters in suffering and in the Heart of Christ, and that in him I love her very much and pray for her. The sufferings she offers up for her dear little ones will do them more good than anything else she could do for them as a mother.

Let me know when you begin your treatment and how effective it is. But just a short note, nothing long. You can't imagine how much I think of you and love you, and how much I thank God for allowing our paths to cross. He has offered me this pleasure along a road that is somewhat difficult and weary.

I often recite the prayer of Blessed Margaret Mary that you sent me.[23] It says everything, and I consider it another bond between us. My handwriting is really poor, since my hand is still swollen, making my writing almost illegible. In spite of this, dear friend and sister, I'm sure you'll be able to decipher all the loving feelings I've put in my letter, my loving thoughts, and my fond hopes for you. With a fond embrace and the assurance of my love in God who is so good.

Your friend,
E. Leseur

Letter XIX

December 1, 1911

My dear little Sister,

Having just returned from Sacré Coeur, where I talked to our Lord about you during my communion, I want to send you a loving message while I'm still feeling overwhelmed by the enjoyment of this holy encounter. I asked to have Mass said for you, and I have entrusted our Lord with the task of restoring your eyesight, your good health, and giving you many good graces. More than ever, we both must draw near to his Heart, finding there great strength and peace, a share in that overflowing love that his Heart pours out on all. In him alone we must find our strength and consolation, because only he truly understands us and knows our needs. Let us learn, dear sister, to be content with whatever he sends us: joy or sorrow, sickness, consolation or spiritual dryness, to accept with pleasure even the most trivial things, and—for myself—those social events and exterior responsibilities so burdensome to one who wants only to be closer to God. Deep within me I have such an intense longing to withdraw, to find that silent, hidden life that the world and many Christians don't understand. This is why I've offered totally to God this "external" life, which I accept and carry out with as much good grace as my poor health permits. It calls for constant renunciation and sacrifice on my part. And since this is offered in the secret of my heart, I trust these gifts will be blessed and will benefit others. My friend, you are the only one who understands this spiritual "exchange," and I know you will pray that for me this will be fruitful and a means of becoming holy.

I'm pleased to learn that your treatment isn't painful; I was so concerned that it would be. However, as long as the doctor doesn't want you to do any writing, you mustn't send me any more letters. Your health and a successful cure are more important to me than my own pleasure. Besides, even though your letters bring me so much—and they do give me great reassurance and consolation—I don't need them to convince me of our deep spiritual bond. We meet in prayer before the tabernacle, in our communions, at the hours of prayer and recollection, and we find ourselves especially united in the heart of Jesus.

If your present treatment is insufficient and you need to come to Paris, if it's all right with you, I could ask the Helpers of the Holy Souls if you could stay with them. They are my neighbors, and I often visit their chapel. We could easily see each other there. If that is the case, let me know if you would like these arrangements.[24] I would love to have you here, and yet I hope this trip won't be necessary, since that would mean you're getting better. We'll be at Beaune this summer, and I'll plan to spend at least two days with you, so we'll be able to talk at length. I think I'll be able to speak more freely than I did the first time.

All here are fine. My husband is well, although he's extremely busy. I'm not bad myself, really as good as can be expected. However—and this is between us—little by little the presence of my interior enemies is gradually affecting my state of health and I sense that the coming years will be decisive ones for me. This will be according to God's will, and I will welcome all that comes from him. I ask him only to grant my deepest wishes, hear my prayers, claim for himself the souls I offer to him, and to do with me *everything* he desires. Help me to obtain this, my beloved sister.

Your love for me has become the joy of my life. Until now, I've experienced little spiritual consolation from the love that has been shown me. The people I've encountered in my life all seem to have been in need of whatever I could give them. And now in this interior desert nourished only by the waters of divine life (and they are truly sufficient), I've been given a beautiful small drop of water, so clear and refreshing, and so good for me. I can't help thinking that this is a gesture of attentiveness, a loving touch from God who wanted to give a bit of human kindness, love, and spiritual support to one whom he alone has been guiding. Having given him a tremendous thank you, I send one now, a smaller one, to you, whom he has chosen as his beloved instrument for me.

I'll end now, my friend, so as not to tire you. Besides, I don't want to leave my mother alone for too long a time since I'm writing from her home. She sends her love, and my husband wishes to be remembered to you as well. Give our respectful good wishes to your superior, and ask her and the Marion sisters for their prayers. My loving embraces to you, my dear little sister.

Your friend,
E. Leseur

Letter XX

December 15, 1911

My dear little Sister,

Although I'm a little hesitant to write to you because of your eyesight, I don't want to let this anniversary of dear little Marie's first communion and also her departure for heaven pass without sending you an affectionate message. I have faithfully prayed for her, although I have every confidence she is happy, and the thought of her brightens my life. She was, in a totally innocent and charming way, the intermediary between the two of us, becoming the unknowing means chosen by Divine Providence to give me the great joy of your unique and deeply Christian love and the comfort of your God-filled heart. There is no reason for me to believe you will ever abandon me, since my soul has been put into your hands from on high. Our friendship, a gift of our common Master, is being perfected by him and will flourish in heaven. Don't you find that if we didn't have such an intimate union with our Lord, if we had no Eucharist, which is truly the bread of strength and joy, we would at times feel nostalgic for heaven? The times when we despise the world and its "pleasures," when we feel completely isolated in spiritual matters and our closest relationships are not spiritually grounded, when life, outwardly filled with deep affection and the comfort of material things, is really filled with self-denial and a self-imposed silence about the very things one longs for, it is then we turn our gaze more and more to our heavenly homeland. And yet none of these is the greatest reasons or the most important; what matters above all is God's love, the tremendous desire to see him, to love him totally, to be one with his loving heart, with that thirst for him which enables even our poor hearts to understand and cry out with Saint Teresa, "O Jesus, isn't it time for you to see us?"

I have spoken to you about God, dear sister, and neglected to talk about you. However, I do not believe you will hold that against me. I want so much to hear about you, and to find out how the treatments are going, since they must be almost over by now. If Sister Germaine Marion could let me know through just a short note, I would be so grateful, since you must not write to me yourself. Being deprived of your letters is an offering that I can place at the crib of the Divine Child. We will meet there during these days, both of us asking for the humility, docility, deep peace, and purity of heart, all that Jesus in the crib teaches us. We will bring to Jesus, at the same time so great and so little, all our weaknesses, our difficulties, our feelings, as well as our love and good will. What a great joy, my friend, to remember that on this holy night the angelic messenger sent by God promised the rewards of peace not only to the saints but to all people of *"good will."* We're not saints, by any means, but our Christmas gift to our all-loving Friend will be our total, joyous good will.

My health has been fairly good for some time, and I have only to put up with those chronic ailments that will be with me until my dying day. They are, after all, excellent companions, since as God's helpers they've brought me many good things, and I consider them my friends.

All my dear ones are quite well at present. My husband is very busy and sends you his best regards. My niece often speaks lovingly of you, which pleases me. How is your dear mother? Please assure her of my best wishes and loving thoughts, and tell her one of the reasons I love her is because I love her daughter so much.

In the next few days I'll send you a money order for twenty francs. This will be my New Year's gift for your poor or your work, to use as you see fit. My best regards to your superior and the Marion sisters. And as for me, I embrace you, my beloved little sister, and send you the renewal of my love in the Lord.

Your friend.

E. Leseur

Please pray to the Infant Jesus for all my intentions, and I will do the same for you.

Letter XXI

December 28, 1911

My dear little Sister,

I'm taking advantage of some free time to tell you what a wonderful Christmas night I had. My husband was thoughtful enough to come with me to Midnight Mass—perhaps it was your good angel and mine that inspired him to do so. Instead of going to the parish church, which would have been too tiring for me, we went to a suite of rooms that was actually in the building where I went to school. One of the rooms has been converted into a chapel. A Jesuit celebrated the three Masses, and it was all very intimate and contemplative. It's not hard to guess what my prayers were: first, for the church; then for those I love and wish to love even more, and for all God's concerns; then for all those dear to me, for my "new little sister," which is how my heart knows you; for all the poor people I encounter in my life's journey who know nothing of God or who are in need. I asked the loving infant Savior to take my beloved husband totally into his love and his service. That hour of deep prayer on Christmas night was, and I hope will be, good for me.

Dear sister, on that holy night the Child was born again in our hearts. Let us assist in his mystical development within us through our prayers and sacrifices and work. May his growth within us achieve the fullest measure of human perfection so that he can remain with us forever. May he share the divine life with us, enabling us, poor and weak as we are, to become messengers of his love in his church and for others. Then during these forty hours let us remain close to the crib, the source of all beauty, joy, and holiness. Let our hearts be molded and transformed by the pure hands of the divine Child. Then we shall return with joy to those near us, replenished with serenity and love, and able to share our spiritual gifts. Let us try to joyfully put into practice the great lessons of the crib: humility, purity of heart, gentleness, mortification, and spiritual poverty. Let us love Jesus, so good and so giving, and let us express our love for each other in him, and we will do so forever, since passing things are no longer of interest to us, but rather only those that will last into eternity.

I'm so happy to know that you have less pain in your eyes and that your vision is improving. May our Lord grant me your cure as a Christmas gift. Perhaps because of your good prayers, I feel I've been "spoiled" these past few days both physically and spiritually. This won't last, nor should it, for then I would have nothing to offer to God. This little respite, however, enables me to gain my spiritual breath, giving a new impetus to prepare me for future sacrifices. In truth, dear sister, when our divine Master draws aside the veil that separates us from him, coming closer to us, don't we have a real glimpse of eternity, however slight, alas, and fleeting? It's like a whiff of heavenly perfume bringing love and desire into our heavy hearts, so often deprived of air. Won't it be lovely someday to inhale freely the air of heaven, allowing us to expand forever and finally to live only for God and for others?

As you can see, my "spiritual whiff" has taken me far afield. Tomorrow I'll probably be weak again, under the weight of my usual problems. Nevertheless, with the help of God's grace, I will try to remain joyful and will serve God in suffering more than in consolation. I've resolved to no longer be disgruntled with him, to be joyous as I offer my humble gifts to him, and for him and for others, increasingly to conceal my physical and mental problems under a veil of smiles and graciousness. This, my dear sister, is what I intend to do, but how many lapses there will be before achieving the success that only God can bring.

Pray for me, for *us*. You are with me as I approach the tabernacle and the Heart of Jesus. It's good for me to think about you, since that helps me to be one with God. You know how dear you are to me, since you love me in a similar way. How can we express our gratitude for this Christian love if not by greater dedication to the One who has created this gift for us, and to the poor souls who are not able to love since they have little or no Christian charity.

Dearest sister, I embrace you warmly, and entrust my guardian angel with my loving thoughts and good wishes for you. Have a happy, holy new year. Healing and good health to you, and for your interior life, charity and a blessed ministry. Pray that I won't be a useless worker and that my sufferings may be beneficial.

Your friend and sister,
E. Leseur
My husband sends his greetings and good wishes.

Part 2

Letter XXII

January 12, 1912

It's been so long since I've chatted with you, and I've decided this...cannot continue. True, we're never really separated, since we live and work for the same beloved Master and are one with him in front of the tabernacle or at other times of prayer. And yet I experience such a deep calm, truly a consolation, when I'm able to open my heart to you, fully one with you in spirit. Although we're not near one another, it is so good to know I'm united with a true spiritual sister who prays for me, and that in God there is no distance, since all hearts meet together in the heart of Jesus.

Has the year begun well for you? Is your eyesight good, and does the treatment continue to be effective? I pray for that each day, asking God also to shower you with abundant blessings. May God make you holy, dear sister, becoming ever more your companion, your living light, and a guide that you may always hear and follow. Let us go wherever he leads us: in darkness or light, to the splendor of Tabor or the foot of the cross. It makes no difference as long as he is with us, and we will always be able to hear him when he speaks to us. There is great peace in this sort of total abandonment, and in the gradual detachment from all consolation and self-seeking that little by little God allows to take place. I'm far from that point, but God is working in his poor little servant and will lead her there, since she surrenders all to him.

How reassuring it is to feel surrounded and wrapped in divine love, realizing that our all-loving father is bringing us to the eternal shores, letting us occasionally breathe in from afar their life-giving scents. And then, if the path becomes more difficult and our guide less visible, we surrender ourselves blindly to his gentle direction, waiting in self-forgetfulness until God's presence can be felt once more. Earth is not heaven, after all, and were we always surrounded by spiritual consolations, we might find it difficult to understand the difference. We have been given the grace we need to help us reach the joys of our much desired heaven.

...For the moment, all are well here. I hope you can say the same for your good mother. Be sure to give her my best wishes and respectful remembrances. For the past two months our weather has been downcast and rainy, making Paris less than a desirable place to be.

Whenever I wish to make a spiritual visit to the Blessed Sacrament, I frequently allow myself to be transported in mind to your little chapel, placing my heart before our Savior. In this way we must meet frequently in God's presence. In the course of each day I often repeat Blessed Margaret Mary's prayer reaffirming our total gift to God. Generally speaking, I prefer the beautiful liturgical prayers most of all, since they unite us with the entire life of the church. The Christmas season is particularly conducive to this.

Please pray for four of our friends whom God has called to heaven recently, and also for a sick young man for whom I've been asked to pray. Remember also a few special people whom I've encountered who are in great need of our prayers and sacrifices. How is poor Louise? Has she really left the hospital, and, if so, does this mean she's better or worse?[25]

...This morning, as always, I remembered you in my communion prayers. My warm embraces, my dearest sister. My husband too sends you his best wishes. I end with an *A Dieu*, as you say with such feeling, and also with an *au revoir*—until we meet again in the heart of Jesus.

Your friend,

E. Leseur

Letter XXIII

January 24, 1912

My dear little Sister,

There is some good in everything God gives us, even the mild flu I have, which happily allows me to write you today. I hope you haven't caught it and also that your eyesight is as good as it can be. Let us agree that if I don't hear from you, that means all is well. But if there is anything wrong, no matter what, you will tell me or ask one of the sisters to be kind enough to let me know. My little sister, I so need to know that you're feeling well. I am at peace and always united with you in spirit, and even when I don't actually hear from you, I know the Sacred Heart is transmitting your profound messages to me. In spite of the distance between us, and the duties that demand our attention, we are never separated, and we find each other in the blessed meeting places provided for Jesus' disciples: communion, prayer, meditation, as well as visits to the Blessed Sacrament, where we can take a deep breath and renew our courage and serenity.

At times I might even envy the good you do in your life of prayer and charitable deeds, if I did not know that the all-important thing is to do God's will no matter how monotonous or distasteful things may seem. At times I really yearn for greater solitude and recollection as well as being able to work for God. And certainly God knew what he was doing when he gave me a life filled with multiple responsibilities, where I have to stretch myself well beyond the limits of my own inner capabilities, and where at the same time I must conceal the deepest desires and needs of my heart. My whole spiritual life has been spent alone with God, supported for some years by the priest that Providence sent me at a precise moment of need. When I reflect on my past, I see clearly God's will, how God has so perfectly planned and accomplished things for me, and I am so filled with joy and gratitude that the rest of my life should be a song of thanksgiving. It is truly cause for astonishment and joy when I think of where I was when God took hold of me, and the point to which he has brought me, with the only merit on my part being that I followed his loving voice. Can one even call it merit when the voice is so loving? Dearest sister, help me to express my gratitude and to respond to so many graces. Were it not for our Savior's goodness, I could be overwhelmed by the responsibility imposed by such a blessed calling. In the future I hope to answer the divine call better than in the past, by giving myself humbly and joyously to all that God asks of me, including this worldly involvement that I find so difficult and that weighs so heavily on me, if that can serve God's glory and contribute to the well-being of others.

You will pray for me, won't you? Let us be completely united as we offer together our prayers, sufferings, and acts of self-denial, knowing that we will follow different paths as we carry out our daily lives. You have been especially chosen by God to dedicate yourself completely to the poor and the suffering who come into your life, whereas I must take on the ways of the world in order to reach those around me, a duty I find most oppressive. It is important that I remain peaceful and calm in dealing with those around me who hear me but who do not understand the language of Christians. As Paul had to preach an unknown God before he could make the known God loved, I must slowly and gradually reveal the divine light to those blinded by the false light of the world. And, dear friend, carrying out this task doesn't allow for any egoism or pride, but rather much renunciation and self-forgetfulness, and more reliance on the power of grace.

But even in our daily lives, isn't it true that our paths are basically not so divergent? We have the same Friend on our journey, are led by the same light, and pursue the same goal. At the end, we will be together in love and happiness, adoring the One that we both are striving to love and serve here on earth.

I'm reading Madame de Flavigny's life of Saint Bridget of Sweden. What obstacles she encountered in her life without ever seeing any positive results from her prayers and deeds! I've also read the life of Saint Catherine of Siena by the same author. After Saint Teresa, Catherine is my favorite saint. It is so easy to see how she was able to convert so many through her charm and meekness! Isn't it wonderful to think how much the Holy Spirit accomplished in her and through her? That depth of humility can be most disconcerting to human eyes. No matter how insignificant we think we are, we still desire to reach the heights where Truth, Goodness, Love, Beauty gently attract those who don't feel "at home" in this world. Dear sister, may we allow ourselves to be led wherever God wants. Let us think of ourselves as small, insignificant stones that God has placed where he wished in his grand building plan. It is only in this way that we will be able to do his work and carry out his will. God, who acts only out of love, will use us as he wishes.

How I have gone on in speaking with you, although I don't think I'm mistaken. Clearly, God has sent you to me to give me comfort and joy on my lonely journey. Wouldn't it be wrong not to recognize or take advantage of the support that God gives me through you? For this, let me not be ungrateful.

Maman, except for her woes, is feeling well this winter, and our young people are doing well too, as is my husband, who keeps busy and stays in good health. So, from a human perspective there is much to be grateful for. Spiritually, however, there are so many things they all need, and this is what I'm giving you as a mission of charity.

Aside from the flu and other normal ailments, I'm doing quite well. I hope never again to be dragged down by my illnesses but rather to endure them with a joyful heart, in union with the cross of our dear Savior.

Have a peaceful Christmastide. Let us be united often in the presence of the divine Child, who will teach us gentleness and humility. I leave at the crib my loving greetings and thoughts for you. Our friendship has come from God and will last forever. I place all our intentions in God's loving heart, asking that they may be granted and we ourselves blessed.

My husband asks to be remembered to you. A warm and loving embrace for you, my Sister and friend.

Your friend,

E. Leseur

Letter XXIV

February 1912

My dear Sister and friend,

...Your last letter came when I was experiencing great spiritual dryness, a condition which continues. You've experienced similar difficulties, and you know how little we can offer the One who alone gives strength and joy. Everything seems bleak, without any consolation, and we are humbled by the realization of our helplessness when we are deprived of light. As a peaceful thought in this time of emptiness, perhaps we can offer a little more to God in the struggle and boredom than we formerly gave with a joyful heart. Since he himself chose the worst forms of distress and interior abandonment, isn't it appropriate that we should unite ourselves to his anguish and his cross and accept with a willing if not joyful heart the spiritual trials through which he leads us to greater love and self-sacrifice. The point of all this is to tell you that since God treats us both more or less the same, I feel more than ever your beloved and loving sister.

I am convinced, my friend, that in some people God takes over completely. True spiritual direction is a precious but rare thing. One can be comforted and strengthened by the guidance of a holy priest and yet never achieve that fullness of direction God sometimes reserves to himself. We have depths reserved to God who alone fully knows our hidden weaknesses, our secret desires and needs. In simplicity and docility we should simply ask our spiritual guide for more insights into our weaknesses, some general direction for our spiritual life, comfort when we are suffering or depressed. However, it's only in the heart of Jesus that we will find the ultimate support, profound strength, and complete understanding of what we need in order to grow closer to him. One thing is sure, namely, the Divine will always wants what is good for us, whether in giving, refusing, or measuring out for us whatever we truly need. We are so fragile that we need to be guided and sustained either by those sent to us by God or by God himself when his representatives are lacking or have not yet come our way.

You tell me you are becoming more and more aware of "your powerlessness, your poverty, and your ignorance." Dear sister, this proves that in contrast to what is occurring with your human vision, your spiritual vision is becoming sharper and stronger. Do we not make another observation when we examine ourselves seriously, in good faith? The saints themselves—and we are not saints—cried out in distress and humility when they measured their misery against God's greatness and beauty. How great and how infinite is the abyss between the Creator and the creature, God's limitless strength and our weakness, God's being and our insignificant selves. So, dear sister, how peaceful and even joyous it can be for us to examine ourselves with such humility. Yes, let's rejoice in being *nothing* since for us God is *everything*. Let's be happy in being truly poor, begging for the help of the one who is rich, and let us take pleasure in being ignorant, since divine wisdom knows us and provides for our needs. Let us be glad at the very thought of our powerlessness. It is because of this that we can ask our Lord to take on the entire task, using our sufferings, our poor work, and our miserable prayers. It is only in heaven that we will realize how wonderfully God made use of the labor of these little workers: the multitude of small duties, the daily acts of self-sacrifice, the acceptance of pain, offered to the heavenly father, poor worthless metal transformed by God into gold for others, that pure gold of love enriching others and ourselves.

See how I preach to you, my friend, when I'm really talking to myself? I must also face life more courageously, and I make many humbling observations. In spite of my weaknesses and failings, I'm not discouraged. I tell myself that since God has chosen me and claimed me for his own, he will not abandon me. Trials, times of darkness, and even times when he seems not to be there, all are different ways that he is dealing with me. Wouldn't it also be the same for you, even more so since you are closer to his heart through your consecration to him, and because he wants to mold you, as Saint Catherine of Siena has said, into a more precious jewel?

I'm feeling better on the whole, in spite of some fatigue and other ailments. I've been going to see Maman, who is crippled with arthritis in her back, and I'd like to see the end of that. I was saddened this week by the downfall of the parents of a friend of mine. She is a good and holy woman, totally dedicated to charity, and now perhaps her whole way of life will be changed by this situation. How strange the will of Providence, which always seems to join suffering with even the holiest of good works. Nothing great or lasting is accomplished without the cross.

...I'm so happy to hear that the doctor is pleased with your eyes. Take good care of them. Already, you're able to do a little more, and soon I hope you'll be able to participate in the Office. Speaking of this, please remember a poor friend who died last night who wasn't much of a Christian. God, however, can show great mercy at these final moments.

I hope I haven't taken up too much of your time. I find it so helpful to be able to talk with you. You'll receive with this letter my loving thoughts, just a token of what is always in my heart for you and which I use to talk to God about my beloved sister. I embrace you with a profound and Christian love.

Your friend,
E. Leseur

My husband sends you his best wishes. Please remember us to your superior and the Marion sisters.

Letter XXVIII

April 20, 1912

My dear Sister and friend,

How kind of you to send me that lovely remembrance of Juliette's anniversary![26] It was so comforting to me to realize that our three souls have met close to God, in his heart, and that my sister has blessed the adopted sister that Providence has given me.

How good it is to love and to know that these important loving relationships come from God and will return to him, and that after having grown through sorrow, they will end in joy and in the most radiant union! When you look beyond yourself, beyond all the sorrows and the heavy burdens of life, you feel comforted, happy, ready for any sacrifice. These are the shining lights, the interior illumination through which the good God gives back the little courage that we need so much in our great weakness. Don't you think so, sister?

But afterward we come back down to earth; the divine face turns away slightly from us and then we feel the full weight of the burden, all the weariness, our great misery, and our worthlessness.

It's this last phase that I have recently gone through, because for several weeks God has seen fit not to treat me too gently physically and morally. After having been treated by God like a spoiled child, it's only fair that I be led along a rougher road, and for almost two years that's the way it has been. My dear sister, how well I understand now what the ascetic authors say about this straight and painful path that must be walked in order to reach the First Light. I'm catching quite a glimpse of the "dark night" of Saint John of the Cross! When God drew me to him, by some wonderful means without any human intermediary, he *lavished* me with such graces, flooded me with such ineffable joys that I have been completely conquered forever. But until now he was the perpetual giver, doing everything for me who had never done anything for him, who had, on the contrary, worked against him. That was all well and good. It was just that the time came for personal work, for labor, for effort; the time for self-giving, for self-denial, for sacrifices; the time when I would finally be able to offer something to the one who had given me so much. I had already suffered when my sister died and because of my health, but to suffer in the joy of the spirit is nothing. That's why the trials of the soul, the most intimate and subtle heartaches had to come to purify and transform. This divine work continues, and I daily offer my sorrows or my efforts to my unique Friend, the one who alone knows my depths. Pray that I may know how not to lose any of these precious graces of sufferings, better and more fruitful than any joy.

Pray also that this blessed flower of spiritual joy may blossom in me and bring forth all its fruit.

How open I can be with you, my friend, so easily and simply. The atmosphere in which I live is hardly favorable, from a religious point of view, to this kind of self-disclosure. I run into people in distress, suffering hearts, and hostile or indifferent minds every day. And from this contact arises considerable suffering and at the same time the intimate consolation of trying to do a little good. But, if I try to give a little to others (how badly and how imperfectly!) I scarcely receive anything in return, and my heart open to others is only open to receive from God. Besides, isn't that the story of all those for whom God has done so much! They have received so much from God that nothing human can fully satisfy them.

And yet a little light, ignited from the divine source shines for us here below, and these are our precious human loves, all that I feel for my loved ones, and for you.

I thank God because my husband understands, from a religious point of view, things that before were foreign to him. However, it is still not the faith; that will come from God eventually in God's time. Pray that it will not delay any longer and that this conversion will be accomplished more quickly. God only needs an instant to change a heart and to attach it to himself forever.

You are the only person with whom I talk about myself like this and about the deep desires of my heart. I hope this is not selfish. This sharing is very good for me, and I find it extremely comforting. So then, that will lead you to pray more for me and for all my intentions. But when we see each other, you will make up for it and you'll be the one who talks, giving me advice and comfort, telling me a little about your own interior life and about anything that is not for the divine Friend alone.

Physically, I am well at this moment, after a very mediocre period due, they think, to my liver. The young and the middle aged all around us are very well, but my poor mother is not as strong or as lively as usual. She really needs activity and suffers from not being able to give as much as before. Pray that, for her, interior action will make up for it and that God will fill up the void that life and old age have created for her; that a great faith will turn her immense goodness and her devotion to duty toward the supernatural.

What a horrible thing–the sinking of the *Titanic!* I pray for those so quickly called into eternity and for those who mourn them. How quickly the thin line that separates us from eternity is crossed! At least, by an immense mercy, we know that a loving God awaits us with open arms after this difficult passage and that after an act of expiation, he will open heaven to us. How insignificant our sufferings and our struggles must be when seen from the other side of the veil! It seems to me that there one must only regret not having suffered enough, not having loved enough here below, having offered so little for all that one receives.

How are your eyes, my friend? Are you taking reasonable care of them? Don't write to me; reserve your sight for your spiritual reading, for your patients, for all the good that you can do. I know your love for me, and that you speak of me to our Lord, and that we find each other in his heart. That suffices, and if I am deprived of your kind letters, that will give us both the opportunity of denying ourselves.

So I'm going to stop tiring out your poor eyes with this long letter. Excuse me. Please remember me to your good mistress, your mother, and the Marion sisters. Aren't the latter supposed to come to Paris? If so, I shall see them with joy to talk about you.

My husband sends you his respectful regards. I embrace you, in Christ's love.

Your friend,

E. Leseur

P.S. My regards to poor Louise.[27] Tell her that I think of her, and that one day we will be happy together in heaven after so much suffering.

Letter XXXI

June 5, 1912

My dear Sister,

I would have liked to write sooner but was prevented from doing so by my daily tasks. But, I also remained very lovingly, very closely united to you in our Lord and this in the midst of many interior upsets, because the good God has treated me for some time with a tender harshness and led me along rather rough roads. At the same time, because in God joys and sorrows are inexplicably mixed, he gave me the deep feeling of his protection, of his love, and of the mysterious work of reparation and of the austere renewal that he was accomplishing in me. Really, it matters little whether God acts through joy or suffering; what is important is that he acts, and if because of my great weakness I was afraid of being presumptuous, I would even say that "the sorrows that strengthen me are better for my soul than the joys in which my misery could take too much delight." But I add simply and with great abandonment to this beloved will, "Whatever Jesus prefers is best for me: joy or suffering, because what he sends me is what I spiritually need at that moment." No doubt he thinks it good for me to "shake me up" a little bit recently.[28] And then this trial of mind and body was perhaps an answer to the gift that I made of myself to him and to the graces that I wanted from him *at any price*. And you, my dear sister, have been able to surrender yourself entirely to God. It's a great grace! The response from God will be all the good that you will do for these poor suffering members of our Lord, for those who have been entrusted to your care by him. I will see you at this new post of honor. It will probably be about the middle of July that we will get to Beaune, and the thought alone is already a joy for me. As soon as my husband has decided on the date of his vacation, I will write to let you know.

My little nephew is getting better and better, and we hope that this accident will not leave a trace. Only one finger still remains a bit stiff.[29] The holy Virgin will, I hope, make even this last trace of the accident disappear. We are hoping, without yet being entirely decided, to be able to leave for Lourdes on Tuesday, the eighteenth. In that case we would stay three days and I would receive communion there, for my triple thanksgiving on Thursday, Friday, and Saturday. But I will let you know before we leave.

…Everyone in the family is healthy right now. Maman moves with great difficulty but is less discouraged than she was at the beginning of winter; perhaps I owe that to your good prayers. Likewise I am noticing with respect and deep feeling what the good God is doing spiritually in my dear husband; you would say that God is preparing the soil for faith. But in order to attain this last request, we shall have to unite our prayers and our sacrifices more than ever. My dear sister, help me to give this soul to God and to the church; he will do a lot of good, and you will be doing something very fruitful by working for this conversion. As for me, I would give *all* with joy to obtain it and perhaps—since our God knows the intensity of this desire—it is the hidden reason for so much of suffering, both physically and morally, that he has given me as a precious gift.

...Is it the fruit of so many prayers, of sacrifices offered by holy people? But I am really struck by the movement right now that is bringing back or attracting gifted people from every class toward God. I recently heard of a civil service worker, formerly a Freemason, who was converted along with his wife. A university professor, one of our friends, is being worked on at this moment and is a lot closer to the faith than a while ago. Some writers are transformed, and I recently read a very beautiful poem by a poet who was at one time an unbeliever and is now filled with the most unassuming and sincere faith.[30] God's enemies are forgetting only one thing in their way of thinking: the power of the cross, the strength of the Precious Blood, and the fruitfulness of prayer. And after having seeded the ruins, they are very surprised to hear rising from them a joyous *Alleluia*, to hear the murmur of prayers on the soil that they had hoped to make into a spiritual desert. Isn't it comforting how good God is!

My dear sister, it is to him that I entrust your eyes, your health, and even more your soul, which is very dear to me. Pray for us and believe that I love you very much.

Your friend,
E. Leseur

Letter XXXIII

June 30, 1912

My dear Sister and friend,

During our stay in Lourdes I could only send you a quick note, but you were constantly being remembered. I took you with me to the holy grotto, near our Lord in my communions, everywhere that

I prayed, and one prays everywhere in Lourdes, as you well know. What consoling moments I spent in that peaceful city of Mary, an unforgettable time that leaves a deep mark on one's life forever. It seems to me that I love the holy Virgin ever more as her daughter, that I have a greater desire to serve the good God. I also have more of an attraction to the poor, the sick whom he so loves, a greater willingness to work for the spiritual good of others through suffering or action, according to God's will.

At Lourdes I received communion four times, once at the grotto; we attended the candlelight procession in the evening, and took part in Benediction of the Blessed Sacrament. It's truly an awesome sight, with the sick vividly representing all human miseries. The nurses are so full of compassion. What a spirit of ardent faith and charity; and for a few days how far we felt from all human pettiness, raised above all that is transitory and all that causes suffering! How well one prays, almost without words when praying alone, and with the words of the Hail Mary when praying in common! My dear sister, don't you find that to spend a few days in prayer, thinking of those you love, in the contemplation of the unique interests and joys of the spiritual life, don't you think it's a glimpse of a little corner of heaven?

Now, I am "back" in daily life and taking up the big and little burdens, but I'm wrong to use the word *burden* to express something that the gentle Savior carries with me, the piece of his cross that he rests a little on my shoulders and on my heart. This cross seems heavy only when God hides the comfort of his smile, and even then you know that in the absence of all consolation the divine presence is nonetheless real. Say a joyful "thank you" to the good God with me for the spiritual strength that he gave me, and ask him for an increase of faith, of love, and of interior and exterior serenity.

My husband was very moved by the great scenes of Lourdes. I asked the holy Virgin for his conversion and also asked for it as a special gift from the Heart of Jesus at the end of this month. We're thinking of a stop-over at Paray-le-Monial from Beaune. You see that we are taking a liking to pilgrimages. Can you tell me if there is a hotel or a convent that takes male guests and that is clean (that's the important thing)? What a shame that you have already made that trip![31] It would have been so nice to do it with you.

...I shall not forget you tomorrow on this feast of the Visitation that I love so much and that speaks so much of humility and fraternal charity. On Friday, I'm asking you for a special prayer for my dear sister Marie; it's the anniversary of her death, and since she got me another sister Marie in you, you won't forget her, will you?[32]

Your friend,

E. Leseur

Letter XL

Jougne (Doubs)
August 16, 1912

My dear Sister,

I hope you received my letter from Vallorbe; we had some delightful guests at the time and an outing planned at the last minute prevented me from writing. I am sending you belated loving wishes for your feast day; yesterday I thought of you and I prayed for you; in the morning we were united in the heart of our Lord. I love the feast of the Assumption, which is so full of the triumph of Mary and of her joys. My present life, in which the role of Martha takes precedence over the role of Mary, did not allow me to meditate yesterday as much as I would have liked on the holiness and beauty of our mother Mary. I will, though, this month, and near her, with God's help, acquire humility, tenderness, and inner joy. Ask for that grace for me, dear sister, as I shall ask it for you.

With your feast day as an excuse, let me tell you again how deep my affection is for you. How can I thank God enough for having put you on my path and for having given me your affection? By arranging for our meeting each other, he wanted, no doubt, this friendship to help us spiritually and to bring us closer to him. What a joy to think that we are forever united in his heart! A day will come, dear sister, when having shaken off our heavy, clumsy body, we will soar toward the One who is our great love, where we will immerse ourselves in his holiness, his infinite beauty. There, knowing his very gentle humanity, penetrated with the joy of heaven, we will let the great flow of divine love bathe our souls. Then in the radiant company of the angels and of the holy people of all times, reunited with those we have loved so much, we will both be together forever in that dear heaven, where our love can be fulfilled. Doesn't that thought transform our lives and help us to accept with a joyful heart all its sorrows, its burdens, and its troubles?

I am asking you to pray very specially for my dear niece, Marie; the thought of her future is beginning to worry me. Entrust her to God and ask for health, happiness, and a successful future for her, especially a graced Christian life. More than ever pray for my dear husband, for all those that I love so much.

We have friends here at this time, so I am quite busy and scarcely have any leisure time. It is a sacrifice for me, who loves good moments of solitude and for whom meditation is a necessity. But this activity is really a duty for me, so I have no choice but to deny myself, relying on God to take care of me while I do my daily tasks. Really, there is still consolation in this renunciation of spiritual joys for a loving purpose, in this abandonment to the divine will instead of to our own miserable will.

I am reading the life of Saint Bernard by Abbé Chevallier and find it very interesting. What a magnificent figure he is, this austere and yet tender monk, passionate for solitude and yet living an incessantly active life by his strong will. His holiness has influenced so many all this time. In spite of our own insignificance, we can profit a great deal from contact with saints like him; they teach us to do generously the much more modest work God wants of us, without looking at the apparent result, without looking at ourselves, in a simple, joyful, and strong way. They teach us, above all, that suffering is the lot of the friends of Jesus, that nothing great is done without suffering, that it obtains everything and hollows out the channel through which the great river of grace flows on its way to others. Finally, they reveal to us the power of prayer and its hidden action. There, dear sister, are the lessons that Saint Bernard is giving me at this time; I am sharing them with you because you will know better than I how to profit from them.

...How is your dear mother? Your dear departed mistress is not forgotten in my prayers. I understand your deep sorrow. My sister and friend, let us look for these beloved dead close to God and let us tell ourselves again that the separation is only apparent. That assumes lots of sorrow, I know, but behind this veil that hides eternal realities from us, these beloved ones are alive, nearer to us than our weak minds can imagine. Your spiritual mother loves you better and more than ever; her legacy to you is the continuation of her work on earth through your prayers and sufferings, as well as through that untiring charity of which she gave you the example. Live with her memory, no doubt, but look ahead or rather upward where she is waiting for you.

Give the Marion sisters my very affectionate regards and share with them my husband's respectful greetings. I embrace you, my very dear sister, with all my great and Christian love.

Your friend,
E. Leseur

Letter XLI

Jougne (Doubs)
August 20, 1912

How upset I am to know that you are ill, my dear sister, and how happy I will be to learn that you are completely well. If you can carry out your plan to go on a pilgrimage to Ars, you will bring my prayers and the deepest desires of my heart there. If, on the other hand, you are still in Beaune because of your health, you will offer a small part of that disappointment for all these dear intentions. I can imagine you alone in your room meditating. And I say to myself, remembering my own experiences, that these times of illness are not among the hardest in life because they bring with them some very consoling compensations—a more complete union with the crucified Jesus, and a more loving intimacy of heart with him. For my part, during these times of physical suffering I have known the best spiritual joys; I also have a sort of weakness for those periods of illness, a weakness that I would not dare admit to everyone. Really, physical suffering is the least of all; emotional sufferings are far greater, but those of the soul surpass them all. It is truly the latter that try us and purify us, which bring us along an obscure path, so well described by the great mystics, to the spiritual region where we are finally fulfilled in God. Both of us are probably not involved with this dark path; that is a great grace and there will not be enough sufferings, enough effort on our part to respond to that grace. So let us accept the cross, under whatever form it comes, since the same divine hands are offering it to us, helping us carry it, and sustaining us along the road. Illnesses, heartbreaks, deep and painful spiritual trials let us know how to want it all, offer it all, love it all, through love for God.

How can you reproach yourself for showing your affection for me? I refer you to the very words of Saint Bernard on friendship, and to what the Abbé Chevallier says about it in his book. How could you be concerned about disedifying me? If you only knew what joy I feel at the thought that this little book,[33] the fruit of sorrow and tenderness, can do you some good. Isn't it my beloved sister who does you good, or rather, who obtains it from the great divine Goodness, and isn't there a very sweet and powerful link among the three of us? So, do not have any more scruples and be sure that your friendship is a comfort and a joy to me.

So much the better that your new mistress is the way she is. Your sorrow will not be lessened, but you will still be able to have good, strong support. What you tell me about the beginnings of your vocation touch me deeply. That is the way it should be: a breaking-off of all that is purely natural, the suffering caused by all that you leave behind, by the loves from which you distance yourself and which nevertheless do not diminish. All that will be returned to you a hundredfold. And if I did not firmly wish the divine will be done, I would be tempted to envy you for having given so much to our Lord. He has not allowed me to do that for him. I will not have the place near his heart reserved for those who are totally consecrated to him, but the example of your generous gift of self fills me with the desire to do something for God, and I am going to try very hard to be more courageous in his service.

Let me hear from you or have someone let me know what the doctor thought of this illness. I am still feeling as well as possible; my family news is rather good, although I do not think Maman is as well as I would like. Keep up your prayers for her.

Perhaps we will leave by car and go to Annecy on a pilgrimage to Saint Francis de Sales and Saint Jeanne de Chantal for whom I feel a strong attraction. When I am in Paris, I will send you the book by Mme. de Flavigny on Saint Catherine of Siena, if it is not sold out. I want you to get to know and love my dear Saint Catherine.

We had better weather for a few days; today it is raining again. What a nasty summer!

I love you and repeat that my affection for you is tender and Christian; my husband sends you his respectful regards, and I will meet you near our Lord at communion times or during quiet meditation.

Your friend,
E. Leseur.

Letter XLIV

September 24, 1912

My dear Sister,

Here we are back in Paris, after two days spent in Seine-et-Oise with Maman, whom I found to be very ill and very different. After the peacefulness of summer and the enjoyment of a few days spent in some beautiful countries, it is back to daily life and the taking up of the cross again. Maman had never completely left my heart, because I suffered knowing she was far from me and imagined her sad and gloomy. I was not wrong, and now I am very upset about her. Her health is bad, and she is going to begin the winter in a mediocre state; then, what pains me even more perhaps, she is very depressed, discouraged, thinking too much. Dear sister, I beg you, pray for her a lot; ask God for good health for my beloved Maman, but especially, most of all, ask him for peace of heart, spiritual consolation, a faith deep enough to transform her sufferings, a strong and active spiritual life. I am suffering in my inmost being over the physical and especially the moral state of Maman. Oh! That our Lord would consent to having me suffer in her place and cure this sad person by teaching her to love him; may he take possession of this heart that I would like so much to give him. Let us pray, my sister and friend, and let us offer up our

263

trials. Pray also for my dear niece, Marie, so that a distant intention may be fulfilled,[34] so that she may be happy one day, and that she may become a great Christian saint. I give you these two intentions along with the so ardently desired one—the conversion of my husband.

...Are you still in Savigny? If so, give your dear mother my respectful sympathy and tell her how happy I will be to learn of her complete cure. If you are back in Beaune, my heart will follow you again in the midst of your apostolic work and it will be united to yours in the chapel where I often pray with you by transporting myself there.

Now the existence that is so contrary to all my tastes and inner aspirations is going to resume. It is the moment of inner renunciation, of hidden sacrifices. More than ever I want to love Jesus Christ, "and Jesus Christ crucified." More than ever I want to try really hard to make him known and loved. If you knew, dear sister, how I long for meditation and prayer, how I long to flee the world and to no longer live except for dear, close ties and for those already in the tender company of God! And it is for him, in order to accomplish my task, that I want to give myself to the world and cover with a smile my efforts and my sacrifices. Pray that I may know how to forget myself and do my work with a joyful heart through all the displeasure, all the distaste and weariness.

How I go on talking to you about myself! It is because I am weaker and you give me so much in our spiritual sharing. May God grant you, my dear friend, his best joys and finest graces and make you a saint, so that you can be a saint for the two of us, a saint after his own heart, full of charity, loving him for himself, without seeking his gifts and making him radiate around you.

I feel very weak, very small. And at the same time, I feel that his strength can do all things in me, and I repeat with Saint Paul: "I can do all things in him who strengthens me."

My dear sister, I am sending you a tender kiss and my Christian love.

E. Leseur

P.S. Respectful regards from my husband.

Letter XLV

October 7, 1912

My dear Sister,

How sorry I am that you are experiencing such anguish over your dear mother.[35] Nothing quite equals the pain we feel when those we love suffer; no doubt that is why God sends it to us, because if we only experienced our own sufferings, we would not really know *suffering;* and that is also perhaps why Jesus wanted to suffer the sorrows of his mother and of his friends, in order to experience this emotional pain and thereby serve as a model for us in everything. Let us raise our eyes toward him, when sorrow or anxiety overwhelm us, and let us place our burden gently in his blessed hands and it will seem less heavy to us. Then let us take our miseries, our anxieties, our private heartbreaks and put them in his heart, so that from that heart they may go to God, then shower down on souls by that same royal road of love and become for others spiritual graces and joys.

You have been lucky to meet two saintly people,[36] don't forget to speak to them about me. Yes, it is truly consoling to meet such people. The stoics used to say, *"Suffering is nothing,"* and they were not telling the truth. But, more enlightened, we Christians say, *"Suffering is everything."* Suffering asks for and gets everything; because of suffering God consents to accomplishing all things; suffering helps the gentle Jesus to save the world. At times, when I feel overwhelmed by the immensity of my desires for those I love, by the importance of what I want to obtain for them, I turn toward suffering. I ask suffering to serve as the intermediary between God and them. Suffering is the complete form of prayer, the only infallible form of action. So, my beloved sister, may suffering accomplish what we desire, may it obtain the realization of our desires, may it benefit these dear people and praise God!

So then, my sister and friend, when you leave your beloved mother, look at the cross, think that this trial will do more good for her than even your loving presence, and you will lift her with you high above earthly sorrows, up to the heart of God.

To you alone, my friend, am I able to say that my detachment from the world is increasing, that I have a real thirst for recollection, prayer, and solitude. This profound need really comes from

God, since it is not the result of anything human or external; it fits in well with my growing love for my dear relatives and, far from causing me to flee action and work, it urges me to desire them only for God and with God alone. But until I receive a new directive, I must not change anything in my life, and no one knows how certain responsibilities weigh on me and represent sacrifices. No one must know that except the One who wishes these sacrifices for me, and on the outside I want more and more to conceal them with good grace, with a smile, and with joyous kindness.

Tell me in a quick note when you will be back in Jougne so that I can follow you again in spirit into your chapel. Maman returns to Paris today or tomorrow. She is better, but not strong yet. The children are back at their studies, my sister back to her active life and my husband to his work. Paris is noisier than ever, and that is not a rest for prayerful souls who must, like Saint Catherine of Siena, create "an interior cell" for themselves. Speaking of Saint Catherine, do you still want me to send you her biography?

Félix asks me to give you and your mother his respectful regards, and I send my deepest sympathy to your mother. I embrace you, my dear Sister, and I love you *in Corde Jesu*.

Your
E. Leseur

Letter XLVIII

November 3, 1912

My dear Sister, every day I was hoping for, and at the same time fearing to get a note from you. Is your silence a good sign? Or are your anxieties still the same? I remain deeply united to you; these consoling holy days have brought us closer in the heart of Jesus, have united us to our beloved departed in him. I hope God has given great graces to your dear mother during these days; as for you, my dear sister, the only thing I ask for you, whom I love so much, is the knowledge and accomplishment of the divine will. You are consecrated to God, dedicated to love and reparation for souls. In a very simple way I too have received the gift of God. From that time on, we both have not been able to love, want, or do anything other than what our adored Father wants for us. Let us accept everything from his hand, the unpleasant and the pleasant, suffering or tenderness, spiritual abandonment or consolation. Let us look at heaven beyond the cross, the resurrection beyond death, the open heart of Jesus beyond sorrow. Let us offer ourselves; humbly joined to the oblation of the Savior, ours will work for the good of others and to the glory of God. Let us forget ourselves so as to think only of the beloved Master, of those he wishes to save and for whom he asks for our prayers and our sacrifices.

When you can, without too much physical fatigue or emotional pain, tell me about your dear mother. Since I am not near enough to help you carry your burden, I am offering it from afar to our Lord. I pray for your beloved patient; I love her with you and suffer your sorrows, my sister, my friend.

You must be physically exhausted and that disturbs me. May God give you all the physical strength and spiritual peace and consolation you need....

Your sister

E. Leseur

Letter XLIX

November 5, 1912

What joy your letter brought me, my dear sister.[37] May God be blessed for leaving your mother with you, for giving you such happiness. My heart sings with yours a canticle of thanksgiving, and it seems to me that this good God, after having answered our prayer, will still give us the other graces we desire so much. Oh! may he wish to illuminate my dear maman with his supernatural lights, to take for himself my beloved husband, to give to all I love so much the temporal goods and the spiritual graces that I desire for them. Your recent sufferings that are ending in joy will contribute toward this great project; more than ever I wish to work on it also through my prayers and sufferings.

Tell your beloved mother how happy I am, how much I have thought and do think of her, how intense my prayers are for her. I dare to ask you to kiss her very respectfully and affectionately for me. My being your sister makes me a little bit her daughter through love.

What a debt of gratitude we owe the good God! We are going to pay it back by an increase of love, abandonment, and generosity! We are going to live closer to the heart of Jesus, more united to him, more given over to his will. How the love of souls is going to fill us and prompt us to make all kinds of sacrifices, to make every effort for them! How the love of our Lord is going to penetrate our hearts and teach us total self-forgetfulness, along with the gift of ourselves for others. How we will strive to be gentle, unassuming, and to radiate the gentle peace of the divine heart on all. My dear sister, may there be nothing more for us, as for Saint Paul, than "Jesus Christ crucified," and in him and for him all these loving relationships that will last into eternity.

Take good care of yourself now, because you need your health for your mother; later it will be for your patients. During this month let us pray together for…"our" souls in purgatory. What a grace and what a joy the communion of saints is!

I also thank God for having brought us together; life and duty separate us, but along different roads we are walking toward the same blessed end. A day will come when there will be no more distance, separation, and sorrow. Heaven awaits us, and then we will be together again forever, we will find God, we will know him, and we will be able to love him fully at last!

What consolation your dear mother's faith is for you! Perhaps, complete union with those I love would have given me too much joy. May God give it at least in eternity! God wanted to be my only guide, friend, and confidant, and because I am weak and he is good, he put you on my path, like a gentle ray of sunshine, while I await the great sun of his eternity.

My sister and friend, I am sending you along with the respectful and affectionate regards of Félix for your mother and you, a kiss and my sisterly love. United *in Corde Jesus*,

Your sister and friend,
Elisabeth

Letter L

November 20, 1912

My dear Sister, first of all let me thank you for your wishes on my feast day. It was very lovely to feel you united to me, to know you were praying with me for my intentions. May my patron saint repay you and become your protector. Next, let me also send you my most sisterly wishes, the most affectionate wishes for your birthday. The day after tomorrow I will be with you in spirit; my communion will be for you, for your beloved mother, for all your intentions. I will ask for the abundant graces you need and the most interior spiritual joy.

Finally, my sister and my friend, I want to assure you of my profound compassion in the painful crisis that you are going through.[38] I understand it thoroughly. But if the waves of suffering and bitterness are violent, do not let yourself go under, especially under the influence of a physical and emotional depression that is very natural after such a shock. Do not let harmful imaginings and debilitating thoughts invade your heart. You answered the divine call long ago, responded to your providential vocation. Religious life brings with it such security, provides such help, and procures such great comfort that without exceptional self-denial, and some heavy crosses, it would already be the vestibule of heaven. Having come to Jesus to share in his sacrifices and his passion, you have experienced this and continue to go through an agony similar to the one the Savior knew in Gethsemane. Do you know that these anxieties, these dilemmas are not unknown even in the world? It is enough to have received these choice graces and to know at the same time the deep call, the mysterious vocation of suffering. Consecrated people, both those in the cloister and those outside have the same task: to suffer, and through suffering to make reparation and obtain graces for others.

If you consider the possibility in your mind, attractive to be sure and very human, that you had chosen another path, are you sure that would have been better for your mother? From a material point of view, situations change quickly, and then a woman cannot devote herself to her mother any more than a religious could; her husband, her children come before everything else, and the same kind of "division" of heart occurs. You cannot relive your life in your mind and imagine that all would have been easier and better in another direction. No, the cross is planted everywhere, in the world as well as in the monastery. And if the cross plunges more deeply into God's chosen ones, it is because he has himself prepared favorable soil.

But how I understand what this trial must be for you and how I share a daughter's feelings. Your poor heart suffers less for yourself than for your mother. The most difficult sorrow is to cause those you love to suffer. In a lesser way I understand and know what it means personally. If you were married, my dear sister, and living far away, perhaps you would not have been able to give your mother such long-term care and you would have had to return to your husband already. The One to whom you have given your life will also help you understand his call and that it will cause you some suffering and heartache. You surely will not do less for him than you would for a beloved husband. A priest said about a woman who was struggling with her feelings: "There are times when you have to take your heart, throw it at God's feet…and step on it." How hard that is, but how mysterious! At that moment, miracles of grace take place, and one hour of such suffering is equal to a life given over simply to doing the good.

Can your mother consider moving closer to you? She is perhaps held in Savigny by what she still has there; or else she is too weak now to withstand the change. It is very hard for me to give you advice on the subject from a distance and not knowing everything. How I would like to at least be able to provide something for you materially, but (strictly between us) for us too the future holds many uncertainties and I am obliged to be very prudent. Tell me, however, very frankly, if I can in some small way help you, and next month I will arrange it. All this, very simply, and as your sister.

Let me know when you have to return to the Hôtel-Dieu, so that my thoughts may follow you there. My beloved Sister, since you do not seem to have a spiritual guide right now who can help and enlighten you, turn toward the only Friend, the incomparable Councilor, so that he may speak to your heart, inspire you, let you know his will. Without sacrificing any of your deep feelings, banish as quickly as possible any looking back and any regrets or vain desires—the overly "sensitive" impressions of your delicate nature. I know how much you sometimes have to struggle against your sensitivity, with an entirely spiritual intention in order not to lose any of its deep strength. When we go to God, in his dear heaven, our sorrows and our efforts will endure, not human feelings, not even the best and most legitimate. Let us make of our sufferings steps upon which to climb higher.

Oh, my dear sister, how easy it is to preach and how weak I would be if I were in your place! I am sorry for you, I love you, and I am going to pray for you more than ever...I am already doing that!

My health is better right now; my liver is behaving itself; but the good God is substituting something else for that. And since that "something else" is the pain of a loved one, it is harder than a liver attack...and there is also your pain, which is mine. In all of this, let us say together: *Fiat.*

Maman is not very well, but everyone else is in good health.

Tell your mother that I think of her, I feel sorry for her and share her sufferings. Tell her of my respectful and deep sympathy. How much good she must be doing now by her sufferings of body and soul!

My husband sends you his respectful remembrances; I give you a hug and the usual tender reunion (especially at the painful times that I live in spirit with you) in the blessed heart of Jesus.

Your sister and friend,
Elisabeth

Letter LI

December 4, 1912

Not having received any word from you, my dear sister and friend, I am wondering how your mother is, and if you are not paying now for the pain and fatigue of these past months; at the same time I am worried a bit about your reaction to my last letter. If my letter seemed too hard to you, my dear friend, do not think there is any lack of tenderness or deep compassion. You are always in my heart, and your present heartaches resound sorrowfully in my heart. It was my love for you that impelled me to talk to you so frankly. Faced with a painful situation and profound decisions,

271

you have to ask for all the light of the Spirit of love; you have to ask for divine grace and the graces of each hour; then, armed with proper advice, you have to act in all simplicity, even against your human affections, with all your moral energy. That is what I had wanted to say. I leave the rest to those who are near you and who have the responsibility to act and to you the responsibility to discern your duty and to accomplish it fully.

My dear sister, suffering is the great law of the spiritual world. God's chosen ones escape it less than others; they pay the ransom for others, sometimes at a very high price. We will know only later the work accomplished by our suffering and our sacrifices. It all goes to the heart of God, and there, joined to the redemptive treasure, it expands in souls in the form of grace. We can convert, sanctify, console without going out of our home or out of ourselves. Ceaselessly united to the One who acts in all of us, we offer and obtain without flagging. And God lavishes our humble gifts on others. When we present to him the most intimate heartaches, this "blood of the heart" that makes spiritual martyrs, we become very powerful with him. There is almost nothing our recent trials cannot accomplish, my friend. They will pass away, and you will obtain heaven; your dear mother will be there for all eternity with you, and there will be no more conflict between our love for God and our human affections. Divine love will enfold and take delight in all our loves.

If you can write just a note without getting too tired and without neglecting any of your duties, give me some news about your mother and the rest of your family. I am afraid of a physical reaction in you after so much fatigue and so many emotions, and I would like to be reassured of your well-being.

Last week Maman was very ill with an attack of emphysema; her health is always a great worry for us. The rest of the family is fine, even I am doing all right, at this moment.

...However, I also have my troubles, very intimate and profound, not the physical suffering, which is sweet, but those of the heart and soul. The good God, little by little, is stripping me of everything earthly in my affections, consolations, and supports. He is taking everything away from me, leaving emptiness; perhaps, or rather, surely, he intends to fill it. And I really think that he already lives alone in me, blessing my human affections.

I embrace you, my dear sister and friend, while sending you respectful remembrances from my husband, those of both of us for your mother, while telling you again how much I love you in spiritually, profoundly, sisterly, for always.

Your friend,
E. Leseur

Part 3

Letter LV

January 8, 1913

My dear Sister,

You must have found my note of January 1 inadequate. Even more than you, I felt I had not expressed to you, as I would have liked, my love and my good wishes. Multiple activities have overtaken me, and I am being disciplined by living in a way so contrary to my tastes. My dear sister, closely united to God in my depths, I take refuge as often as possible in that "interior cell," the only one possible, where I make provisions for peace and serenity, near my unique Friend. Externally, I was battered by all my duties, the upsets of life, and this time of year. My thoughts went out to you, but I did not have time to tell you of my deep love for you. No one around me knows how much deprivation and self-denial result for me from worldly distractions and Parisian life. I am so thirsty for recollection, for a deep interior life, for an existence directed entirely toward God and the well-being of others. But until I receive new orders, duty lies in these trifles that crucify my will: Alleluia! Perhaps one day I will know an existence more compatible with the deep desires of my interior life, or even perhaps God, unwilling to give me that joy here below, will reserve for me in heaven his sweetest compensations and the happiness of total union with him. Whatever it may be, blessed be his will and may it completely replace mine.

Ask him, my dear sister, for three special graces for me this year: the conversion of my beloved husband, the holiness of my dear mother, and the best and happiest future for my dear niece,

Marie. Those are really my most ardent desires at present, the ones that I entrusted to the Christ Child, to our sweet Jesus. *At any price* I want to obtain the answer to my prayers. Help me with your prayers.

How I go on talking about myself! It is true that because I love to hear you talk to me about yourself, it seems that the opposite must be true. I realize with great empathy the moment of your sad separation is approaching. How sorry I am for you, my friend, or rather how sorry I would be if I did not think that this magnificent cross is given to you as a gesture of immense love by the one who carries our crosses with us. What wonderful graces he wants you to obtain by accepting the cup of sorrows: graces for your mother, for those for whom his heart is so thirsty, decisive graces, who knows, for my loved ones. How self-centered I am, my dear sister, since I am trying to profit from your very sufferings, but this is allowed, isn't it, since it is based on our admirable communion of saints?

Your mother, in her generosity, will also know how to accomplish her difficult sacrifice. For both of you, I wish her many more years of life; but, finally for all of us, the years will pass quickly, in spite of everything. Eternity draws near and with it an endless reunion. In this joy of union, in this blessing of divine contemplation, in this supreme endless joy, what will our most bitter separations of earth and all our troubles be, if not the fruitful material of our eternal happiness? Then, if we have one regret, it seems to me that we would only be able to regret not having done enough for God, not having given him enough.

...In spite of frequent malaise and the limitations that being a shut-in entails, Maman is quite well at this moment, as are my sister and her children. My husband is very busy; the commercial and industrial world is suffering a lot from the outside situation, and we all strongly feel the consequences. You tell me that materially you also are feeling the effects; it is only because of your mother that you consider the situation to be painful and distressing. God willing, everything will turn out for the best for her, and therefore for you. The accident that happened to your dear patient must have been another source of anxiety.[39] My friend, I carry both of you with me to our Lord in my communions and in my prayers, and I speak to him tenderly about you.

...My dear sister, give your mother our respectful regards; may she allow me to embrace her through you. Félix sends you his best regards, and I tell you once again while embracing you of my deep love and also of my union with your heart in the blessed heart of Jesus.

Your friend and sister,
Elisabeth

Letter LVI

February 6, 1913

Your silence bothers me, my dear sister and friend, and I would have told you so sooner but my multiple duties and occupations have deprived me of the joy of writing to you. Where are you at this moment? What arrangements have you made for your dear mother and yourself? Are you at peace in the midst of the painful challenges of life and of suffering? I am talking about substantial, deep peace, compatible with agitation, with all our daily upsets. May God grant you that grace, may he make you see in his pure light what he wants for you and what you can do for his glory and for those who are so dear to him. The will of God! That is the only important thing under whatever form it presents itself, often that which is the most repugnant to our nature. This dear, good God is a marvelous artist; he knows how to knead us, to work us in view of the work that he wants to do in us and through us. Everything is good to him: suffering, illnesses, the events of our lives, the joy even, when he wishes it, although that is not the usual way. He detaches us from the world, from ourselves, from spiritual consolations, and leads us to loving him alone and into the happiness of which he is the principle, without any searching for his gifts. When you have left everything for him, you are sure of finding him, aren't you?

So, what will that mean for you, my dear sister, you who offer him the most complete sacrifice of a daughter's affection and the most complete self-renunciation. Ask him to do for your dear mother what is impossible for you and to lavish on her his best graces. How is your beloved patient? Has the incident you told me

275

about left any traces? I would like to be sure about it and to know that you are calmer. Lent is already beginning, and I really want it to be fruitful for me and for my dear sister. Let us unite our sufferings, our self-denial, our sacrifices; let us pray a lot; let us act in complete union with our Lord; and let us ask him to use our poor gifts for those we love and for his church. May this time of recollection be a time of preparation; when Lent is over, we must be ready to go to heaven or to begin a new life of labor and struggles.

Maman has been in bed for a few days, suffering from varicose phlebitis; she got up the day before yesterday but always has a lot of pain and does not leave her apartment. Poor Maman, how I wish for her the spirit of faith and all the sweetness of love for God. Pray also for that, my friend.

The young people are fine; my husband is a bit overworked. As for me, I have a few little pains; for Lent one could bear considerably more. I do not know if I will be able to go on retreat. You know how much I want to. The preaching in the parishes around me is not to my liking, and that at my little convent would perhaps be too absorbing for my lay vocation. Ah! The duties of my state in the world, there is the real daily cross, heavy at least for my shoulders. What a source of self-denial, of deprivations that no one knows about, but Jesus counts and collects them! How many times I do without the Lord in order to accomplish his will!

My dear sister, as soon as you can, tell me about yourself and your mother in a quick note. Do I have to tell you again of the loving union of my heart with yours? Let us both be servants and friends of the heart of Jesus, even though to different degrees, but with an almost equal love. Let us become women of prayer, apostolic women. I pass on to you this little prayer, inspired by a brochure that I read: "My God, give me an adoring soul, a reparation soul, an apostolic soul." An apostle, you are one both through action and through suffering. I can do nothing as far as works go. May the good God use my little hardships and my very poor prayers.

...I love you and tell you again of my deep Christian love for you.

Your

E. Leseur

Letter LIX

March 13, 1913
[Letter written in pencil][40]

Be assured, my dear sister, I am getting better. The headaches and the vomiting have stopped, and if this improvement lasts a few days more, it will be possible for me to resume a little of my usual life.

The doctors have not clearly diagnosed what I have. But the opinion that makes sense to me is this one: my gall bladder, which once was overflowing, probably retracted on some stones and that would have caused those pains; what is more, it would have led to or aggravated those terrible headaches. Will that come back? I abandon myself to the divine will in that, as in everything else. What seems more than probable is that I will have for one or two years various pains, so many that I will not see old age. With my various illnesses that is only natural.

Yesterday I had the great joy of the most tender and dearest of visits. Our Lord came to me, and you can guess what comfort he brought. Truly, with him, suffering is nothing anymore. For some time now I have never been more deprived of real consolation, more tested by discomfort and physical pain; and never have I felt at the same time such efficacious action of God in my depths. It is for these miseries, alleviated by him, that he promises us his heaven! That is enough to make you confuse it all with love and admiration.

Thank you for the holy card and relic of Bernadette Soubirous, which brought a sweet unction to my heart. I am going to keep it near me until I am completely cured. I would really like to be able to go to church a little next week, Holy Week. But I surrender all to God—that is so good…and so sure.

…Take care of your precious eyes as much as possible. *Do not write to me!* That will be a sacrifice for me, and I feel you are so united to me that I can offer it to God. Did your dear mother receive the letter that I dared to write her? I always pray for our three mothers: mine, yours, and my good mother-in-law.

I hope to be able to begin to stand up soon, perhaps a short while today.

Regards from both of us. Love and kisses from

Your friend and sister,
Elisabeth

ELISABETH LESEUR

Letter LXI

April 10, 1913

Your letter was received with joy as always, my dear sister and friend. The only drawback is your eyes, which you must take care of and be careful with,[41] be very prudent and immediately do *everything* that they tell you to do. I think that that is the best thing for you as well as for me: to take good care of oneself as if by doing so one were to recover and leave the result to God. How consoling it is to say to oneself that whatever happens, it will be good for us, since it will be given to us or imposed on us through love. During the Easter season we must make a special resolution about interior joy, ask God for it, and try to make it radiate around us. If you knew how clearly I saw my weaknesses during this last illness! It provided me with some very fruitful insights; so now I count only on God to transform me. As these spiritual mists move away and this physical onslaught lessens.... I am beginning to see that the good God has not been inactive and that he is doing his work in me. But now I can no longer let him act alone, and of all things— sufferings, prayers, and this bit of action that is possible for me— it is necessary that I do some apostolic work Let us together, dear sister, be unassuming apostles of the Sacred Heart and let us become holy with his help. He allows us this desire, since we feel our weakness, our misery. Let us put our entire, joyous, tender confidence in "the One who strengthens us."

Until I get new instructions, I have been able to resume my usual communions and you can guess with what joy.

My health is better, and yesterday, and I was able to go to Maman's, where I shall return tomorrow, but lots of prudence is needed or I shall certainly experience the offensive return of my diverse enemies. Maman is also a little better with the same uncertainties. Everyone else around us is well.

How is your dear mother? Is that crisis that you told me about over?[42] Give her my best regards and all our cordial respect.

My sister and friend, do you think that those distractions, dullness, and heaviness in prayer and in union with God are unique to you? For our consolation, I like to think that the saints were familiar with these distractions. Only with courage and through humble supplication did they surmount them. If we poor weak ones cannot do

278

as much as they, we can at least place ourselves at the feet of Jesus, and through acts of love or surrender draw toward us his gentle regard, which illumines everything. I believe that we are often too agitated in his presence instead of staying there very peacefully just as we are, letting him see our distress and our needs, whether we talk about it or not. After all, there is immense consolation just being near someone we love, even without talking. In our daily work let us practice charity, affection, and humility through the accomplishment of our normal duties, and then let us come to the feet of Jesus with all that. He will know how to see all, to accept all, and will transform what needs to be improved in us. Just the thought that he is there, in the tabernacle, and that his heart bends toward our heart is enough to nourish our intimate contemplation.

How your love creates illusions on my account, my dear sister! I would like to substitute my conscience, which sees deeper than you, for yours. How many hidden defects we discover in ourselves ceaselessly, and how much a struggle it is to always start again. It is good that we have this distress, because without it, pride is always ready to intervene and would be able to have free reign. How subtle the enemy and how alert we need to be! May the good God give us humility and also that meekness that he said would possess the earth. The conquest of hearts can only be accomplished with gentleness.

I ask you for a special remembrance in your communion the day after tomorrow and your prayers for my dear sister Juliette. It will be eight years since she died. May God give us his heaven, with her, one day. Time passes quickly, and we will scarcely have time to suffer and work a little for our Lord before reaching port.

Félix sends you his respectful regards, and I embrace you tenderly, my dear Sister, giving you our usual meeting place, *in Corde Jesu.*

Your friend,
E. Leseur

Letter LXIII

May 26, 1913

My Sister and friend, my niece will write herself in a few days, but I want to tell you that her engagement is now official. She is happy, and so are we, because our future nephew possesses all the qualities that give promise for future happiness. Continue your good prayers for them, and on Friday entrust them very specially to the heart of our Lord; put them also under the protection of the holy Virgin during these last days of the month of Mary. Finally, my dear sister, do not forget to pray to Mary and to the divine heart for my dear ones and my deepest desires for them.

...How are your eyes? You do not have to write if you have been forbidden to do so, but perhaps one of the good Marion sisters can let me know your news in a short note. To be stricken with eye trouble, what a suffering, and how I feel for you, my friend. At the same time, I think that God must really love you since he is transforming you like this through suffering. Ah! Suffering! How truly it is his messenger and the surest means that he uses to transform us in the most interior part of ourselves. And it is so fruitful, more than all our poor activity. Do good; lots of spiritual good for others; for us, through your present trials; do some good for me, who does so little. Pray, suffer, act in a loving union of hearts with the love-filled heart of our Savior. When you are not able to act or read, rest in his dear company, and you will see that he will tell you more profound things than any book. Thus, you will act more effectively during the hours of inactivity willed by him than during the busy hours that he would not have wanted for you. To want what God wants, that is it! To see each day what God wants and to ask him for it in the loving intimacy of prayer; then to accomplish his will, no matter what the cost, that is the invitation. It is up to him to bring forth the good and fruitful results of our efforts, our trials, and our prayers.

...Today I am a bit tired and slightly conscious of my nasty headache. We do not know how the summer will turn out; no doubt, we will not stay as long in Jougne as last year, but unless something unexpected happens, we will go for a little while and I will pass through Beaune to give you a hug. You know what a joy that will be for me.

My dear sister, on June 28, the day of Marie's twentieth birthday, Maman will give a family dinner for the engaged couple. You will think of us that day, I hope.

My husband asks me to convey to you his respectful regards, and I will give you a hug while sending you this expression of my deep love, my sister and friend.

Your friend,

E. Leseur

Letter LXVI

July 14, 1913

[Letter written in pencil]

I am writing you from my bed, my dear sister and friend. Having left Paris in a far from perfect state of health, I came back here really in pain.[43] For one week I have been in bed again with terrible headaches and vomiting. It is getting better, but this attack leaves me very tired again.

The departures are about to begin. My mother, my sister, and the engaged couple are going to leave for the seashore at Wissant, in the Pas-de-Calais, next to the Hochart family. My brother-in-law and his children will be going to Jougne with us for a few days before going to join them. Mr. Hochart Sr. told my sister what a fine welcome you gave him. Thank you. In this regard a Dame Knarzer, whom I met at the home of some friends, will be going to Beaune toward the end of the month. I am warning you, if she resorts to your goodness, that I do not have any relationship with her; in addition, she is also not a believer. But I know that you will have all the necessary vigilance and tact.

We intend to leave Paris toward the twenty-sixth or twenty-eighth, more likely the latter; please tell us if you will be at Beaune then. If we can, we will stop there two days, whichever would be the least trouble for you. You know what joy I will have seeing you again and visiting with you. For some time God has been offering me lots of trials, and through lots of weakness, pains, and distasteful things of all sorts, my union with him grows and I experience this strange mixture of suffering and of profound joy (intangible) that made Saint Paul say: "I am overjoyed in the midst of tribulation." How good our God is and what a friend he is; with him, the pain really does not exist anymore, or rather, it is absolutely transformed. I ask him, my dear sister, to help you understand more

281

and more and sometimes feel all that. Your life is consecrated to him and that creates a beneficial unity; that is what is missing in my life, so fragmented right now. The important thing is to do not what one would have wanted, but what God wants. Let us ask him to no longer take notice of us, to forget us, to no longer see anything but our neighbor, souls, and his own glory. There is a saying of Jesus that touches me deeply and on which I meditate with joy: "If anyone wishes to be perfect, let him renounce himself, take up his cross every day, and follow me." That is the whole program of the spiritual life.

How are your eyes? Are you being very prudent? Only send me a note giving the date of your coming to Beaune. Félix sends you his respectful regards. I embrace you very tenderly, my dear sister and friend, and assure you of our usual meeting in the heart of our Lord.

Your friend,
E. Leseur

Letter LXXI

September 18, 1913
[Letter written in pencil]
It is very nice, my dear sister, finally to be able to tell you again of my love and prove to you by this note that I am getting better: I eat well, can sleep again, and feel myself reborn day by day.[44] In a little while we are going to leave for Versailles by ambulance, to go to the nursing home of the Franciscan Sisters, on Maurepas Street; we will stay there as long as necessary, since Félix will be able to come and go from there to his business in Paris. There is a park where I will be able to take "my first steps."

You know, my dear sister, that I have just gone through a great test. It was really total prostration and suffering, not leaving room for a thought, a prayer, the stripping away of everything. The good God, I think, looked with compassion on his poor crushed child. I was receiving communion like that, so it was really he who was carrying everything, because I offered only my suffering, but is not that what he prefers? I have suffered terribly, but no use going back over that. At one moment I thought I was dying of starvation. So many prayers, your dear prayers, have brought about this improvement. I will still need lots of care, lots of rest, a strict diet, because these abnormal conditions of the gall bladder, of the pylorus, and of the stomach still linger on. But I will do all that I have to. My dear husband has shown admirable tenderness and dedication. You know all that I have to obtain for him, for Maman, for those whom I love, my engaged couple, and also for many others. This illness seems to be a response from Providence. May it obtain all that I want more than anything. You will help me do it with your prayers, won't you?

In this sort of coma in which I lived, thoughts of you were floating in my heart; since I have revived, thoughts go to you with all the strength of my love. Let me tell you again, my dear sister, how much I feel my soul united to yours. God has just made me pass through a dark and painful tunnel; perhaps when I get out of it, I am going to find myself in different spaces and I will have progressed without feeling it. Pray for that for me.

Respectful regards from Félix and a tender kiss from

Your,
Elisabeth

Letter LXXIV

November 6, 1913

My dear Sister and friend,

This convalescent is happy to send you one of her most loving thoughts and to tell you that she feels very deeply the union of her soul with yours. I have had the joy of attending Mass and receiving communion on the feast of All Saints, on Sunday, and again yesterday. I am afraid I will not be able to tomorrow and will have to wait until Sunday, because, if my health is as good as today, I will go to Maman's to avoid tiring her with a trip to my house. The good God will forgive me for sacrificing him to a daughter's duty, so much the more since there will be a sacrifice for me to make. We will not be less united in heart because I will find you in the blessed heart, to whom all our prayers and all our love will go tomorrow. How good God is, my dear sister! I am more aware of his goodness than ever after this painful attack. Upon emerging from the dark tunnel where I have trudged heavily along during these last few months, and where I have experienced in an overwhelming way the sense of my powerlessness and my nothingness, I am coming back to fresh air and facing new horizons, and I acknowledge that, whereas I was doing nothing but suffering, God was acting in me. However, I still have lots of personal dislikes, lots of deep sufferings, many hidden deprivations, but so what? A deep sense of the divine presence has returned, that tender union with the adored Master, and I want to try to do the work that he wants of me, as little and as humble as I am.

How are you, beloved sister? My husband is slowly getting over the shock that he has had. Maman is aging and is sometimes in pain. The others are fine. Pray for us all, okay? I recommend to your prayers our dear old servant who raised us all, our Mamie, whom I talk about in my little book.[45] She is very ill in her own country, and I regret I cannot be near her, to take care of her. May God give her at the end of her life all that she did for us and repay her devotion to us in supernatural grace and joy.

...After a glorious month of October we begin November in the rain. These are the three most difficult months of the year for me, at least, who so loves the sun and the brightness. Last summer did not exist for me; may the next one be more pleasant, but I still see lots of complications and uncertainties about duty and *"the best,"* which are a real torture.

How is your dear mother? Give her my respectful regards. Thank you again for your prayers....

A kiss, my dear Sister, with all the love from your friend,
Elisabeth

Letter LXXVII

February 6, 1914
[Letter written in pencil]

My very dear Sister,

I am sending you a note, as soon as I can and without expecting a relapse. First of all, I want to tell you that after some bad days, I am now again in a period of calm, for which I thank God; then to tell you again how much I love you, deeply, tenderly, in a very spiritual way. I felt myself less separated from you during this attack; when you have a meeting place in the heart of our Lord, you are no longer ever entirely separated. Today, my dear sister, we are together there more than ever.[46] My next communion will be on next Wednesday, February 11, the feast of our Lady of Lourdes. I intend very humbly to ask the holy Virgin to obtain for me a rapid cure and to receive communion for this intention. My sister will also. Will you join me and pray for your little sister, who has great love and confidence in Mary?...Thanks in advance. I rejoice over this solid spiritual union and believe nothing is impossible to our Savior and that his blessed Mother can obtain everything from her son.

Maman is not very well and cannot move. We do not see each other; this separation would be less painful if I felt a spiritual union with her. Pray, my dear sister. There, too, nothing is impossible to God.

...Félix sends you his respectful friendly greetings and I embrace you with all my heart. Let us always love each other in the one whom we could never love too much.

Elisabeth.

Letter LXXVIII

March 12, 1914

My dear Sister and friend,

A very short note because writing still tires me.[47] I have had a very bad time after our union of prayers. For two weeks the aches and vomiting have ceased, and although I still have a great deal of pain, and am able to rest a very short time each day on my chaise lounge, I feel for the first time a little, a very little, impression of health and foresee (in the distant future) the end of the tunnel. Alas! I will have fresh painful attacks, no doubt. Pray for me to the holy Virgin and the Sacred Heart.

Félix is fine, the others also, only Maman is not very well. And you? I think of you, I love you, and I was united to you this morning in my communion. A kiss, my dear sister.

Elisabeth

NOTES

Introduction

1. For an earlier and more expansive treatment of these themes, see Janet K. Ruffing, "Elizabeth Leseur: A Strangely Forgotten Modern Saint," in *Lay Sanctity, Medieval and Modern: A Search for Models*, ed. Ann Astell, 117–29 (Notre Dame, IN: University of Notre Dame Press, 2000).

2. Mm. Gavignot reported the immediate chemistry all in the room felt around the young couple on their first meeting in her home (unpublished papers).

3. Elisabeth Leseur, unpublished letter to her mother (Christiane Schmitt, *"Elisabeth Leseur: une femme dans l'église de son temps,* 1997," Dominican Archives, Bibliothèque Saulchoir, Paris, 6, photocopy).

4. Léon Gambetta (1838–82), a Freemason and a leader of the moderate Republicans, founded this militantly anticlerical journal and was briefly prime minister of France. The journal was the official organ of the "opportunistic" faction within the Republicans.

5. Félix Leseur, *Vie d'Elisabeth Leseur* (Paris: Gigord, 1930), 106–7.

6. Their travel was extensive. In 1896 they went to Carthage, Tunisia, Egypt, Algeria, Iran, and Turkey. In Carthage, Elisabeth met the White Fathers, who showed her the sites associated with early Christianity. Félix was overseeing the building of a mosque in Paris, which justified this trip. In 1897 they went to Munich, Bayreuth, Nuremburg, Bamberg, Berlin, Dresden, Prague, Vienna, Budapest, Bucharest, Iasi (Romania), Carpathia, Moldavia, Salzburg, and Innsbruck. In Bayreuth they attended four Wagnerian operas in addition to Parsifal twice. In 1899 they went to Russia, Finland, Constantinople, Athens, Smyrna, Patras, Brindisi, and Venice.

7. Elisabeth only had Chanoine Weber's version of the New Testament and a separate version of the Psalms translated from the Hebrew (not the Septuagint). Lay Catholics did not have full editions of the Bible yet (Schmitt, *"Elisabeth Leseur,"* 17).

8. Edited and published by Félix Leseur in 1917.

9. Jules Charles Marie Hébert, in religion Père Joseph, OP (April 12, 1864–October 7, 1920).

10. Soeur Goby (1865–1922) was a nursing Hospitaller Sister of St. Martha of Beaune whom Elisabeth met through befriending Marie Ballard, a tuberculosis patient at the Hôtel Dieu where Marie Goby was stationed. The correspondence between Goby and Leseur was published in French under the title *Lettres sur la souffrance*.

11. Wendy Wright summarizes the pattern De Sales advocated: "The devout wife of the courtier will move modestly attired among garish finery, attend dances and theatre without attachment to the frivolity and licentiousness that sometimes accompany these diversions, fast on prescribed days but otherwise eat moderately of foods set before her, pray fervently but only as often and as long as the discharge of her familial duties recommends, cultivate friendships that are based on mutual religious aspirations and practice the unobtrusive virtues of meekness, temperance, integrity and humility" (Wendy Wright and Joseph Powers, *Francis De Sales, Jane de Chantal: Letters of Spiritual Direction*, Classics of Western Spirituality [Mahwah, NJ: Paulist Press, 1988], 56). For Francis de Sales on married life, see *Introduction to the Devout Life*, trans. John Ryan (Garden City, NY: Image, 1966), 44, and Part III. Elisabeth had the first fifteen volumes of the *Complete Works of Francis de Sales* in her library.

12. *Journal*, March 11, 1901. This brief journal entry points to the character of their marital relationship. The gift alluded to was a writing desk. Félix in his religiously hostile mind-set had started calling his wife Madam Péchin, a character in a novel by Anatole France. In the novel an agnostic physician makes fun of Madam Péchin, a figure whose belief in immortality is attacked. In the Leseur household Elisabeth took up intellectual pursuits in order to defend a spiritual view of life, and Madam Péchin as a nickname became associated with Elisabeth's intellectual life. Elisabeth responded to her husband with good humor. But when Félix realized he was hurting his wife, he made amends by having this writing desk delivered together with a love letter. Elisabeth responds to his thoughtful and loving gesture, initiating her new desk by writing a love letter to him on it ("sending...from the depth of my little Péchin heart, a feeling of tenderness, in which all forms of love are mixed together, united so that it would be impossible to separate them") expressing the depth of her love for him and her gratitude for "the happiness of being loved by another dear and good person such as you" (unpublished letter, Dominican Archives, Paris, March 9, 1901).

13. *Journal*, July 4, 1905.

14. "An Essay on the Christian Life of Woman" and "A Little Treatise on the Christian Life Written by Elizabeth Leseur for her Nephew, André Duron, at His First Communion," in *The Spiritual Life: A Collection of Short Treatises on the Inner Life by Elizabeth Leseur*, trans. A. M. Buchanan (London: Burnes, Oates, Washbourne, 1922). A fresh English translation of these essays is included in this volume. André was her godson, whom she accompanied to his first communion preparation, taking notes of the talks and going over them later with him just as her mother had done for her. Her sister Juliette had been named Marie Duron's godmother and asked Elisabeth to take her place. Amélie, Elisabeth's sister, was their mother.

15. The Dominican Archives in Paris have more than two dozen of these notes and letters from the children.

16. See Edward Sellner, "Lay Spirituality," in *The New Dictionary of Christian Spirituality*, ed. Michael Downey [CD-ROM] (Collegeville, MN: The Liturgical Press, 2000/1993); and Kees Waajman, "Lay Spirituality," *Studies in Spirituality* 10 (2000): 5–20. Although Vatican I expressed the view that obedience to the clergy is the distinguishing feature of lay spirituality, the actual situation of Catholics in increasingly secularizing societies resulted in a number of creative initiatives by lay people and in an evolving partnership with the clergy.

17. For a more extensive treatment of Elisabeth Leseur as an exemplar of the "mixed life" tradition in Christian spirituality, see Janet K. Ruffing, "Elizabeth Leseur: Wife and Worldly Mystic," *Mystics Quarterly* 19 (March 1993): 17–25.

18. "Notebook of Resolutions," October-November 1906.

19. The entire pattern of Elisabeth's ascetical practices is shown in this first entry in the "Notebook of Resolutions."

20. Ibid.

21. Thomas A. Kselman, *Miracles and Prophecies in Nineteenth-Century France* (New Brunswick, NJ: Rutgers University Press, 1983), 93.

22. See Pierre Pourrat, *Christian Spirituality*, vol. 4, *Later Developments* (Westminster, MD: Newman Press, 1953–55), 469–518; and Ralph Gibson, *A Social History of French Catholicism 1789–1914*, Christianity and Society in the Modern World (New York: Routledge, 1989), 251–67.

23. Thérèse Martin died in 1897, and her *Story of a Soul* was published in France in 1898. Elisabeth had a copy in her library, but she does not refer to her explicitly until 1911 in the *Letters on Suffering* (Letter VI, June 7, 1911, translated herein). She does not refer to Thérèse at all in her *Journal*. Elisabeth essentially adopted the same strategy of unconditional

love in her relationship to unbelievers. Both women drew on scripture as a primary source of their spirituality. Another contemporary of Elisabeth Leseur, Charles de Foucald, became a monk in the Saharan desert, living among the Tuaregs as a loving presence. I think Thérèse of Lisieux, Charles de Foucald, and Elisabeth Leseur independently developed an approach to the Christian life that made loving presence to others central. Each responded to the particular context of his or her own life while being influenced by some of the same external sources. Certainly, Elisabeth would have appreciated Thérèse's emphasis on loving presence in one's immediate social world, which would have reinforced her own convictions on the matter.

24. Kselman, *Miracles and Prophecies in Nineteenth-Century France*, 107.

25. Elisabeth has a Mass said for the intentions of her friend Soeur Goby at the basilica (referred to in *Letters on Suffering*, Letter XIX, December 1, 1911, translated herein).

26. Leo XIII, *Annum sacrum*.

27. *Massime Eterne de S. Alfonso M. De Liguori con Florilegio de Preghiere, Sacramenti ed altre pratiche di pieta, il vespro festivo* (Milan: Winterberg, 1889). This volume included a pattern of mental prayer and suggestions for meditation for each day of the week and for some feast days; an examination of conscience; and many other prayers and litanies.

28. Among Elisabeth's personal possessions is such a missal marking her wedding: *Paroissien de la Renaissance contenant les offices des dimanches et fêtes de l'année selon le rite Romain* (Paris: Gruel Engelmann, 1883). It included the proper Collects for each Sunday in Latin and in French, and the Gospel in French only. The Ordinary of the Mass is in parallel columns of French and Latin. This is an elegant book, with each page enclosed in border designs with many full-page designs as well, gilt-edged, with silk internal lining, and Elisabeth's initials and wedding date printed in gold leaf.

29. Lagrange was the biblical scholar and theologian who founded the *École Pratique d'Etudes Bibliques (École Biblique)* in Jerusalem in 1890. He was very important in the Catholic revival of interest in scripture and ecumenism.

30. Kenneth Latourette, *The Nineteenth Century in Europe: Background and the Roman Catholic Phase*. Christianity in a Revolutionary Age 1 (New York: Harper, 1958), 346. See also, Jordan Aumann, *Christian Spirituality in the Catholic Tradition* (London: Sheed and Ward, 1980) available online, Chap. 10, p. 2.

31. Elisabeth had one volume of Ozanam's personal writings in her library (Elisabeth Leseur, *La vie spirituelle* [Paris: Gigord, 1919], 439).

32. There is still some debate about this issue among historians.

33. *La vie spirituelle*, 411–17.

34. Geneviève Duhamelet, *Le miracle de l'amour chrétien: Elisabeth Leseur 1866–1914* (Paris: P. Lethielleux, 1959), 7–8.

35. Wendy Wright, "Introduction," *Francis de Sales, Jane de Chantal—Letters of Spiritual Direction* (Mahwah, NJ: Paulist Press, 1988), 64.

36. De Sales, *Introduction to the Devout Life*, 161–67.

37. Elisabeth Leseur, *Journal d'enfant*, with an introductory letter by Cardinal Verdier, Archbishop of Paris (Paris: Gigord, 1934).

38. Elisabeth expresses reluctance in her journal to show the journal to Abbé Seguin but is rewarded with praise when she does so. She followed Seguin to Notre Dame de Paris to make her prenuptial confession on July 28, 1889 (official parish slip inside her wedding missal, Dominican Archives, Saulchoir Bibliotèque, Paris).

39. Msgr. Charles Gay, cited in Pourrat, *Christian Spirituality*, 4:494.

40. Ibid., 4:493–99.

41. Auguste Gratry, cited by Robert Morel, ed., in *Dictionnaire des mystiques et des écrivains spirituels* (Limoges: Ateliers Mellottee, 1968), 341.

42. Pourrat, *Christian Spirituality*, 4:451.

43. Jean Verbillion, s.v. Faber, Frederick William, in *The New Catholic Encyclopedia* 5 (San Francisco: McGraw Hill, 1976).

44. Duhamelet, *Le miracle de l'amour chrétien*, 98–99.

45. Unpublished letter of July 1903, cited in ibid., 98.

46. Adrien Dansette, *Religious History of Modern France*, vol. 2, *Under the Third Republic* (New York: Herder and Herder, 1961), 89.

47. Ibid., 113.

48. Duhamelet, *Le miracle de l'amour chrétien*, August 26, 1903, 119 n. 1, translation mine.

49. Dansette, *Religious History of Modern France*, 2:114.

50. For the description of Harmel's social programs within the factory setting, see ibid., 120.

51. Ibid., 124.

52. Ibid, 132.

53. Elisabeth Leseur, *Writings on Christian Vocation*, "The Christian Man," translated herein.

54. *Journal*, September 20, 1899.

55. *Journal,* July 30, 1900.

56. Elisabeth Leseur, *Writings on Christian Vocation,* "The Christian Life of Women," translated herein.

57. James F. McMillan, "Clericals, Anticlericals and the Women's Movement in France under the Third Republic," *The Historical Journal* 24 (June 1981): 365.

58. Msgr. Félix Dupanloup, *La femme studieuse,* vol. 1 (J. Gervais, n.d.).

59. Cited in McMillan, "Clericals, Anticlericals and the Women's Movement in France under the Third Republic," 365.

60. For a description of this development, see ibid., 367.

61. Ibid., 374.

62. Documents related both to the Foyer de la Jeune Fille and her participation in La Ligue des Femmes Françaises are in the Dominican Archives in Paris. See also, Félix Leseur, *Vie d'Elisabeth Leseur,* 260–63, for his description of the home for single working women that Elisabeth was able to sustain only from 1903 to 1905. The project failed because of insufficient funding. In the same chapter Félix describes Elisabeth's work with L'union familiale and with L'Union populaire catholique, a diocesan organization directed by Msgr. De Gibergues and affiliated with La Ligue des Femmes Françaises. Félix's description demonstrates the flexibility of response to the needs of each quarter. He includes dispensaries, soup kitchens, public gardens, and a clinic where professionals such as doctors or lawyers volunteered one day a week. Thus the church responded to both the material and spiritual needs of the poor in working class neighborhoods (Ibid., 269–70).

63. Gérard Cholvy and Yves-Marie Hilaire, *Histoire religieuse de la France contemporaine 1880–1930* (Toulouse: Bibliothèque Historique Privat, 1986), 2:155–56.

64. Ibid., 157, translation mine.

65. Ibid., translation mine.

66. McMillan, "Clericals, Anticlericals and the Women's Movement in France under the Third Republic," 376.

67. Emilien Lamirande, "The Communion of Saints," *The Twentieth Century Encyclopedia of Catholicism,* vol. 26, trans. A. Manson (New York: Hawthorn Books,1963), 125–26.

68. Dansette, *Religious History of Modern France,* 2:318.

69. Ibid., 317: "It was Bergson's philosophy that had the greatest influence over the whole of this period. In 1903, he laid down the main lines of the contemporary revival in metaphysical thinking. Science apprehended things only from the outside, he contended. It made possible only

a relative understanding. Metaphysics, on the other hand, reached the essential, giving an absolute understanding through intuition, considered as the effort of the contemplating mind to grasp the object, not only dispassionately, but in one intellectual movement, excluding any chain of reasoning. Bergson outlined the stages on his road to personal intuition in a letter to Père de Tonquedec, which became famous. 'In my *Essai sur les données immédiates* (1899),' he wrote, 'I stressed the existence of freedom. In *Matière et Mémoire* (1896), I succeeded, I hope, in demonstrating the reality of the soul. In *L'évolution créatice* (1907), I presented creation as a fact. From this, the existence should stand out clearly of a God freely responsible for creation and generator of both matter and life, through the evolution of the species and the constitution of human personalities.'"

70. Félix Leseur, *Vie d'Elisabeth Leseur*, 432. Maritain was one of the principal philosophers responsible for the revival of Thomist philosophy in the first half of the twentieth century. He was baptized in 1906, largely through the influence of Léon Bloy.

71. Lucie Félix-Fauré Goyau was the wife of Georges Goyau and a Catholic feminist and a poet within the Catholic revival. Duhamelet asserts that Elisabeth was familiar with Lucie Félix-Fauré's writings, particularly *Choses d'âmes:* "Toute âme est le levier qui soulève le monde, pas une ne s'élève sans que le monde soit soulève" (Duhamelet, *Le miracle de l'amour chrétien*, 55). Elisabeth paraphrased this line "Toute âme qui s'élève élève le monde," which she wrote in Juliette's journal.

72. Dansette, *Religious History of Modern France*, 2:320. Goyau gave this assessment as cited in Dansette, "With Huysmans and Baumann, this writing acquired an exegesis of suffering. With Léon Bloy, Claudel, and Rette a philosophy of life, and with Péguy an understanding of the life of the Church" (320). Although Dansette disagrees with Goyau and makes more distinctions among the way these writers applied Catholic doctrine to social concerns, Elisabeth was clearly influenced by these Catholic intellectual currents.

73. Dom Germain Morin, cited in Lamirande, "The Communion of Saints," 24.

74. Aquinas, cited in Lamirande, "The Communion of Saints," 29; see Aquinas, *Commentary on the Creed* (1273), concluding section.

75. *Letters on Suffering*, Letter XXVIII, April 20, 1912, translated herein.

76. I strongly contest Valerie Raoul's interpretation of Elisabeth's journal writing and her offering of her sufferings for her husband's conversion as emotional blackmail. Raoul reduces Elisabeth's mystical sense of the communion of saints to purely commercial metaphors. Elisabeth

does not write her journal for Félix's benefit. She agrees to save the journal in order to comfort Félix rather than to coerce his conversion, a strategy that was not in harmony with her deep respect for people's individual paths (see Valerie Raoul, "Women's Diaries as Life-Savings: Who Decides Whose Life Is Saved?" *Biography* 24, no. 1 [2001]: 140–51).

77. *Journal et pensées pour chaque jour de Madame Elisabeth Leseur* (Paris: Gigord, 1927), 322–23, translation mine.

78. Ibid., September 19, 1899.

79. Henri Brémond, *Manuel illustre de la Littérature Catholique en France de 1870 à nos jours* (Paris: Editions Spes, 1925), liii.

80. Ibid.

81. "We complacently scorn those who hold different beliefs and think ourselves scarcely obliged to extend our charity to them. We consider that Jews, Protestants, or atheists are hardly our brothers and sisters in the true sense, beloved brothers and sisters for whom we should sacrifice ourselves and embrace with a delicate love. In relation to them we seem to think anything is allowed, even calumny sometimes, and we seem less concerned with convincing them than with offending them. The gentle words of Jesus, and of Saint Paul, too, declare that in the future there will be neither Jews nor Gentiles; all that will be forgotten (Gal 3:28). Let those who have inscribed the great law of love on their hearts at least learn to practice it toward all their brothers and sisters, whoever they may be" ("Daily Thoughts," p. 136 herein).

82. *Quanto conficiamur,* cited in Lamirande, "The Communion of Saints," 97.

83. *Journal,* November 28, 1900.

84. Ibid.

85. See Janet K. Ruffing, "Physical Illness: A Mystically Transformative Element in the Life of Elisabeth Leseur," *Spiritual Life* (Winter 1994): 1–10.

86. *Lettres sur la souffrance,* Letter XLII, September 8, 1912.

87. *Letters on Suffering,* Letter XLV, October 7, 1912, translated herein.

88. John Dunne, *The Reasons of the Heart* (Notre Dame, IN: University of Notre Dame Press, 1979), 56, 62.

89. See Maureen Flynn, "The Spiritual Uses of Pain in Spanish Mystics," *Journal of the American Academy of Religion* 64 (Summer 1996): 257–78.

90. *Letters on Suffering,* Letter XXVIII, April 20, 1912, translated herein.

91. Ibid.

92. *Catherine of Siena: The Dialogue*, trans. Suzanne Noffke (Mahwah, NJ: Paulist Press, 1980), D.3.

93. Ibid., D.4.

94. Ibid., D.5.

95. Ibid., D.7. See David B. Morris's discussion of sacramental suffering versus modern pain in *The Culture of Pain* (Berkeley and Los Angeles: University of California, 1991), especially chapter 6: "Through pain Catherine grasps a vision beyond pain—where nothing matters except bringing the soul closer to an otherworldly truth. Modern pain...chains us down to the material world. It keeps us centered in the flesh. It places us within the secular circles of medical science. The visionary pain of Catherine, Teresa, and Sebastian by contrast, contains the power to transcend the world and the flesh. In providing release into a pure communion with the divine, it becomes not something to be cured or even endured but rather a means of knowledge, offering access to an otherwise inaccessible understanding. Visionary pain employs the body in order to free us from the body. It initiates or accompanies an experience that escapes the time-bound world of human suffering. The visionary, as Saint Catherine cautions, does not court pain but rather welcomes it when it inevitably arrives, unsought as a sign that always points beyond itself. It gestures toward an ecstatic union with God in which suffering is finally indistinguishable from love (135).

96. Pamela Smith describes a narcotic effect of engagement in intellectual or creative work. Elisabeth may have discovered the effect of mental concentration quite early in her life and used it regularly to cope with her pain (see Pamela Smith, "Chronic Pain and Creative Possibility: A Psychological Phenomenon Confronts Theologies of Suffering," in *Broken and Whole: Essays on Religion and the Body*, ed. Susan Ross and Maureen A. Tilley, Annual Publication of the College Theology Society 39 [Lanham, MD: University Press of America, 1995], 166).

97. Dorothy Soelle, *Suffering*, trans. Everett R. Kalin (Philadelphia: Fortress Press, 1975).

98. Patricia Wismer, "For Women in Pain: A Feminist Theology of Suffering," in *In the Embrace of God*, ed. Ann O'Hara Graff, 138–57 (Maryknoll, NY: Orbis Books, 1995). For a very nuanced discussion of these issues, see Kristine M. Ranka, *Women and the Value of Suffering: An Aw(e)ful Rowing toward God* (Collegeville, MN: Glazier/Liturgical Press, 1998).

99. Dorothy Soelle, *The Silent Cry: Mysticism and Resistance*, trans. Barbara and Martin Rumscheidt (Minneapolis: Fortress Press, 2001), 133–56.

100. These are held in the Postulator General's Office of the Dominicans at Santa Sabina in Rome. There are five bound volumes of certified originals. Two volumes are addressed to immediate family members, the third volume to assorted friends and other family members, and the fourth volume to Jeanne Alcan. This volume includes about ten letters not included in the *Lettres à des incroyants*. A fifth volume is devoted to Madame Duvent, the painter's wife. There are 170 letters to Charles Duvent included in the third volume.

101. Réginald Garrigou-Lagrange taught fundamental, dogmatic, and spiritual theology from 1909 to 1960 at the Pontifical University of St. Thomas Aquinas in Rome. He promoted the universal call to holiness, infused contemplation, and the mystical life as normal ways of holiness. These were the views officially adopted by Vatican Council II.

Journal and *Daily Thoughts*

1. These handwritten copybooks had not yet been found in the Dominican Archives in Paris before this volume went to press.

2. Prayer written by Elisabeth Leseur at the request of her sister Juliette.

3. Auguste Gratry (1805–72) wrote *Les Sources* (Dourniol and Tèqui, 1862).

4. Pierre was her nephew, the second son of her husband's brother.

5. Roger was the eldest son of Elisabeth's brother Pierre.

6. Auguste Gratry, *De la connaissance de Dieu* (Paris: Gervaise, 1881).

7. Jougne is a village in the Department of Doubs, near the Swiss border, where the Leseurs spent each summer from 1902 on. Her last summer there was in 1912.

8. Adolphe was Elisabeth's mother's cousin (see her letter to Jeanne Alcan, August 12, 1902, p. 197 herein.)

9. Maurice was her younger sister Amélie Duron's son, who had diphtheria.

10. Abbé Jean Viollet was the founder of the the Association of Christian Marriage and the vicar of Notre Dame du Rosaire de Plaisance. He came for lunch and dinner from time to time at the Leseurs and talked with them about his many projects. Elisabeth helped him organize some musical and literary soirees, involving their friends

performing for these benefits. For names of some who took part, see Félix Leseur, *Vie d'Elisabeth Leseur* (Paris: Gigord, 1930), 257.

11. Elisabeth accompanied Félix to Moulins, where he was involved in a lawsuit. While he was in court, she made the excursion to the Visitation Convent at Paray-le-Monial, where Sr. Margaret Mary Alacoque (1647–90) received her revelations about devotion to the Sacred Heart.

12. The death of her sister Juliette from tuberculosis.

13. Elisabeth did so a year later: *Une Âme (souvenirs recueillis par une soeur)* (Paris-Auteuil: Impriméries des Orphélins-apprentis, 1906). This volume was never sold, but was distributed privately among friends and family.

14. Louis Veuillot (1813–83) was the author of novels, poems, and polemical essays, and editor of the periodical *L'Univers Religieux*.

15. Marie François Xavier Bichat (1771–1802) was a French pioneer in scientific histology and pathological anatomy.

16. This echoes Maxim 38 of Teresa of Avila: "If possible avoid revealing your interior devotion. 'My secret is for myself,' said St. Francis (of Assisi) and St. Bernard" (*Minor Works of St. Teresa: Conceptions of the Love of God, Exclamations, Maxims and Poems*, trans. Benedictines of Stanbrook [London: Thomas Baker, 1908], 194).

17. Previous translations of this phrase would be, "To restore or reestablish all things in Christ."

18. Dates that appear in parentheses were supplied by Félix Leseur.

19. She had just celebrated her forty-first birthday.

20. This is a paraphrase of Maxim 55 of Teresa of Avila: "Be indulgent toward others, rigorous to yourself" (*Minor Works of St. Teresa*, 196).

21. The couple moved from 3 Rue Argenson to 16 Rue de Marignan, where Elisabeth died.

22. Either in late 1910 or early 1911 Elisabeth noticed a small tumor on her chest. Her doctors required her to wear a painfully tight apparatus about her chest, hoping to eliminate the need for surgery.

23. This prayer marks the pact Elisabeth made with God to offer her prayer and sufferings to obtain the conversion of her husband and particular graces for other family members (see especially entries in Part 2 of the *Journal* for October 19 and November 5, 1911; March 6, 1912; and June 14, 1913).

24. Palm Sunday, the day before her surgery for breast cancer.

25. Father Joseph Hébert, OP, instructed a colleague of Félix Leseur's, and Elisabeth served as the young man's godmother for his bap-

tism on March 25, 1903. Shortly after the baptism, Elisabeth began to make her confession to Father Hébert and seek spiritual direction from him.

26. Her sister Juliette's death in 1905.

27. Frederick William Faber (1814–63), English Oratorian and hymn writer, who converted to Catholicism under the influence of John Henry Cardinal Newman. He was the author of many widely read devotional books, including *All for Jesus* (1853) and *Growth in Holiness* (1854).

28. See "Notebook of Resolutions," February 21, 1912.

29. Maurice was her sister Amélie's son. In playing with a toy gun, which he charged with caps, he badly injured his right hand, and complications were feared that would have led to the amputation of his arm. Ultimately, he was cured, and Elisabeth went with her sister and nephew to thank the Blessed Virgin at Lourdes in June 1912.

30. Marie had met the man she would eventually marry in August 1915. When the couple met, he was still a student at the École Polytechnique.

31. During these weeks she experienced the first attack of the metastatic cancer that was to reappear in July and cause her death after ten months of suffering.

32. Marie Duron announced her engagement officially May 14, 1913.

33. Elisabeth had been confined to bed since July 6. When she wrote these lines in bed, in pencil, she had already passed through very painful crises of suffering. She grew worse, and she was seriously ill at the end of August and the beginning of September. In October she was so much better that she was believed to be cured. On November 12 she became very ill again.

34. These were the last lines Elisabeth wrote in the *Journal*. Her condition deteriorated a few days later, although her suffering lasted for four more months. She died on Sunday, May 3, 1914, at ten in the morning, surrounded by her family.

35. This is a paraphrase from memory referring to 2 Corinthians 4:5–7.

36. In this instance, the Douay Rheims version of the scripture differs remarkably from the RSV. The RSV renders this passage, "Get behind me, Satan, for you are not on the side of God but on the side of men" (Mark 8:33).

37. April 13, 1905 is the date of her sister Juliette's death.

38. The version translated here was recopied and slightly modified by Elisabeth on January 26, 1911.

Writings on Christian Vocation

1. Unpublished letter, September 10, 1901, Dominican Archives, Bibliothèque Saulchoir, Paris. In this letter Elisabeth talks about how she sees the spark of God in every human being and encourages her painter friend to use his "artist's glance [that] knows how to discover some corner of light, of harmonious color." She tells him to "become an artist of humanity."

2. Written shortly after Elisabeth's sister Juliette had died in 1905. Juliette was Marie's godmother and asked Elisabeth to fulfill this responsibility for her. Marie's first communion was on May 25, 1905.

3. Elisabeth is citing herself here. She wrote these lines in Juliette's journal.

4. Blaise Pascal, *Pensées*, no. 173. Blaise Pascal (1623–62), a brilliant intellectual and prose genius, recorded a profound mystical experience in 1654 that led him to probe the relationship between faith and reason among other philosophical and religious issues in his writings after his conversion to Jansenism.

5. Molière was the stage name of Jean-Baptiste Poquélin (1622–44), the brilliant seventeenth-century actor and playwright who invented of a new style of comedy that relied on a double vision—the true and the specious, or the normal and abnormal. He was brilliant at juxtaposing the intelligent and the pedantic, often making women represent the pedantic.

6. In this passage Elisabeth offers a Christian interpretation of the revolutionary slogan: *Liberté, Equalité, et Fraternité*.

7. André Duron, Elisabeth's nephew, made his first communion on May 17, 1906.

8. Elisabeth accompanied her nephew to his first communion retreat instructions and took notes for him in another little notebook.

9. L'Abbé Quignard. This motto, "to pray and to work," is taken from the *Rule of Saint Benedict*.

10. Although Elisabeth had only one niece, she had several nephews on both sides of the family. She planned to develop these ideas further in the future as her other nephews grew older. André Duron was the oldest among her nephews.

11. See pages 20–23 in the General Introduction.

12. Montalembert's monument is located quite near St. Germain des Prés, the church where Elisabeth made her first communion and in which she was married.

Letters to Unbelievers

1. Unpublished papers, n.d., Dominican Archives, Paris.

2. Emile and Jeanne Alcan's oldest son.

3. Elisabeth and Félix had just built a home in this village near the Swiss border in a beautiful place and had moved in for the first time with Elisabeth's family and Félix's mother.

4. Elisabeth is referring to a nickname her husband gave her taken from a novel by Anatole France, *The Amethyst Ring*. In the novel the author describes a burial service in a provincial town and reports a conversation among the people following the cortege. The doctor, Fornerol, speaks these lines, which inspired Félix's ironic application to Elisabeth."All my patients, he says, believe in the immortality of the soul, and do not intend to jest about that above. The fine people, like the Tintelleries like the rest, want to be immortal. It would grieve them to tell them that maybe they won't be. You see Madam Péchin, who came from the fruit seller's with tomatoes in her shopping basket? You would say to her: 'Madam Péchin, you will taste the celestial bliss for billions of centuries, but you are not at all immortal. You will last longer than the stars and even when the nebulae formed themselves into suns and the suns become stars, and in the inconceivable duration of these ages you will be bathed in delights and glory. But you are not at all immortal, Madam Péchin.' If you speak to her in this way, she will only think that the point you have made is good news. And if, against all possibility, your discussion relied on such proofs that added faith to it she would be desolate, she would fall into despair, the poor old lady, and weeping, she would eat her tomatoes. Madam Péchin wants to be immortal. All my patients want to be immortal" (215–16). Félix used this passage to ridicule Elisabeth's faith by applying it to her. Elisabeth, in her gentle goodness, bore this attack with good humor and a smile.

5. *Clerical* in the French.

6. Elisabeth refers to the passage of the Associations Law in 1902, which was directed against religious congregations, making it very difficult for them to continue their work, especially their schools. She wrote in more detail about her experience in Jougne to her friend, Charles Duvent, the painter. "Listen to this: The superior general of the Sisters of the Charity of Besançon, when the vote was taken on the law of associations went to find the prefect to ask him what she ought to do. He said to her that given the Congregation had kept the previous laws they had nothing to fear and nothing to do. The superior went to Paris to find Waldeck-Rousseau, who used the same language. She returned with

peace of mind and in ten days they will expel them. What do you say to that?" (unpublished letter, July 27, 1902, Dominican Archives, Paris).

7. This woman had just lost her husband.

8. Alice Sachs was in the process of divorcing her husband, the first divorce in Elisabeth's circle of friends.

9. *The War of the Fortress*, in a series called *The Future War*, written by Commandant Driant under the pseudonym of Danrit. He died in battle during WWI before the battle of Verdun and so did not see the return of Alsace and Lorraine to France that his books had predicted.

10. Jeanne's mother.

11. She refers to her younger sister Amélie's serious illness.

12. This letter was also published by Félix under the title "Advice on Living a Spiritual Life for Unbelievers" in *La Vie Spirituelle*. I have placed it in the context of the correspondence and the letter that immediately preceded it.

13. Blaise Pascal, *Pensées*, no. 173.

14. At the time, she was *Directrice de l'Ecole Municipale Superieur Sophie German*.

15. Aimée replied in part to this letter: "The profusion of beauty, the variety of life, hidden under this transparency, the wondrous transformation of matter that elaborates it in this huge mass, are for you proofs of the existence of God. And you are serene, and you are infinitely tolerant and good. Seeing these waves that, for centuries, follow one another, crashing on the beach, and the huge patterns that erase themselves, I see they move with the same indifference as the wreckage that floats on the surface, plants, animals, and people—in which all mixed together is destruction, life, and death. Here I find supreme equality...It profoundly calms me in showing me the unity of everything around me, and it pushes me to solidarity and to love. In this perpetual movement of the surf, I also see how you conceive of the immortality of the soul; this sustains and comforts you, the future life that you prepare for splendidly in sowing the best that is in you and that renews you endlessly. I do not believe in an immortal soul; I believe that we live our immortality at the same time as we live our lives, and that it is made from that which we have given of ourselves, consciously or unconsciously. This is why I work to give myself only to that which means something to me" (February 8, 1905).

16. This letter was written shortly after Elisabeth's sister Juliette died.

17. Cepoy is located in Loiret.

18. Pécaut (1828–98) was an educational reformer and a liberal Protestant. In 1880 he became deputy inspector general for education

and later inspector general for primary instruction. He organized the *École Normale Superieure* to train women teachers and administrators for primary schools. Aimée Fiévet was one of his pupils at Fontenay and became an inspector of schools. These reforms were interested in removing religious influence from the schools as much as in promoting female education.

19. She had just been appointed inspector of the girls' schools in Paris for 1907 and 1908.

20. The official announcement of Yvonne Le Gros's engagement to Félix Le Dantec was December 26, 1904.

21. Félix Le Dantec had become ill and left Paris for a while in order to take care of himself. This was on the eve of the day originally chosen for the wedding.

22. Mamie was the servant who cared for the Arrighi children and with whom they kept in contact as adults.

23. See reference to Goyau in the General Introduction. He was noted for his books on social Catholicism and on German religion.

24. Elisabeth refers to the serious events that unfolded in three agricultural regions. The people held the government responsible for a drop in wine prices caused, in their opinion, by fraud, which they felt the government and ministries ignored. The regions in question broke off all ties with the central government, and one part of the infantry supported the strikers. Peace was restored with great difficulty and the 17th regiment of the infantry was disarmed and then sent to Tunisia.

25. The cemetery attached to an Augustinian convent in which some of the more illustrious victims of the Terror in 1793 were buried. It is in the 20th *arrondissement* near the Place de la Nation today.

26. This notation is in the original letter. Its significance is unclear.

27. Anne Sophie Swetchine (1782–1857), Russian mystic and writer, who lived in Paris.

28. This letter contains some of Elisabeth's thoughts after she read Félix Le Dantec's book *L'Athéisme*, which appeared toward the end of 1906.

29. Elisabeth refers to a book by Le Dantec published about two years earlier, *Les influences ancestrale.*

30. Elisabeth is referring to a passage in Le Dantec's book: "Why, under these conditions, having written this book, if it displeases so many people, will they turn against me, one group at least among them, up to the present, having received my previous writings favorably? It is difficult for a convinced atheist to have a distant goal; I do not have one; I am not one

of those who thinks that the apple tree has a goal in giving its apples; it gives its apples following its nature: I act like the apple tree" (*Athéism*, 16).

31. In this dialogue with Le Dantec, Elisabeth confronts a new form of intellectual life more characteristic of the twentieth century than of the nineteenth. Renan's agnosticism rejected Catholicism but preserved its moral base. Le Dantec's agnosticism led him to a scientifically based atheism that was more resistant to religious influence. Elisabeth seems to be able to understand his position rather easily and to describe realms of experience to which he has no access.

32. Le Dantec replied to this letter on July 29, 1907: "Moreover, it is certain that we do not understand one another; for you, what is good is inseparable from what is true. For me, truth and social utility are two entirely separate things, often antagonistic to one another. But we will continue to discuss these things joyfully, without hope of convincing one another, because we are both absolutely sincere. Today, let me only say to you that even if your dialectic does not make a dent in my positions, I remain full of admiration at the loftiness of your nature. If there were more people like you, the questions that divide humanity would never be posed."

Letters on Suffering

1. *Extrait du Nécrologe, communauté des soeurs hospitalières*, Archives of the Hôtel-Dieu de Beaune. I wonder if this civic honor was perhaps a result of Sister Marie Goby's expert nursing of war wounded. The plain outside of Beaune was the site of a massive American field hospital, to which the wounded were moved from the front lines. Her necrology explicitly mentions the testimony from the French military at her funeral.

2. This refers to the December 17, 1910, letter of the Sister Marie Goby, in which she describes the first communion and death of little Marie Ballard.

3. Elisabeth's account of her sister Juliette's death.

4. The location of the Leseur's summer home near Switzerland.

5. Elisabeth had surgery on April 10, 1911, to remove a malignant growth on her breast, for which she subsequently had to have radiation treatments. From this time on she offers the suffering caused by this terminal illness for her husband's conversion.

6. Sunday, August 13, 1911. Elisabeth Leseur, her husband, and her niece Marie, who went with them to Jougne, had arrived the night before, Saturday evening, at Beaune. On Sunday morning, Elisabeth went

to the community mass at seven o'clock at the Hôtel-Dieu and received communion there with the sisters. She spent the entire morning at the hospital, alone with Sister Goby, whom she finally met in person. They hadn't met during Elisabeth's first visit to the hospital in 1910. At the same time her husband took her niece on a tour of the town and to Mass at the parish church. Thus it was that Sister Goby came to know the woman who quickly became, as she wrote later, "my soul-sister, a holy woman, and an incomparable friend." Elisabeth, enriched and delighted from the morning visit, returned to the hotel for lunch with her husband and her niece. They all attended Vespers and the community Benediction, and her husband was impressed with the liturgical chant and the simple grandeur of the Divine Office. They spent the afternoon in the hospital garden with Sister Goby. In one letter Elisabeth refers to this day as one of the happiest in her life. See Elisabeth Leseur's letter quoted in her husband's introduction to the French edition, 79ff. (F. L. note). The notation in parentheses indicates translations and sometimes abbreviations of Félix Leseur's original notes in the French edition of the letters.

7. These were patients Sister Goby took care of in the hospital. She was particularly close to them, and through her, Elisabeth became interested in them as well.

8. In sending Elisabeth a photo of the Shrine of Blessed Jean Vianney, the Curé of Ars, Sister Goby wrote in a letter from Ars dated August 28, 1911: "Here I am in Ars with my dear mother; we've just arrived. You're very much on my mind, and I will enjoy praying for you at length in this blessed sanctuary, which is such an incomparable place of prayer and recollection. I will have Mass offered for you on Wednesday and will light a candle at the Shrine of the Blessed Curé of Ars for your intentions. I think I can say 'our,' since your intentions have also become mine" (F. L. note).

9. Félix's conversion.

10. Unknown to Elisabeth Leseur, Sister Goby had been back at the hospital from Ars since August 30 (F. L. note).

11. Sister Germain Marion was a sister at the hospital that Elisabeth hadn't yet met, but she knew how helpful she was and that she was a friend of Sister Goby's. Sister Germain had a sibling who was also a religious at the hospital (F. L. note).

12. A work that gave a thorough and detailed history of the hospital at Beaune (F. L. note).

13. In a letter dated August 16, 1911, Sister Goby wrote to Elisabeth Leseur: "Would it be indiscreet of me to call you my Friend? Tell me very honestly" (F. L. note).

14. Patients assigned to the room under Sister Goby's care and in whom Elisabeth was interested (F. L. note).

15. The religious from this hospital were given two weeks vacation each year that they could spend with their families. Sister Goby planned to spend hers with her mother in Savigny, a small village near Beaune (F. L. note).

16. Elisabeth Leseur and her husband were making a short trip to the shores of Lake Geneva in Switzerland, where her brother-in-law and his wife lived, then on to Lake Thoune by the Oberland Bernois train, then returning to Jougne, once again passing by Lake Geneva (F. L. note).

17. Elisabeth is referring to the lymphangitis in her right arm, a result of her cancer surgery. She was confined to bed for two weeks and brought by stages from Jougne to Paris.

18. This was a relic of a Poor Clare sister who had died, apparently recognized for her holiness, Sister Marie Céline of the Presentation, from the Bordeaux monastery. Sister Goby described the relic in a letter to Elisabeth Leseur dated October 1, 1911: "A friend of mine, a Poor Clare at Paray-le-Monial, gave me a relic of a little saint of her Order who had died recently after performing many miracles. I am hurrying to send it to you to put on your ailing arm. You will wear it, won't you? For my part, I'll continue to pray and have prayers said to this little saint, as well as to her heavenly companion, Sister Thérèse of the Child Jesus" (F. L. note).

19. Elisabeth frequently asks Sister Goby to pray for her mother. The latter, a loving mother, was certainly an excellent Christian and a practicing Catholic. However, her active nature had difficulty adapting itself to the life of meditation as understood by Elisabeth, and her heart, so good and so sorely tried by grief, wasn't capable of the complete acceptance and peaceful resignation that Elisabeth would have wanted. These were the graces that Elisabeth requested and asked for her mother, for whom she had a daughter's loving affection (F. L. note).

20. Sister Goby was having serious trouble with her eyesight. She described this in a letter to Elisabeth dated November 3, 1911. "My eyes have been bothering me for quite some time, but I hadn't mentioned it to anyone. Just recently, as I realized my vision was getting worse, I told our mistress [the superior of her house], who immediately sent me to Dijon to see a specialist. He told me that I had extremely weak eyesight and also said it was a dangerous situation. He prescribed a month's treatment under his care. So I was forced to make a choice, remain at Dijon or take two trains each day to get there. I chose the latter because, even

though it's inconvenient, especially in winter, I won't have to leave my Hôtel-Dieu, my sisters, or my sick. How effective will this treatment be? I don't know, but from the beginning I put myself entirely into the all-powerful hands of our heavenly Father, knowing that everything that comes from him is good and will benefit me. I find myself now more than ever your sister and friend, my dearest Elisabeth, because God has called me to suffer in the same way that you have been called. We are made holy through the cross. Let us pray and accept it with complete confidence" (F. L. note).

21. Community retreat: Sister Goby wrote to Elisabeth on November 3, 1911: "Our retreat begins on the fifteenth and will end the twenty-first. I find such joy in these days of recollection and prayer. Pray for me that I may benefit from them. And you know I will speak often to Jesus about you and those you love in this world" (F. L. note).

22. A patient in Sister Goby's ward and in whom she was interested, as noted earlier. Sister Goby writes about her in her letter to Elisabeth of November 3, 1911: "We had a touching feast of All Saints. All my sick received communion and seemed happy. We took Louise into the chapel on a stretcher on wheels so she could be there for Office, which made her very happy. Yesterday, they brought her little six-year-old daughter to her. As I watched the little one, I thought I might ask you to send her a little apron or some other item for New Year's Day. That would make her mother so happy. She often asks about you. It would be a real act of charity, since they are really very poor" (F. L. note).

23. See Letter XV. These are the words of Blessed Margaret Mary's prayers entitled "Offering of the Merits of Our Lord, Jesus Christ": "My God, I offer you your beloved Son in thanksgiving for all the gifts you have given me; for my petitions, my offering, my adoration, all my resolutions, and finally I offer him to you as my love, my all." "Receive him, Eternal Father, in return for all that you want from me, since I have nothing worthy of you except him whom you have given to me with such love" (F. L. note).

24. Earlier Elisabeth had invited Sister Goby to stay at the Leseur home. At the time, however, most women religious would have been required to stay in a convent. Although Sister Goby's community was more flexible than most, it probably occurred to Elisabeth that her friend might be more comfortable in a convent than in a private home, so she thoughtfully arranged for that possibility.

25. Sister Goby responded to this on February 1, 1912: "Louise for all practical purposes left the hospital to go home. But unfortunately she'll be returning in a few weeks since there's no hope for her recovery.

She wrote this morning telling me how happy she was to be back with her husband, who's a little freer during the winter months, and with her lovely little daughter. The poor woman! Her patience and Christian resignation are admirable. Are you aware that a woman from Volnay who takes care of Louise is someone you know? She is Madame Delaplanche, whose daughter Madame Raoul lives in Paris. This is a happy coincidence because we can talk together about you" (F. L. note).

26. Sister Goby wrote a very loving note to Elisabeth on April 12, 1912, honoring Juliette's April 13 death anniversary.

27. Louise was ill again. Sister Goby had written Elisabeth, March 14, 1912: "Our poor Louise came back to us a few days ago, still ill and still resigned. Jeanne Delaplanche and I have promised to send her to Lourdes with Dijon's pilgrimage."

28. Sister Goby had just been reassigned and had written to tell Elisabeth June 2, 1912: "I have left, not without regret, St. Hugue Hall and its interesting surgical cases and here I am in charge of the women's medical unit. It's a school of patience because these are the worse cases, therefore the most demanding and the most tiring. I'm counting on the good God to help me and to give me that tireless goodness that I want to have for my poor sick. It's really very good to obey because you're sure you're doing God's will, and this certainty eases all the pains. Also, in spite of the fact that I feel regret at leaving and am a little apprehensive about the new duties that await me, a deep sense of peace dominates all" (F. L. note).

29. Elisabeth's nephew, Maurice Duron, injured himself with his capgun, getting some of the cardboard in his finger. This finger became infected and required surgery.

30. *Les Georgiques Chrétiennes* by Francis Jammes, which had just been published (F. L. note).

31. At the same time Elisabeth was at Lourdes, Sister Goby was at Paray-le Monial, whence she sent this note on June 21, 1912: "My dear Elisabeth, more than ever I am very intimately united with you, since I too have the tender joy of spending these two days at the sanctuary of Paray! May the Sacred Heart and the Immaculate Virgin shower on us and on all those who are dear to us the gifts of their tenderness and love! With all my heart I pray for you and your intentions. Thanks for not forgetting me. Yours in the Heart of Jesus" (F. L. note).

32. Marie died July 5, 1887. Sister Goby in her letter of July 11 told Elisabeth: "I did not forget the anniversary of your dear sister Marie's death. She bequeathed me her heart to love you, my dear Elisabeth, I feel it more each day." She also mentioned her patient: "Louise will leave for Lourdes with the pilgrimage on July 30; she will be

going to ask the holy virgin for the cure that the doctors are powerless to give her. What a wonderful miracle if she were to return cured! I recommend her very specially to your loving prayers" (F. L. note).

33. *Une âme*, dedicated to her sister Juliette (F. L. note).

34. Marie had met the young man that she was to marry three years later.

35. Sister Goby wrote Elisabeth on October 1, 1912: "Your fine letter caught up with me in Savigny where I still am with my dear mother, who is only now beginning to be a little better. She has had a very serious relapse, which really upset me. She is recovering so slowly that, like you, Elisabeth, I am really afraid of the winter. And then I dread the moment when I have to leave her, and I am very upset just thinking about it" (F. L. note).

36. In the same letter of October 1, 1912, Sister Goby told Elisabeth: "I have two very interesting patients in Savigny that I go to see whenever it is possible to leave Mother. They are lung patients, both of them very edifying. Two very different situations, but two equally beautiful people. One is a young man, twenty-nine years old, very poor in terms of money, but very rich in merits. He is dying happy and smiling, speaking only of Jesus, talking ceaselessly with him, offering him all his sufferings without ever complaining. He is admirable! The other is [a woman] spending her vacation at her mother's chateau. She is fifty years old and is also suffering from tuberculosis. She is a real saint; perfectly patient and serene, always self-forgetful, thinking constantly of others, and living a most intimate life with our Lord! Oh! how holy and ready for heaven are these two people! I asked them to pray for me and for you too" (F. L. note).

37. Sister Marie Goby had just written to Elisabeth on November 3, 1912: "The good God has had compassion for me and heard my prayer. Since yesterday the doctor tells me my dear mother is out of danger. Oh, what a relief; it seems to me that I am alive again. Despite the fact that I am extremely tired, I do not feel tired anymore. The phlebitis has passed, and the stone that was carried to the lungs and had really threatened the heart seems to be back in circulation. My dear patient is extremely weak, but I hope with skillful care to bring her back up again. No doubt that will be a long and difficult road. But the question of time is nothing; the main thing is to be able to get there. I have confidence in God, and I believe he will finish what he has started and leave my beloved mother with me. Poor Maman! Would you believe that she is almost disappointed to see herself coming back to life? She was so ready to die! She had received the last rites with such peace, calm, and serenity! I spent

some really difficult days during which I truly learned what suffering is! It seems to me that I did not know it until then, and yet I had already suffered! But nothing can be compared with the sorrow that you feel when you see those you love more than yourself suffering and in pain. In those painful moments your two letters were very tender and consoling to me! How well you know how to say the right word to relieve or encourage. With what delicacy you touch the wounded heart and soul. Really, my Elisabeth, you have the gift of knowing how to soothe our wounds and make them sting less! If ever I have loved you and have thanked God for having put you in my path, it was during these times of suffering that I just went through!... While I was suffering, I offered many tears for your dear intentions. Being nearer to Jesus since I was on the cross, I often spoke to him about you and those you love....God be with you, my dear Elisabeth. I am scribbling these lines near my good mother, whom I never leave day or night" (F. L. note).

38. This letter was written to Sister Goby in response to a terrible dilemma that she was going through. She was the beloved, only child of an aging widowed mother, whom she loved dearly. Her mother was more than seventy-six years old in 1912, was living alone in the neighboring village of Savigny, and had just survived a very serious illness, which left her quite weak. Sister Marie Goby cared for her mother with all a daughter's devotion. As a result of the depression that followed, she had a very understandable moment of hesitation when she feared leaving her only recently recovered mother in order to resume her life in the convent and in the hospital. She wondered where her duty was for the moment—to stay with her mother or return to the Hôtel-Dieu. She confided this hesitation to Elisabeth and asked her for advice (F. L. note). Letter L is Elisabeth's response. When Félix wanted to publish Elisabeth's letters to her, Sister Goby gave permission for all except this letter. She worried that her vocational crisis might potentially scandalize others and mar the reputation of her community. Félix assured her otherwise and sought the advice of other religious, including Elisabeth's confessor, Père Joseph Hébert, OP, who strongly supported including this letter because of its potential to help other religious who might read it. For a more detailed discussion, see *Lettres sur la souffrance*, 264–66 n. 1, as well as Félix Leseur's "Introduction" to this volume (Paris: Gigord, 1919). Sister Marie Goby's letter to Elisabeth is not in the Dominican Archives in Paris with the rest of the original correspondence. The community to which Sister Goby belonged had the practice of making renewable annual vows rather than perpetual vows. The founder of the hospital wanted the sisters to be free to leave the community if they no longer

wanted to care for the poor (Alain Roels, *Beaune et ses hospices* [Dijon: Bourgogne Magazine, 1996], 30).

39. Sister Goby's mother had had an accident that could have been serious. On Christmas Eve she had fallen backward and had injured her leg, the one with phlebitis. This complication luckily did not have any serious side effects (F. L. note).

40. Elisabeth Leseur was writing from her bed (F. L. note).

41. Sister Goby wrote a letter to Elisabeth on April 2, 1913: "Here I am again condemned to not reading anymore, nor writing, and doing as little hand work as possible. In about two weeks I will go back to the doctor. What will he tell me? I am a bit apprehensive about this visit. While waiting I am following your advice, and I am taking care of my poor eyes. So why don't I have a more contemplative soul? If you knew how I suffer from my poverty on that point! For at the feet of the Lord, not being able to read, I am more easily distracted and often very sleepy. I am ashamed to tell you this sad truth. Pray for me, my Elisabeth, so that the gaze of my soul may become so luminous that without external help it suffices to fix my inner eye and my heart on our beloved Jesus" (F. L. note).

42. In this same letter of April 2, 1913, Sister Marie Goby told Elisabeth, while speaking to her about her mother: "I have had to spend two days this week near my poor mother because material concerns had caused another heart attack. Moved and grateful for your letter, which was so pleasant and delicate, she asked me to thank you for it and to tell you about all the good you had done for her. Her poor hand shakes so badly that it is impossible for her to write, but often she prays for you. My dear mother does not suspect that I again have tired eyes. Why upset her?" (F. L. note).

43. After a period of fairly good health, Elisabeth was slightly tired at the end of June. Nevertheless, she and her husband believed that it was only a passing incident, and she accompanied her husband to Belgium on June 29, 1913. Her husband was a member of the Jury for the Exposition of Ghent. They both hoped that this little trip and the rest that she would have, together with the change of air, would do her good. In Ghent, fatigue persisted. Sometimes she was better, but the fatigue became more pronounced at the end of the stay. Elisabeth could nevertheless make a little detour in Brussels on the way back to Paris. But scarcely back home, she was seized by the same symptoms she had had in March and became bedridden on July 7, 1913. During the whole month of July these symptoms were not alarming enough to make them think it was a serious illness. Elisabeth and her husband made arrangements for their usual stay in Jougne and for a visit to Beaune, especially since

Elisabeth seemed to improve toward the end of the month. They even left Paris on August 1 to visit some friends in the suburbs for a few days of convalescence, they thought, before reaching Jougne. But all these plans had to be abandoned. It turned out to be the illness that settled in and became particularly difficult in August.

44. Elisabeth was transported by car to the home of friends in the suburbs of Paris, from which, after a few days of convalescence, she and her husband intended to leave for Jougne. The next day she had a violent attack. After ten days she was driven by ambulance to Paris, to the nursing home where she had had her operation in 1911. She became so ill that her husband thought she might die at the end of the month. She improved some at the beginning of September, which allowed her to be taken to Versailles, also by ambulance. She stayed there until October 1. Foreseeing a relapse, she had herself taken back home to Paris, still bedridden. The day after she returned she had another terrible attack.

45. *Une âme* (Elisabeth's book about Juliette's death). This old servant was hard-working, honest, and kind; like a member of the family, having seen the children born, and having taken care of them with devotion; attached to them with her whole being, and deeply loved by them. She survived Elisabeth's death and was still alive when these letters were originally published.

46. First Friday of the month, the day consecrated to the Sacred Heart.

47. This was Elisabeth's last letter to Sister Marie Goby. God called Elisabeth Leseur to himself on May 3, 1914, into the Real Life, from which she watches over us. May his holy will be adored and blessed in his infinite wisdom! From how many sorrows and anxieties the Father's goodness has spared Elisabeth Leseur if she had had to witness the frightful events that we are going through! [World War I]. Yes, may God be adored and blessed each day, whatever his Providence sends us! "Lord, give her eternal rest and let perpetual light shine upon her." She "will be remembered forever; she is not afraid of evil tidings" (Ps 112:6–7) (F. L. note).

Selected Bibliography

Editions of the Writings of Elisabeth Leseur

Une Âme (souvenirs recueillis par une soeur). Paris/Auteuil: Impriméries des Orphélins-Apprentis, 1906.

Journal d'enfant. With an introductory letter by Cardinal Verdier, Archbishop of Paris. Paris: Gigord, 1934.

Journal et pensées pour chaque jour de Madame Elisabeth Leseur. With an introductory letter by Father Janvier, OP. Paris: Gigord, 1917, 1927.

La vie spirituelle (petits traités de la vie interiéure suive d'une âme). With an introductory letter by Cardinal Amette. Paris: Gigord, 1919.

Lettres à des incroyants. With a preface by Father Réginald Garrigou-Lagrange, OP. Paris: Gigord, 1923.

Lettres sur la souffrance. With a preface by Père Joseph Hébert, OP. Paris: Gigord, 1919.

English Translations

Light in the Darkness: How to Bring Christ to the Souls You Meet Each Day. Manchester, NH: Sophia Institute Press, 1998 (based on *The Spiritual Life*, 1922).

My Spirit Rejoices: The Diary of a Christian Soul in an Age of Unbelief. Manchester, NH: Sophia Institute Press, 1996 (based on *A Wife's Story*, 1921 edition).

The Spiritual Life: A Collection of Short Treatises on the Inner Life. Translated by A. M. Buchanan. London: Burnes, Oates, Washbourne, 1922.

311

A Wife's Story: The Journal of Elizabeth Leseur. With an introduction by her husband, Félix Leseur. Translated by V. M. London: Burnes, Oates, and Washbourne, 1921.

Secondary Literature

Aumann, OP, Jordan. *Christian Spirituality in the Catholic Tradition.* London: Sheed and Ward, 1980.

Brémond, Henri. *Manuel illustre de la Litérature Catholique en France de 1870 à nos jours.* Paris: Editions Spes, 1925.

Catherine of Siena: The Dialogue. Translated by Suzanne Noffke. Mahwah, NJ: Paulist Press, 1980.

Cholvy, Gérard, and Yves-Marie Hilaire. *Histoire religieuse de la France contemporaine 1880–1930.* Vol. 2. Toulouse: Bibliothèque Historique Privat, 1986.

Dansette Adrien. *Religious History of Modern France.* Vol. 2, *Under the Third Republic.* New York: Herder and Herder, 1961.

De Sales, Francis. *Introduction to the Devout Life.* Translated by John Ryan. Garden City, NY: Image, 1966.

Duhamelet, Geneviève. *Le ménage Leseur.* Brussels: Foyer Notre Dame, 1955.

———. *Le miracle de l'amour chrétien: Elisabeth Leseur 1866–1914.* Paris: P. Lethielleux, 1959.

Dupanloup, Msgr. Félix. *La femme studieuse,* Vol. 1. J. Gervais, n.d.

Flynn, Maureen. "The Spiritual Uses of Pain in Spanish Mystics." *Journal of the American Academy of Religion* 64 (Summer 1996): 257–78.

Gibson, Ralph. *A Social History of French Catholicism 1789-1914.* Christianity and Society in the Modern World. New York: Routledge, 1989.

Herking, Marie. L. Elisabeth Leseur nous parle. Paris: Gigord, 1955.

———. *Le père Leseur:* Paris: Gigord, 1952.

Jonas, Raymond. *France and the Cult of the Sacred Heart: An Epic Tale for Modern Times.* Berkeley and Los Angeles: University of California Press, 2000.

SELECTED BIBLIOGRAPHY

Kselman, Thomas A. *Miracles and Prophecies in Nineteenth-Century France.* New Brunswick, NJ: Rutgers University Press, 1983.

Lamirande, Emilien. "The Communion of Saints." The *Twentieth Century Encyclopedia of Catholicism.* Vol. 26. Translated by A. Manson. New York: Hawthorn Books, 1963.

Latourette, Kenneth. *The Nineteenth Century in Europe: Background and the Roman Catholic Phase.* Christianity in a Revolutionary Age, Vol. 1. New York: Harper, 1958.

Lenzetti, Fr. Benedict, OP. *Articles du procés Informatif de béatification et canonisation de la Servante de Dieu Elisabeth Leseur.* Paris: Imprimérie Auxiliaire, 1936.

Leseur, Félix. *Vie d'Elisabeth Leseur.* Preface by Père M. S. Gillet, OP. Paris: Gigord, 1930.

Livre D'Or des Âmes Pieuses ou Cinq Livres en un Seul: Imitation de Jésus-Christ, Choix de Prières pour tous les temps de l'année, Indulgences avec exercises spéciaux, Paroissien Choisi, Neuvaines et Pratiques de Dévotion, Méditations et lectures pour les dimanches et fêtes et vies des principaux saints medités par M. L'abbé J.R. Desbos. Paris: Roger et Chernoviz, 1894.

Manuel des Catéchismes ou Recueil de Prières, Billets, Cantiques, etc. by M. l'Abbé Félix Dupanloup, Bishop of Orleans, published with the approval of the Archbishop of Paris. Paris: F. Rocher. Adopted by the parishes of Saint-Germain-des Prés, Saint Bernard chapel, Saint Ambrose.

Manuel du Chrétien contenant Les Psaumes, Le Nouveau Testament L'imitation de N.S. Jésus Christ précédés de l'ordinaire de la messe, des vêpres et des complines. Tours: Mame et fils, n. d.

Massime Eterne de S. Alfonso M. De Liguori con Florilegio de Preghiere, Sacramenti ed altre pratiche di pieta, il vespro festivo. Milan: Winterberg, 1889.

McMillan, James F. "Clericals, Anticlericals, and the Women's Movement in France under the Third Republic." *The Historical Journal* 24 (June 1981): 361–76.

Morel, Robert, ed. *Dictionnaire des mystiques et des écrivains spirituels.* Limoges: Ateliers Mellottee, 1968.

Morris, David B. *The Culture of Pain.* Berkeley and Los Angeles: University of California Press, 1991.

Paroissien de la Renaissance contenant les offices des dimanches et fêtes de l'année selon le rite Romain. Paris: Gruel Engelmann, 1883.

Phillips, C. S. *The Church in France 1848–1907.* New York: Russell and Russell, 1936, 1967.

Pourrat, Pierre. *Christian Spirituality.* Vol. 4, *Later Developments.* Westminster, MD: Newman Press, 1953–55.

Ranka, Kristine M. *Women and the Value of Suffering: An Aw(e)ful Rowing toward God.* Collegeville, MN: Glazer/Liturgical Press, 1998.

Raoul, Valerie, "Women's Diaries as Life-Savings: Who Decides Whose Life Is Saved?" *Biography* 24, no. 1 (Winter 2001): 140–51.

———. "The Diary of Elisabeth Leseur (1866–1914): Suffering as Life-Saving." In *Proceedings of the Western Society for French History* 25, 229–37. Boulder: University of Colorado, 1998.

Roels, Alain, and Dominique Bruillot. *Beaune et ses hospices.* Dijon: Bourgogne Magazine, 1996.

Ruffing, Janet K. "Elizabeth Leseur: Wife and Worldly Mystic," *Mystics Quarterly* 19 (March 1993): 17–25.

———. "Physical Illness: A Mystically Transformative Element in the Life of Elisabeth Leseur." *Spiritual Life* (Winter 1994): 1–10.

———."Elizabeth Leseur: A Strangely Forgotten Modern Saint." In *Lay Sanctity, Medieval and Modern: A Search for Models,* edited by Ann Astell, 117–29. Notre Dame, IN: University of Notre Dame Press, 2000.

Schmitt, Christiane. *"Elisabeth Leseur: une femme dans l'église de son temps,* 1997." Dominican Archives, Bibliothèque Saulchoir, Paris. Photocopy.

Sellner, Edward. "Lay Spirituality." In *The New Dictionary of Christian Spirituality,* edited by Michael Downey, 5–20. Collegeville MN: The Liturgical Press, 2000/1993. CD-ROM.

Smith, Pamela. "Chronic Pain and Creative Possibility: A Psychological Phenomenon Confronts Theologies of Suffering." In *Broken and Whole: Essays on Religion and the Body,* edited by Susan Ross and Maureen A. Tilly, 159–87.

Annual Publication of the College Theology Society 39. Lanham, MD: University Press of America, 1995.

Soelle, Dorothy. *Suffering.* Translated by Everett R. Kalin. Philadelphia: Fortress Press, 1975.

———. *The Silent Cry: Mysticism and Resistance.* Translated by Barbara and Martin Rumscheidt. Minneapolis: Fortress Press, 2001.

Verbillion, Jean. s.v. "Faber, Frederick William." In *The New Catholic Encyclopedia* 5. San Francisco: McGraw Hill, 1976.

Verbillion, June. "The Silent Apostolate of Elizabeth Leseur," *Cross and Crown* 11 (1959): 28–45.

Waajman, Kees. "Lay Spirituality." *Studies in Spirituality* 10 (2000): 5–20.

Wismer, Patricia. "For Women in Pain: A Feminist Theology of Suffering." In *In the Embrace of God*, edited by Ann O'Hara Graff, 138–57. Maryknoll, NY: Orbis Books, 1995.

Wright, Wendy, and Joseph Powers. *Francis De Sales, Jane de Chantal: Letters of Spiritual Direction.* Classics of Western Spirituality. Mahwah, NJ: Paulist, 1988.

INDEX

Alcan, Jeanne, 192; Elisabeth's
letters to, 27, 41, 45, 47,
192, 193–206
Alphonsus Ligouri. *See*
Ligouri, Alphonsus
Ame, Une (Leseur), 46
Aquinas, Thomas. *See* Thomas
Aquinas
Arrighi, Juliette, 71, 72, 73, 74,
77–78, 82, 88, 89, 182,
208; death, 2, 38, 42, 46,
80–82, 85, 208–9
Asceticism, 7, 8, 16, 34, 94–95,
115–16
Augustine, St., 171
Au milieu des sollicitudes, 21
Austerity. *See* Asceticism

Ballard, Marie, 44
Bergson, Henri, 28
Bernard, St., 260, 262
Bérulle, Pierre de, 18
Bichat, Marie Françoise
Xavier, 84
Brémond, Henri, 32
Bridget of Sweden, St., 13, 249

*Catechism of the Council of Trent,
The*, 29
Catherine of Siena, St., 13,
39–41, 249, 252, 263

Catholic Action, 26
Chantal, Jeanne de, St., 263
Chevallier, Gustave, 260, 262
Cholvy, Gerard, 26–27
"Christian Life of Women"
(Leseur), 167–78
"Christian Man, The"
(Leseur), 179–90
Church and society. *See* Social
Catholicism
Communion. *See* Eucharist
Communion of saints, 27–30,
42–43, 84–85, 86, 177;
and feminism, 42–43;
friendship within, 43–46

Daily Thoughts (Leseur), 51;
text, 135–62
Dansette, Adrien, 21, 22, 28
DeChantal, Jane Frances, 14
*De la vie et des vertus chrétiennes
considérées dans l'état
religieux* (Gay), 18
Delcassé, Théophile, 3
Desrez, Mlle., 25
Dolorism, 42
Duhamelet, Geneviève, 14, 20
Dupanloup, Félix, 25
Duron, André, 179
Duron, Marie, 24, 46, 166,
167–68

Duvent, Aline, 166–67
Duvent, Charles, 45, 165–66

Eucharist, 2, 12, 17, 96–97,
    129–30, 154, 188

Faber, Frederick William, 14,
    19–20, 123, 228
Faith, 33, 171–72; and reason,
    24, 171
Falloux Law, 23
Feminism. *See* Women
Fénélon, François, 11
Fiévet, Aimée, 45, 191–92;
    Elisabeth's letters to, 45,
    206–14
Flavigny, Catherine de, 249,
    263
Francis de Sales, St., 6, 14,
    15–16, 107, 263

Gambetta, Léon, 3
Garrigou–Lagrange, Reginald,
    48
Gay, Charles, 14, 18–19
Goby, Marie, 5–6, 12, 14, 17,
    38, 44–45, 222–23;
    Elisabeth's letters to, 6,
    34, 37, 38, 44, 47, 222,
    224–85
Goyau, Georges, 13, 21–22,
    28, 217
Gratry, Auguste, 14, 19, 61, 67
Guéranger, Prosper, 2, 12

Harmel, Léon, 22
Hébert, Joseph, 4–5, 6, 32, 47,
    72, 222

Hilaire, Yves-Marie, 26–27
Holy Eucharist. *See* Eucharist
Hope, 53

Interior Castle, The (Teresa of
    Avila), 39
Introduction to the Devout Life
    (Francis de Sales), 14

Jaricot, Pauline, 12, 13
John, St., 171
John of the Cross, St., 36, 37,
    39, 253
*Journal d'enfant d'Elisabeth
    Leseur* (Leseur), 48
Journal et pensées chacque jour
    (Leseur), 4, 17–18, 43, 47,
    51–52; text, 53–91; *see also*
    "Daily Thoughts"
    (Leseur); "Notebook of
    Resolutions" (Leseur)
Justin Martyr, 25

Knowledge of God (Gratry), 67
Kselman, Thomas, 9–10, 11

Lagrange, Marie-Joseph, 12
Laity, 2, 43, 165; *see also*
    Vocation
Lamirande, Emilien, 27
Lavigerie, Charles, 20
Le Dantec, Félix, 45, 192;
    Elisabeth's letters to,
    45–46, 192, 215, 219–21
Le Dantec, Yvonne, 45, 192;
    Elisabeth's letters to,
    45–46, 192, 214–19

Leo XIII, Pope, 69–70, 100; and Sacred Heart, 11; social teachings, 2, 20–21, 22, 27

Leseur, Albert-Marie. *See* Leseur, Felix

Leseur, Elisabeth, 1–49; canonization, 47, 48; devotional life, 7–8 ; education, 25–26; friendships, 43–46; influences on, 9–20; marriage and family, 1, 3, 6–7; religious tolerance, 32, 64–65; social concerns, 20–23, 59–60; spiritual testament, 162–64; spirituality, 6–8; vocation, 31–33, 43; writings, 13–15, 46–48; *see also* specific headings, e.g.: Asceticism; Suffering; and titles of individual works, e.g.: *Journal et pensées chacque jour* (Leseur)

Leseur, Félix, 3–4, 6, 8, 12, 16, 60, 62, 75, 81–82, 85, 192, 197, 199, 200, 222; conversion, 2, 5, 30, 47, 93, 122–23, 258; and Elisabeth's reading, 13, 28, 29; and Elisabeth's writings, 45, 47–48, 52; and Soeur Goby, 45; priesthood, 5, 47

Letter on Frequent Communion (Fénélon), 11

Lettres à des incroyants (Leseur), 45, 191–92; text, 193–221

Lettres sur la souffrance (Leseur), 45, 47; text, 24–85

Ligouri, Alphonsus, 11, 17

Ligue des Femmes Française, La, 26

Loretta House, 13

Maistre, Joseph de, 13, 23, 186

Marian devotion, 9

Maritain, Jacques, 28

McMillan, James, 26

Montalembert, Charles de, 13, 23

Mortification. *See* Asceticism

Mun, Albert de, 22

My Spirit Rejoices (Leseur), 52

"Notebook of Resolutions" (Leseur) 7, 51–52; text, 91–117

Oeuvres des Cercles, 22

Ordinaire, Maurice, 3

Ozanam, Frédéric, 12

Pascal, Blaise, 171, 203

Paul, St., 18, 19, 85, 149, 248, 268, 281

Pécaut, Félix, 45

Penance, 5, 11, 88

Pius IX, Pope, 23, 32

Pius X, Pope, 2, 11–12, 27

Pourrat, Pierre, 19

Quanta cura, 23

Reason, 24, 171, 203
Religious tolerance, 32, 64–65
Renan, Ernest, 4, 51
République Française, 3
Rerum Novarum, 22
Révue Biblique, 12

Sacred Heart, 11, 12, 98
Saints, communion of. *See*
    Communion of saints
Ségur, Louis Gaston de, 11
Siècle, 3
Silence, 8, 87, 89–90, 94, 109,
    120, 147, 149, 151, 161
Social Catholicism, 13, 20–23,
    26–27, 43
Society of St. Vincent de Paul,
    12–13
Soelle, Dorothy, 42
Suffering, 10–11, 33–43, 146,
    149, 152–53, 155,
    222–23; dolorism, 42;
    Elisabeth's letters on, 45,
    47, 224–85; Elisabeth's
    sufferings, 1–2, 33–34, 73,
    75, 76, 83, 84, 87, 114,
    119, 120, 128 133–34;
    radical suffering, 42; of
    women, 42–43
Syllabus of Errors, 23

Teresa of Avila, St., 13, 16, 39,
    183, 249
Thérèse of Lisieux, St., 10
Thomas Aquinas, 24, 29–30

Ultramontanism, 19, 23
Union of Prayer in Reparation
    to the Sacred Heart, the,
    13

Vatican Council II, 43
Veuillot, Louis, 82
Vie d'Elisabeth Leseur, La
    (Leseur, Félix), 48
Vie de Jésus, La (Renan), 4
Vie spirituelle, La (Leseur),
    47–48
Vincent de Paul, St., 174
Viollet, Jean, 71
Vocation, 31–32, 53; of men,
    179–90; of women,
    165–78

Wismer, Patricia, 42
Women, 54, 65; role of, 24–27,
    58; suffering of, 42–43;
    vocation, 165–78
Wright, Wendy, 15